UNIVERSITY OF NORTH CAROLINA AT CHAPEL HILL
DEPARTMENT OF ROMANCE LANGUAGES

NORTH CAROLINA STUDIES
IN THE ROMANCE LANGUAGES AND LITERATURES

Founder: URBAN TIGNER HOLMES

Distributed by:

UNIVERSITY OF NORTH CAROLINA PRESS

CHAPEL HILL

North Carolina 27514

U.S.A.

NORTH CAROLINA STUDIES IN THE
ROMANCE LANGUAGES AND LITERATURES
Number 206

THE POETRY OF CHANGE:

A STUDY OF
THE SURREALIST WORKS OF BENJAMIN PÉRET

THE POETRY OF CHANGE:

A STUDY OF
THE SURREALIST WORKS OF
BENJAMIN PÉRET

BY

JULIA FIELD COSTICH

CHAPEL HILL

NORTH CAROLINA STUDIES IN THE ROMANCE
LANGUAGES AND LITERATURES
U.N.C. DEPARTMENT OF ROMANCE LANGUAGES

1979

Library of Congress Cataloging in Publication Data

Costich, Julia F.
 The poetry of change.

 (North Carolina studies in the Romance languages and literatures; 206)
 "Works by Benjamin Péret": p.
 Bibliography: p.
 1. Péret, Benjamin, 1899-1959—Criticism and interpretation. I. Title.
II. Series.

PQ2631.E348Z59   841'.9'12   78-27311
ISBN 0-8078-9206-8

I. S. B. N.: 0-8078-9206-8

IMPRESO EN ESPAÑA

PRINTED IN SPAIN

DEPÓSITO LEGAL: V. 739 - 1979   I. S. B. N.: 84-499-2593-2   .

ARTES GRÁFICAS SOLER, S. A. - JÁVEA, 28 - VALENCIA (8) - 1979

TABLE OF CONTENTS

INTRODUCTION

Surrealism is completely and fully realized in the works of Benjamin Péret. Just as the Surrealist movement is marked by his contribution from 1922 [1] until his death in 1959, so his "audace, fidélité, surréalisme" [2] continue to be a major influence upon the contemporary international Surrealists. Other founding members of the movement [3] either left the group or were expelled by André Breton for violation of its principles, but Péret remained loyal. [4] For those who participated in the activities of the Surrealist group at all stages of its development, Péret stands as an example of Surrealist heroism of unequaled loyalty, authenticity and purity. [5]

---

[1] Péret joined Breton in breaking from Dada in 1922. For an example of Péret's rejection of Dadaism, see his essay "A travers mes yeux," *Littérature,* nouvelle série 5 (1922), 13. This essay is reprinted in Jean-Louis Bédouin's *Benjamin Péret* (Paris: Seghers, 1961), pp. 31-32.

[2] Philippe Soupault uses these words as the title of his obituary article on Péret, *Arts,* 446 (1960), 4.

[3] Breton notes in *Entretiens 1913-1952* (Paris: Gallimard, 1952) that "un noyau éprouvé pour sa cohésion et sa solidité est constitué par Aragon, Eluard, Ernst, Péret et moi" (pp. 70-71). Of the four men listed by Breton, only Péret remained a member of the Surrealist movement throughout his life.

[4] Péret spent the years 1929-31 in Brazil, August 1936 - March 1937 in Spain, and 1941-46 in Mexico. Claude Courtot, in his *Introduction à la lecture de Benjamin Péret* (Paris: Le Terrain Vague, 1965), pp. 11-57, gives a detailed account of Péret's life, accompanied by letters from Péret to Breton written during these periods. In *The Surrealist Revolution in France* (Ann Arbor: University of Michigan Press, 1969), Herbert Gershman dates Péret's return from Brazil in early 1932 (p. 194). During these absences from Paris, especially the long stay in Mexico, Péret authorized the use of his name for the signing of various Surrealist documents; consequently his name appears along with those of other Surrealists during periods when he was not actually present in Paris.

[5] The series of homages published in *Arts,* 442 (1959), 3-4; *Preuves,* 9 (1959), 82-84; *Les Lettres nouvelles,* 7ième année, 24 (1959), 36-37; and

Fearless intransigeance, scandalous invective with the underlying support of unswerving courage, and the forceful expression of love and hate mark his Surrealist years. The love of the *merveilleux* in city or jungle combines in his work with an absolute unwillingness to compromise in literature or politics, to bend to the shape of bourgeois France or to that of the Stalinist Soviet Union. For his epitaph, Péret chose a statement which is the title of one of his collections of Surrealist poetry, "je ne mange pas de ce pain-là." His unique devotion to André Breton is paralleled by Breton's constant admiration and support of Péret: the final manifestation of this spirit was Breton's request to be buried next to his most faithful comrade. The relationship between Breton, the great theorist of Surrealism, and Péret, its most consistent practitioner, is not merely that of leader to follower, but rather the complementary status of defender and illustrator.

To those who knew Péret, the power of his poetry was immediately obvious; in "Une Vague de rêve" (1924), for example, Louis Aragon speaks of him in the following terms:

> Mais celui qui est capable de tout, celui qui est le plus simplement dans le plan héroïque, celui qu'on rencontre au Soleil Levant, celui qui défie le bon sens à chaque respiration, c'est Benjamin Péret, aux belles cravates, un grand poète comme on n'en fait plus, Benjamin Péret qui tient en laisse une baleine, ou peut-être un petit moineau. [6]

For André Pieyre de Mandiargues, Péret stands as "le poète surréaliste par excellence," and he adds that "nul autre que lui ne peut ou ne pourra prétendre à représenter pleinement et purement la poésie surréaliste." [7] Jehan Mayoux recounts that "Eluard . . . un jour, dans une conversation, a dit 'Péret est un plus grand poète que moi'," [8] while Philippe Soupault stated in 1962, "moi, je don-

---

Cahiers des saisons, 19 (1960), 414-15, ranges through the movement from its inception (Breton) to the present (Gérard Legrand).

[6] Louis Aragon, "Une Vague de rêve," *Commerce,* 2 (Fall, 1924), 118.

[7] André Pieyre de Mandiargues, "Benjamin Péret," *Deuxième Belvédère* (Paris: Grasset, 1962), pp. 82 and 83.

[8] Jehan Mayoux, "Benjamin Péret, ou la fourcchette coupante," *Le Surréalisme même,* 2 (1957), 153. Eluard expresses his admiration for Péret in the essay "L'Arbitraire, la contradiction, la violence, la poésie," originally published in *Variétés* (1929) and reprinted in Eluard's *Œuvres complètes* (Paris: Galli-

nerais toute l'œuvre d'Eluard pour un seul poème de Péret." [9] Critical awareness of Péret's importance in the Surrealist movement is growing, and three works on Péret have appeared as of 1973. [10] French critics and those connected with the Surrealist movement have greatly contributed to the public's awareness of his life and work. Octavio Paz's remark is typical of their approach to Péret: "J'aime beaucoup Benjamin Péret, qui à mes yeux est comme un exemple moral, une attitude de vrai poète devant la vie." [11] The three books which have appeared on Péret are valuable as general surveys of his work, but they rarely discuss specific texts.

So large and so diverse is the written legacy of Péret that failure to mention it in a discussion of Surrealism risks the misrepresentation of the movement. [12] While the relative scarcity of critical material on Péret's texts may indeed by attributable to the difficulty of obtaining his works in the past, the problem is being overcome through the efforts of the Association des Amis de Benjamin Péret. [13] Péret's poetry appears both as separate texts as-

---

mard, 1968), II, 817-25. A *prière d'insérer* for Péret's *De derrière les fagots* (1936) is also highly laudatory.

[9] Quoted in Courtot, p. 69n.

[10] Criticism of Péret falls into three divisions: those few articles which appeared before his death, the proliferation of homages immediately after he died in 1959, and the few studies which have been published since 1965. The only major articles in the first of these divisions are those by Eluard referred to in note 7 *supra,* and the article by Jehan Mayoux cited in the same note. The critical comment of the homages is slight. In more recent Péret criticism, the work of Mary Ann Caws, Elizabeth Jackson Hanchett and J. H. Matthews in the United States, along with that of Jean-Christophe Bailly, Jean-Louis Bédouin and Claude Courtot in France had contributed to growing awareness of Péret's prose and poetry. Courtot's study combines biographical information with textual analysis. Jean-Louis Bédoin's volume in the *Poètes d'aujourd'hui* series is also largely devoted to biography and includes a selection of texts. Jean-Christophe Bailly's *Au-delà du langage* (Paris: Losfeld, 1971) is valuable for its concentration on Péret's texts. Pierre Prigioni's *Conte populaire et conte surréaliste* (Urbino: Argalia Editore, 1970), an attempt at structural analysis of Péret's tales, is not generally accessible.

[11] Claude Couffon, *Hispano-America en su nueva litteratura* (Santander: La isla de los ratones, 1962), p. 76, quoted by Danièle Musacchio, "Le surréalisme dans la poésie hispano-américaine," *Europe,* 475-76 (1968), 275.

[12] As recently as 1972, a study entitled *Surrealism: Theater, Arts, Ideas* by Nahma Sandrow (New York: Harper and Row, 1972) omits any mention of Péret.

[13] *Œuvres complètes* I (1969) and II (1971) contain all of Péret's poetry and all references to his poetry are to this edition. Most of the prose tales were published in *Le Gigot, sa vie et son œuvre* (Paris: Le Terrain Vague,

sembled in a collection and as long poems centered about a single topic. His prose also takes varying length and form: he produces tales, essays, scenarios and a "natural history." In the area of non-fiction, Péret wrote a number of ethnological articles and other works in collaboration with other Surrealists and Trotskyites. [14] He was also responsible for the translation and edition of works in Spanish, Portuguese and Italian. [15]

The concept of change as it is perceived and revealed by the poet is the dynamic constant in Péret's Surrealist texts. In the privileged position of being able to see change in life and death, the poet finds the world to be a place of organic metamorphosis caused by the sublimated force of desire. The freedom of desire is the most important aspect of revelations vouchsafed by the non-rational mind; Péret continually defends "l'inconscient, individu cosmique où siège le désir, souverain phénix qui s'engendre indéfiniment de sa propre fin." [16] Péret's theory of desire, to which he gives the name *l'amour sublime,* extends desire beyond the realm of sexual relationships. As the force of desire takes on verbal form in poetry, the principle of sublimation becomes immediately applicable to words. Breton says of Péret:

> Lui seul a pleinement réalisé sur le verbe l'opération correspondante à la "sublimation" alchimique qui consiste à provoquer "l'ascension du subtil" par sa "séparation d'avec l'épais." *L'épais,* dans ce domaine, c'est cette croûte de signification exclusive dont l'usage a recouvert tous les mots. [17]

Through the action of his prose and poetry, Péret changes the world by liberating potential in both verbal and physical domains.

1957), and the complete Surrealist prose is to appear in volumes III and IV of the Association des Amis de Benjamin Péret series. For those tales which were not included in *Le Gigot,* I have used typescript copies which were generously given to me by Vincent Bounoure, the editor of Péret's prose.

[14] Along with other Surrealists, Péret joined the Communist party in 1927, but he rapidly became disillusioned with the Stalinist line and converted to Trotskyism. His activity in the realm of revolutionary politics continued until his death, and he produced a number of political tracts and essays.

[15] For further information on these works, see Appendix.

[16] Benjamin Péret, "La Pensée est UNE et indivisible," *VVV,* 4 (1944), 12.

[17] André Breton, ed., *Anthologie de l'humour noir* (Paris: Pauvert, 1966), p. 384.

The continual metamorphosis which is shown in his work is a glimpse of the real powers inherent in nature and in words, powers which the poet alone can demonstrate through his privileged status as observer from within the living world.[18] In "La parole est à Péret," he speaks of the primitive or poetic mind:

> Le soleil, la lune, les étoiles, le tonnerre, la pluie et la nature entière lui ressemblent et si, de matière à matière, son pouvoir est faible, il est compensé, d'esprit en esprit, par une puissance qu'il postule sans limites.[19]

In the interaction of man with nature, each participant takes on the powers of the other. From the primordial beginnings of time to the present moment, the process of change and generation continues with a hidden freedom which denies the reality of the boundaries and divisions which appear to exist in the world.

Although Péret writes on the relationship of the poet to his society, he does not formulate poetics in treatises or manifestos. The principles which rule his work are elaborated in "Le Déshonneur des poètes" and "La parole est à Péret" and occasionally in other essays, but the process of composing texts is not discussed. Péret's single explicit reference to the act of writing appears in "L'Ecriture automatique" (1929),[20] and even this treatment of the subject is limited to two paragraphs which are followed by a long example of automatic writing. The introduction is presented as instruction to those who wish to practice automatism:

> Il suffit donc de chasser cette chienne de raison et d'écrire. . . . Prenez une main, du papier, de l'encre et un porte-plume avec une plume neuve et installez-vous con-

---

[18] In *L'Un dans l'autre* (Paris: Losfeld, 1971), Breton notes that in the course of a game "on demande à Péret de se définir comme fenêtre alors qu'il s'est précisément conçu comme fenêtre (une telle coincidence ne s'est produite qu'une fois)" (p. 28).

[19] Benjamin Péret, "La parole est à Péret," *Le Déshonneur des poètes, précédé de La parole est à Péret* (Paris: Pauvert, 1965), p. 25. Originally published in Mexico City: Poésie et Révolution, 1945.

[20] "L'Ecriture automatique" was written for the Brazilian journal *Diario da Noite* in 1929 but is not to be published until *Œuvres complètes,* IV. These instructions are very similar to those given by Breton as "secrets de l'art magique surréaliste" in the "Manifeste du surréalisme," *Manifestes du surréalisme* (Paris: Pauvert, 1962), pp. 44-45.

fortablement à votre table. Maintenant oubliez toutes vos
préoccupations. . . . Ecrivez le plus vite possible pour ne
rien perdre des confidences qui vous sont faites et surtout
ne vous relisez pas.

Péret's Surrealist texts are their own justification. His complete faith
in the validity and efficacy of poetry (which, as applied to all creative work, includes his prose) as a means for constructive change
is evident in his contention that poetry is "le véritable souffle de
l'homme." [21] In view of Breton's limited poetic output and the
defection or banishment of the other founding Surrealists, Péret
emerges as the most faithful representative of Surrealism.

---

[21] "Le Déshonneur des poètes," p. 71.

I

THE MOBILE METAMORPHOSIS

Benjamin Péret's first published collection of poetry, *Le Passager du Transatlantique* (1921), appears as a manifestation of the Dada movement, but two pre-Dada texts have come to light. Noting the rarity of early extant works, Jean-Louis Bédouin remarks that "il m'a confié lui-même . . . qu'il avait commencé par écrire des poèmes inspirés de Mallarmé." [1] The two texts from Péret's teens show that he was aware of literary movements in the period immediately after World War I and that he experimented with poetic styles through the early stages of his involvement with the Parisian avant-garde. "Je rêve d'une musique indolente et fanée" [2] is an ex-

---

[1] Jean-Louis Bédouin, *Benjamin Péret* (Paris: Seghers, 1961), p. 25.

[2] By 1971, only one post-Symbolist poem had been found; it is included in *Œuvres complètes,* II. This untitled text begins with the line "Je rêve d'une musique indolente et fanée" and, as Péret's statement to Bédouin suggests, it reflects Symbolist style. The editors of the collected works qualify the early text as "mystification" or "pastiche," implying that Péret's status as a highly contestatory individual does not allow for this text's positive valuation of words such as "fanée," "mièvre," "madone," "bergère" (the piece of furniture), and "invocation." In response to the contention that the use of Symbolist vocabulary might mark "Je rêve d'une musique indolente et fanée" as a hoax, it may be argued that this text also includes usage which later became typical of Surrealist poetry: "rêve," "image," "l'eau s'écoulant," "mort," and "herbes folles." The sincerity of this text may also be questioned because Péret expresses a love of music which is contradicted in his later work. However, the music in question is not real but dreamed, and music itself is an important element of Symbolist poetry theory.

The editors of Volumes I and II, which contain Péret's poetry, present themselves as participants in a collective effort. "Je rêve d'une musique indolente et fanée" and the commentary on this text appear on pp. 334-35 of *Œuvres complètes,* II.

ample of Péret's writing in a symbolist vein. The status of this text in relation to Péret's orientation at the time of its composition must remain unresolved, but it is nonetheless valuable as evidence that Péret did not spring forth into the Dadaist movement without prior poetic experience.

Another pre-Dada poem, "Importé du Japon," [3] is intriguing as a bridge between post-Symbolist and Dadaist expression. Two lines of this text make it appear to be a prediction, twenty-five years in advance, of the atomic bombing of Japan: "Qui a sali les viandes de Nagasaki / le vent perdit la fin de la chanson." The vocabulary is a startling mixture of the genteel delicacy of Symbolism, in such images as "un chrysanthème blanc" and "une coupe bleu de roi," and the brutality which will reappear throughout Péret's works:

> Dans la coupe bleu de roi le chrysanthème blanc
> D'un coup sec on déchire une soie
> Des taches rouges et de l'eau sur le parquet
>
> Demain matin le chiffonnier
> Avec les viandes à son chapeau
> Causera de Nagasaki.

The elevated stance and diction of the Symbolist poet are rejected for an intensely carnal vision. References to a Papuan in the first and last lines point to Péret's later interest in primitive cultures. "Importé du Japon" is doubly prophetic in its startling reference to Nagasaki and its presentation of a phase in the development of the young poet in which the vision of the future is evident, albeit still clouded. Before this poem had appeared in print (July, 1920), Max Jacob had written Francis Picabia asking him to help Péret establish himself in Paris. [4] Although Péret moves from a vaguely defined point outside the Parisien avant-garde to acceptance as a

---

[3] It is to "Importé du Japon" that Herbert Gershman [*The Surrealist Revolution in France* (Ann Arbor: University of Michigan Press, 1969), p. 216] refers when he remarks that "another avant-garde literary review of the type Breton would presumably have vomited was *Action, cahiers de philosophie et d'art*.... In addition to Aragon and Eluard, it published Apollinaire, Cocteau, Malraux, Centrars, Jacob, Pascal Pia — and Artaud, Rigaut and Péret (no. 4, July 1920)."

[4] This letter is reprinted in Michel Sanouillet, *Dada à Paris* (Paris: Pauvert, 1965), p. 557.

member of Tristan Tzara's group in 1920, his poetic vision is present in this text written independently of Dada, and his vision will be elaborated rather than created through his contact with his new Parisian friends.

According to Michel Sanouillet, Péret's first public appearance as a member of Dada took place in early 1920:

> C'est au cours de la manifestation de la Salle Gaveau que Benjamin Péret fit sa première apparition, non sur la scène avec les Dadaistes, mais dans la salle où il se signala à l'attention des acteurs en criant à pleine voix: "Vive la France et les pommes de terre frites." [5]

As a member of Dada, Péret participated in manifestations and other activities: during 1920 and 1921, he signed the manifesto "Dada soulève TOUT," attended the lecture by the Italian futurist Marinetti, took part in the black humor of the tour of Paris and played the part of the neck in Tristan Tzara's *Cœur à gaz*. [6] His role in the Procès Barrès (May 13, 1921) was considered the most scandalous of all. Wearing a German uniform and a gas mask (he had recently been employed in a factory making them), marching in a goose-step, Péret "jeta un froid dans la salle où éclatèrent bientôt de violentes manifestations d'hostilité." [7] The uproar which followed the unpatriotic gesture of this recent *cuirassier* led to Picabia's leaving the movement. [8]

Although Péret is not known as a plastic artist, he exhibited two items in the 1921 "Salon Dada," one entitled "Une Belle morte," made up of a nutcracker and a rubber sponge, and a second showing the Venus de Milo with a man's shaved head on her shoul-

---

[5] Sanouillet, p. 178n.

[6] *Ibid.*, pp. 235, 238, and 245. Sanouillet adds the following comment to his account of the visit and demonstration at Saint-Julien-le-Pauvre: "Rapportons cependant les dires de plusieurs témoins selon lesquels Benjamin Péret, déjà fidèle à cet anti-cléricalisme qui devait devenir pour lui un style de vie, aurait insisté pour que la manifestation se déroulât à l'intérieur de l'église" (p. 246n). This example supports that of the Unknown Soldier incident at the Procès Barrès in showing that Péret was capable of outdoing the Dadaists in the audacious behavior that was their specialty.

[7] Sanouillet, p. 261.

[8] This event may explain the absence of Picabia's name from the dedication of *Le Passager du Transatlantique*.

ders. Both creations exemplify Lautréamont's theory of beauty, especially in their union of images with male and female connotations. Péret's contributions to the Dada journal *Littérature* date from the June-August issue of 1920. [9] Among his texts in the new series of this periodical, under the direction of Breton, is "L'Auberge du cul volant," certified as having been written "la première partie avant de faire l'amour et la seconde partie après." [10]

Another early prose text published by *Littérature* is the first of Péret's many tales, "Au 125 du boulevard Saint Germain." [11] The consistency of Péret's Surrealism and his true independence from Dada are evident in these tales, which are remarkably similar from the first one to "Midi," which is dated 1950. No break is apparent between those composed prior to the "Premier Manifeste du surréalisme" (1924) and those written after the constitution of Surrealism as a separate movement, although fewer were composed in the late 1920s. The Surrealist tale, which is an example of the Surrealist experimentation with forms which transcend generic

---

[9] Work by Péret also appeared in the second number of the first series and in all numbers but the fourth of the second series until the rupture between Breton's followers and those who remained with Tzara, which occurred after the combined publication of issues eleven and twelve.

[10] *Littérature,* nouvelle série 3 (May 1922), 16.

[11] Published as a separate text by *Littérature* in 1923. See Appendix for further information on publications.

Henri Michaux mentions the effect of this tale on his view of poetry and refers to it as a voyage, which links "Au 125 du boulevard Saint Germain" with *Le Passager du Transatlantique.* Michaux's allusions to specific Surrealist works and authors are rare; hence, the impact of this tale must have been especially strong. He mentions it in the same breath with Lautréamont's *Chants de Maldoror,* and, although he finally rejects the point of view of both works, his equation of Péret with Lautréamont reflects the Surrealist reverence for the latter author: "Quel voyage ce fut pour leurs premiers lecteurs que 'Au 125 du boulevard Saint Germain' de Benjamin Péret, que les *Chants de Maldoror* du comte de Lautréamont! .... Les métamorphoses, les transsubstantions, les bilocations, les impossibilités physiques devenaient la chose du monde apparemment la plus facile. Le plaisir était si grand, si libérateur." Henri Michaux, "Les Poètes voyagent," *Passages* (Paris: Gallimard, 1963), p. 65.

Herbert Gershman makes the same link between Lautréamont and Péret: he notes that the *Chants de Maldoror* posed a challenge and that most of the Surrealists, while acknowledging its value, ignored it in their writing. He adds that "only Péret, of the early Surrealists, rose to this challenge of automatism carefully controlled so as to give the desire and result, with the content of the Gothic novel: a combination of deliberate sensory and logical confusion with a matching subject. All this in impeccable syntax" (p. 43).

boundaries, differs radically from Dadaist distortion and explosion of language in such texts as Louis Aragon's "Persiennes." Before 1924, prose appears to have been Péret's favorite medium; seventeen tales date from this period, while *Le Passager du Transatlantique* (1921) is his only contemporary collection of poetry. "Au 125 du boulevard Saint Germain," despite its date and publication by *Littérature,* is not a Dadaist text. It is written in complete sentences with standard vocabulary and punctuation and follows the form of a *roman policier*; although it includes attacks on contemporary society and French culture, they are mild when compared with the active violence of the Procès Barrès and the Dada manifestoes. The story of "Au 125 du boulevard Saint Germain" is resolved when the man who throws bathtubs from windows at eleven thirty at night is found and identified. Other early tales are in the same mode and form, which is uniquely Péret's.

A.   THE DADA PASSAGE

Despite his complete participation as a "dadaiste convaincu" [12] in manifestations and soirées, Péret is no more a Dadaist poet than he was a Symbolist poet. *Le Passager du Transatlantique* contradicts the anti-publication stance of the movement, yet it is indubitably under the aegis of Dada. [13] The four woodcuts by Hans Arp, one of the founders of the movement, and a review by Philippe Soupault in *Littérature* eight months after the publication give the volume official credentials, as does a dedicatory list which includes most of

---

[12] Max Jacob to Francis Picabia, Sanouillet, p. 557.

[13] *Le Passager du Transatlantique* was published in July, 1921 by Au Sans Pareil in their "Dada" collection. Because of the confiscation, copies of this edition are extremely rare; there is none in the Bibliothèque Nationale. The title appears with a capital T in Philippe Soupault's review of the poems (*Littérature,* nouvelle série 1) as it is reprinted in the *Œuvres complètes,* I, p. 295, and in Breton's letter to Picabia of December 6, 1922 as it appears in Sanouillet, p. 525. In the Gallimard reedition of *Passager du Transatlantique* along with *Le Grand Jeu* in their "Poésie" series (Paris: 1969), the reading is *transatlantique.* Although the word refers to an ocean-going vessel with both upper and lower-case spelling, only the lower case allows for the reading of "transatlantique" as a folding deck-chair. In either case, it may be hypothesized that this title exists in contrast with Blaise Cendrars' "Prose du transsibérien et de la petite Jeanne de France" (1913).

the movement's adherents. [14] The Soupault review, while showing that Péret's work was warmly applauded by the group, is puzzling: he speaks of Péret as being distant from the Parisian scene ("Je ne parle pas de notre cher Benjamin qui vit tranquillement à Nantes. Lui aussi est très gentil"), [15] yet pictures and documents attest to his active participation in the Parisian movement as early as April, 1920. [16] Despite Soupault's enthusiasm, *Le Passager du Transatlantique* was not successful, and a letter from Breton to Picabia of December, 1922 notes Péret's chronic poverty and that the entire edition of the collection "lui a été confisquée par le Sans Pareil et séquestrée." [17]

The title of Péret's poetic contribution to the Dadaist movement further indicates an ambivalent impermanence. As the transatlantic passenger, he is on board only until the liner carries him to his destination. The transatlantic ship is itself in passage upon the ocean, and this body of water is in turn in a state of flux. The second meaning of "transatlantique," a deck chair, would denote the poet as an "armchair traveler," one whose voyages are mental rather than corporeal. Yet in *Le Passager du Transatlantique,* the traveler moves constantly in order to describe movement about himself, as for example in "Passagers de seconde classe et leurs cheveux":

> J'y cours
> Où courez-vous
> Nulle part
> Moi aussi
> Alors.

This obsessive movement by the speaker, in combination with the implicit movement of the title, is reduced to stasis when the law of relativity is applied. A problem of Dadaism is reflected in this

---

[14] Picabia's name is notably absent from the list, and that of the mysterious Henriquez Zimmern-Zacholorpoulos is included.

[15] *Littérature,* nouvelle série 1 (March 1922).

[16] See, for example, the photographs from the visit to Saint-Julien-le-Pauvre, April 14, 1920, or those taken at the vernissage of the Max Ernst exhibit at the Au Sans Pareil gallery in May of the same year. The letter from Max Jacob introducing Péret to Francis Picabia, and presumably to Paris, is dated "le 9 mars, 1920" (Sanouillet, p. 557).

[17] Sanouillet, p. 525.

paradox: the invalidation of all reference points leads to movement which takes place in a referential void and which therefore cannot be perceived by an observer who is himself designated as being in motion. In contrast, André Breton's Surrealist command, "Lâchez tout," [18] far from demanding the extinction of that whole, enumerates its elements. Change takes place in relation to that which is transformed or rejected, and real movement is possible.

In view of the positive value given to movement in *Le Passager du Transatlantique,* it is significant that in Péret's next two collections of poetry, *Immortelle Maladie* and *Dormir dormir dans les pierres,* the speaker is physically immobile in dream or death. Vision is itself productive of movement, because the eye must constantly readjust to changes in illumination. The artist Gyorgy Kepes, for example, finds that this property of the sense of sight produces a world which sounds very much like Péret's own: "Things grow and disintegrate; they change their shapes, size and position relative to themselves, to each other, and to us." [19] Péret's poetic optic in the early collection can be compared with a movie camera constantly in search of the effective travelling shot, while in the second and third volumes the poet is equipped with a more probing lens which can penetrate the surface of reality like an X-ray or detect change where none is immediately apparent, as does a time-exposure.

Péret's passage through Dadaism is a process of purification and redefinition which purges him of symbolist and other traditional literary remnants. As Jean-Louis Bédouin notes, "l'absolue pureté de ces poèmes que ne contamine nulle 'littérature' " is such that "il ne prend même pas la peine de faire de l'anti-littérature." [20] Two texts in *Le Passager du Transatlantique,* "En avant" and "Chaufferie mélancholique," describe this process through the metaphor of explosion. In "En avant," impediments to forward motion are destroyed, even when this process leads to self-destruction. "Chaufferie mélancholique" advances the metaphor of explosion to a more concrete level; it appears as a danger to be averted through action.

"En avant" begins with a verbal arrangement which gives the

---

[18] *Littérature,* nouvelle série 2 (April 1922).

[19] Gyorgy Kepes, *The Nature and Art of Motion* (New York: George Braziller, Inc., 1965), p. ii.

[20] Bédouin, p. 46. This avoidance of anti-literature further distinguished Péret from his fellow Dadas.

text the formal appearance of an analysis. The two words of the
title recur in the opening lines: "En avant disait l'arc-en-ciel ma-
tinal / En avant pour les soupiraux de notre jeunesse." The second
and third of the poem's four divisions each begin with one of these
two words, and their implications are explored individually. The
manner in which this dismemberment is performed relates "En
avant" to "Pont aux cygnes," which also presents a group of elements in the first line, then treats them in separate divisions. In
"En avant," this analytic approach results in the replacement of
an unsatisfactory response to the initial statement, "Nous avons
éclaté / et tout ce qui était bleu est resté bleu," with one that has
the desired result of avoiding disaster:

> Avant casse ta tête
> ou celle de ton voisin le plus proche
> en sorte que tous les deux
> nous prendrons l'Orient-Express aux prochaines vacances.

"Chaufferie mélancholique" also shows progress from an unsatisfactory activity to one that prepares for the accomplishment of the
desired goal. The first action, "J'ai rêvé à toutes les étoiles / et
elles en font autant," builds up pressure in the emotional boiler
room of the title. Explosion is imminent because of immobility:
"Nous sommes perdus / nous sommes perclus"; but the catastrophe
is avoided by action:

> Soupirer ou regarder
> pas du tout je ne rêve plus et je m'en vais
> Nous ne sommes pas perdus.

Forward movement in "En avant" is accomplished only after passage through an intermediate state, and even then it assumes the
romanticized aspect of taking the Orient Express, while in "Chaufferie mélancholique" this movement is immediate and unqualified.
As a response to the situation at hand, displacement in space is a
means of self-preservation which changes the speaker from dream
to actor and maintains his physical integrity. In contrast, the "casse
ta tête" of "En avant" is destructive of the physical self in the
cause of fidelity to the dreams of youth, among which the actual
movement may be counted. The interaction of tenses is also indicative of this shift. "En avant" contains five verbs in the past tense,

followed by two imperatives which imply future action and one concluding verb in the future tense. On the other hand, "Chaufferie mélancholique" begins and ends in the present, with the future indicated by one verb, "va éclater," which denotes an event avoided by the speaker. Movement is no longer projected into the future: it is an immediate condition of survival.

In other texts in *Le Passager du Transatlantique,* man is defined as a function of his movement. The "mystère de l'homme" in "Homme de quart homme de demi" is diminished by stasis or identification with the present state: "Pour diminuer que faut-il / être sûr de son age." Human increase is a form of movement which links man with telluric mystery:

> Pour augmenter que faut-il
> Marcher ou descendre ou monter
> C'est un mystère
>
> Terre.

Samuel Altiber, the precocious protagonist of "Passagers de première classe et leur teint frais," is a prodigy of growth and development, speaking his name at the age of one day. His social progress is exemplified by his father's introducing him to fine tobacco: this acculturated activity contrasts with the gratuitous movement of "Passagers de seconde classe et leurs cheveux." The activity in the latter poem is Dadaist in its willful lack of direction.

Rubber, a metaphor for human change which recurs in Péret's later works, appears in "Emigrant des mille milles"; the title of this text is yet another use of the concept of spatial displacement. Dedicated to Jacques Vaché, the poem contains an allusion to Germany and recalls the internationalism of the Dada response to the chauvinism of its time: "Boulevard Sébastopol ou Wilhelmstrasse / nos sœurs sont deux putains." After denying spiritual progress as a function of age, Péret puts forth the idea of an internalized movement which is change without spatial progress:

> Qu'est-ce qu'un cancer
> Qu'est-ce que le génie
> C'est la même chose
> et le caoutchouc aussi
> mais dites-moi ce qu'est le caoutchouc.

The human mystery is preserved; any apparent progress toward man's definition is illusory because, like rubber, he is potentially multiform and in a continual state of change. An additional movement, that of human life toward death, is also presented as a condition of life to be accepted in "Alarme mal calculée":

> Pourquoi avez-vous crié si fort
> vous voyez bien que nous allons mourir
> moi je n'y tiens pas.

When the subject of death reappears in the next poem, "Bar pour bar fumoir pour fumoir," the ambiguity of the reference is heightened by a religious context: "Mais vous quand aurez-vous votre jour C'est simple mourez d'abord." Integration of death into life is an important concept in Péret's later work, and its appearance at this early stage shows that it is one of his fundamental concerns. The focus on death is still vague; it is a reality to be included in the general picture but not yet a subject for deep exploration.

In *Le Passager du Transatlantique,* images are linked and lines of poetry are made continuous by repetition; some poems are based entirely on a repeated word or phrase. "Passerelle du commandant," an early example of Péret's fascination with proverbs,[21] is constructed upon a strict parallelism in which each line begins "Il faut être" and continues with a one-syllable adjective and three syllables which are verbal except in line three: "Il faut être riche pour tous les temps." This text moves from acceptable ideas to new concepts according to a cumulative principle. An implicit bourgeois interlocutor, having acquiesced to the first five statements, will automatically agree with those that follow because they are similarly cast in the imperative. The turning point is line six, "Il faut être bien pour supporter." As the Dadaist is not "bien," he will not tolerate the repressive axioms of the first lines, which exalt chastity,

---

[21] Péret's affection for proverbs is also apparent in his collaboration with Eluard on *152 proverbes mis au goût du jour* (1925). This work is reprinted in Eluard's *Œuvres complètes* (Paris: Gallimard, 1968), vol. II, pp. 155-61. As the notes to this edition indicate, Eluard and Péret composed their contributions to the volume separately; sixty-nine are by Eluard, while the remaining eighty-three are by Péret. Péret also collaborated on the editorial board of *Proverbe,* a review directed by Eluard from February, 1920 to July, 1921.

age, wealth and size. The first line to follow this shift replaces the linear system of cause and effect with circularity, the only valid measure on the scale of the transatlantic traveler: "Il faut être rond pour mesurer." In the last three lines there emerge paradoxical statements concerning the opposition between solitary action and the need for love. Solitude, though necessary for operation, is not sufficient to human life; exaggerated individualism is opposed to the tenderness of concurrence with other and to the acceptance of a partner.

"Babord pour tous" is also built on a pattern of repetition. The first ten lines follow a sequence which includes an initial "Babord" and a verb in the imperative. The pivot line, "car nous passons," marks the end of this pattern, which is relinquished for a more complex series of duplications:

> Nous passons et les hirondelles passent avec nous
> mais nous crachons en l'air
> et les hirondelles crachent sur nous.

Another involved repetitive structure appears in "Petit Hublot de mon cœur"; it is based on a willful confusion of the country called Canada with the Canada apple, a variety of rennet, and the French word for rennet, "reinette," affords another pun. Forms of "Canada," appropriate to the collection as it lies across the Atlantic, appear eight times in the eighteen lines of the poem. The confusion of queen and country with apples and species is performed through a series of transformations worked on a simple visual image of the queen in a hat with the apple in a basket under her arm. In the eighth lines she becomes "la reine dans son panier." The simple, folksong tone of the text relates it to the first poem in *Le Grand Jeu* (1928), "S'essouffler," which also rearranges words in simple lines to produce a new meaning. Within the narrative context of "Petit Hublot de mon cœur," a second series of repetitions emerges: "Elle chantait / Lorsque le pélican lassé d'un long long voyage long voyage long voyage"; but this series is not allowed to persist: "et partit du pied gauche." Whether the line from Musset [22]

---

[22] This line is a modification of the following verse from the "Nuit de mai" as published in *Premières poésies, poésies nouvelles* (Paris: Gallimard, 1966): "Lorsque le pélican, lassé d'un long voyage" (p. 249). The poetic theory

is intended as an improvement on the original or as a continuation of the romantic tone of the text as set by the title, Péret's use of repetition to replace and intensify adjectives adds to its simplicity. As Claude Courtot points out, most of Péret's later poetry is based on subordination and qualification,[23] but in *Le Passager du Transatlantique* this poetic technique is exploited only rarely and is never used in lengthy sequence.

The ruling metaphor of shipboard travel eliminates all distinctions of rank among objects and levels of poetic diction; whatever their class, all the metaphorical passengers sink or float together. In his *Entretiens 1913-1952,* Breton remarks:

> *Le Passager du Transatlantique* témoigne d'ores et déjà de tous ses dons: une liberté d'expression sans précédent. Comme Hugo avait aboli la distinction entre les mots "nobles" et "non nobles," Péret abolit la distinction entre les objets "nobles" et "non nobles."[24]

These classless objects do not proliferate in *Le Passager du Transatlantique* as they do in *Le Grand Jeu* (1928) or in the later collection *De derrière les fagots* (1934), but they are present, and they act as ironic counterpoints to abstractions and traditional poetic imagery. In "En avant," the "arc-en-ciel" and "soupiraux" are deprived of worn associations by their juxtaposition with "petits oignons." Other texts rely upon the unexpected appearance of one of these objects, for example the "pralines" in "Pont aux cygnes" and "caoutchouc" in "Emigrant des mille milles." Eggs are raised to the poetic height of being an attribute of the flag in "Drapeau des mains sales," and along with an alarm clock they constitute an important element of a world that has become chaotic in "Tribord asiatique":

---

presented in "Nuit de mai," with the lute-playing poet in conversation with his Muse, is diametrically opposed to the principle of the inner voice which directs the writing of the Surrealist automatic text. To the opposition between external and internal inspiration may be added the formal difference between the free, simple style of "Petit Hublot de mon cœur" and the closely-knit alexandrines of "Nuit de mai." In view of the gulf between Péret and the poet he quotes, the use of this line by the queen is, as Péret indicates, "gauche."

[23] Courtot, pp. 133-54.

[24] André Breton, *Entretiens 1913-1952* (Paris: Gallimard, 1952), p. 68.

Les œufs sont cassés
et le réveille-matin ne sonne plus
Veux-tu me dire pourquoi
tu veux rester tranquille.

The inelegant human ear, one of Péret's most consistently used images, profits from the same technique:

Il était un petit drapeau
il avait deux deux œufs sur l'oreille l'oreille l'oreille
("Drapeau des mains sales")

Je n'ai qu'un œil et deux cerveaux
Et vous comment va votre oreille.
("Timonerie des vieux génies")

Poetic diction undergoes the same leveling as object status in this collection. The use of an idiomatic expression in the last line of "En arrière" reduces the stature of the prince and princess: "C'est pourquoi le prince / voulait qu'on fasse machine arrière." Dialogue is relatively rare in Péret's later work and even in his tales, but it dominates *Le Passager du Transatlantique*: six texts [25] contain statements and responses in some form and seven more [26] are addressed to a second person who does not respond in the text. The poet as passenger is constantly in a social situation. Even "En arrière," which has no verbal exchange, has human protagonists. External to the poems, a group is constituted by the individual dedications of five of the texts to Georges Ribemont-Dessaignes, Théodore Fraenkel, Hans Arp, Jacques Rigaut and Jacques Vaché.

The exotic atmosphere created by the title and internal references to distant places in *Le Passager du Transatlantique* enter into conflict with a constant use of the banal or commonplace so that the impression of unity created through travel imagery finally ap-

---

[25] The following texts use dialogue: "Pont aux cygnes," "Timonerie des vieux génies," "Tribord asiatique," "Homme de quart homme de demi," "Passagers de seconde classe et leurs cheveux," and "Bar pour bar fumoir pour fumoir."

[26] The second person is used in the following texts: "En avant," "Petit Hublot de mon cœur," "Passerelle du commandant," "Chaufferie mélancholique," "Babord pour tous," "Passagers de première classe et leur teint frais," and "Alarme mal calculée."

pears to have been imposed *a posteriori* and from without. In 1921, Péret had not crossed the Atlantic although he was to do so three times during his life, in 1921, 1941, and 1955. When he does write poetry specifically about foreign countries, most notably in *Air mexicain* (1952), he does not speak as an outsider, but rather as one who exists within the context of these places. Apart from the titles, the only references to foreign countries in *Le Passager du Transatlantique* are the proper nouns Canada, Orient Express and Wilhelmstrasse. They are deprived of foreign connotations by their integration with French phenomena: the Orient Express, the dream of French schoolboys in "En avant," originates in France; Canada, aside from being a former French colony, becomes a French apple in "Petit Hublot de mon cœur"; and the Wilhelmstrasse is designated "sœur" to the Boulevard Sébastopol in "Emigrant des mille milles." Within the context of the collection as a whole, these three references would lose their importance were it not for the cohesion of the imagery of ship travel in the titles of the poems, for each title refers to a part of a ship, to its movement or to those on board. The identities of these shipboard elements, however, are penetrated by the poet and are found to be quite landbound. The ocean, which appears frequently in later volumes of Péret's poetry, is entirely absent, and the only water mentioned is "l'eau potable" in "Babord pour tous" and "Alarme mal calculée." Even "Tribord asiatique," exotic beyond the transatlantic scope of the collection, contains commonplace images of eggs and an alarm clock. As this is one of the rare poems in which the action explicitly takes place on board ship, the banality of its references is especially noteworthy. When "le bateau penche sur tribord," order on this mundane level is restored.

"Bar pour bar fumoir pour fumoir," the final poem in *Le Passager du Transatlantique,* is a text so unlike the others that it stands as a bridge between Péret's Dadaist phase and his Surrealism. Composed of nine paragraph-like divisions, labeled "exercises," which range in length from one to seven lines, this text uses a technique which does not reappear in Péret's work until 1928 with *Le Grand Jeu,* and then only rarely, as for example in "Le Sang et les arrêts" and "As de pique." Lack of punctuation combined with the use of capital letters conveys to each division a continuity and an urgency which are belied by the final line: "Au surplus je ne vois pas pourquoi nous causons de cela." The apparent lack of consistency in the text as a whole is denied: "Passons à un autre exercice et avouons qu'ils ne sont pas variés." They must be the same because they are exercises in logic and "le rocking-chair ou la logique ne sort jamais d'un certain espace car il s'endort." Movement in place, which characterizes the image of the collection's title, is thus projected to its end. Instead of examining changes from a mobile point of view as he does in the other texts, in "Bar pour bar fumoir pour fumoir" Péret collects images of minute movements which define objects in situation and attempts to discover the wider order in which they participate. The action which takes place in the largest space in this text is the breaking of a table in the third section: "Brise une table et dis que c'est l'œuvre de ton ami." However, the actual execution of this motion is placed in doubt, and others are much smaller: "votre café fait des petits bonds saccadés," "tournez la tête," and "vous sentez vos cheveux pousser" are examples. An eagerly awaited apocalypse is defined by a generalization of movement: "Alors vous allez voir que tout sera changé les objets animés auront des mouvements convulsifs votre fourchette dansera devant vous le fox-trott du jour."

The extension of the designation "objets animés" to things like the fork, which were previously immobile, is generally characteristic of Péret's work. Breton notes that "il n'est pas jusqu'aux objets manufacturés que les objets naturels ne réussissent à entrainer dans leur sarabande." [27] The agitation described does not, however, denote the end of the world: "tout brûle et tout s'éteint l'éternité n'est pas de ce côté." Péret's new world is different; it is an "ici" where human logic fails: "ce serait peut-être vrai ailleurs mais ici où les clowns sont des banquiers et des évêques qui ont la peau dure et les souvenirs amers." In this sense, the ship, detached from shore and floating freely, is in accord with a more generalized phenomenon; the transience of the passenger and the ship in their media is reflected in the fact that "l'éternité n'est pas de ce côté." Eternity will be found when the poetic optic is focused on specific events, not on the wide, diffuse movements of a ship, a train or an explosion. "Bar pour bar fumoir pour fumoir" expresses larger move-

<hr>

[27] André Breton, *Anthologie de l'humour noir* (Paris: Pauvert, 1966), p. 385.

ment in temporal rather than spatial terms by referring to borders and blocks in time, for example "XIᵉ siècle," "jeunesse," "l'éternité," "l'équinoxe du printemps" and, more indefinitely, "il est temps" and "ce sera le jour." Allusions to death in this text and "Alarme mal calculée" also depict man within time. Time is no longer an exclusively human system, and movement in relation to time becomes a form of interaction with external realms of signification.

Le Passager du Transatlantique is best approached as an aspect of Péret's total poetic work rather than as an atypical caprice of his youth. Between this collection and those that follow, there are bases for comparison which help to delineate its place as part of the corpus to which it belongs. A highly positive valuation (if not an accident of copyright) is implied by the inclusion of *Le Passager du Transatlantique* with *Le Grand Jeu* in Gallimard's only publication of Péret's work.[28] The texts which comprise *Le Passager du Transatlantique* are quite brief in comparison with Péret's later works; of the sixteen poems collected in this volume, only "Bar pour bar fumoir pour fumoir" exceeds a single page in length and the others are considerably shorter, "comme autant de pistes brusquement coupés."[29] Unity is achieved in the volume as a whole through the use of titles which join disparate texts in a vision of ocean travel.

In contrast, *Immortelle Maladie* and *Dormir dormir dans les pierres,* Péret's second and third collections, are presented as series of intrinsically linked texts separated by Arabic numerals. The Surrealist objection to long poems was still in force at the time of their composition; they can be treated as separate entities which stand alone.[30] When Péret moves from the transience of the passenger to the permanence of the immortal illness, his style changes. The six texts in *Immortelle Maladie* are quite short, but they form

[28] Benjamin Péret, *Le Grand Jeu, suivi du Passager du transatlantique* (Paris: Gallimard, 1969). Gallimard holds the copyright to this collection, which it originally published in 1928.

[29] Bédouin, p. 43.

[30] Bédouin includes the first and fourth sections of *Immortelle Maladie* along with the second and fourth sections of *Dormir dormir dans les pierres* in his selection of texts (pp. 79-86). *Dormir dormir dans les pierres* is more than four times as long as *Immortelle Maladie,* and its five texts are less uniform in length than the six which make up the earlier collection.

a coherent whole of seventy-six lines, a continuous effort not evident in *Le Passager du Transatlantique*. The word-play on which four of the texts in the 1921 collection are based is entirely abandoned; only the third poem, "Le doigt dans l'eau," [31] in *Immortelle Maladie* uses the folksong tone which characterizes many of the earlier poems. Vocabulary is expanded and sentence structure is more complex. The use of three successive dependent clauses in the *Le Passager du Transatlantique* text "Drapeau des mains sales" is prophetic of Péret's future style, which is largely based on such chains of subordination. The longest sentence in the early collection appears in the last nine lines of "Petit Hublot de mon cœur," but its structure is paratactic, using only two coordinating conjunctions. In all the poems except the third in *Immortelle Maladie,* sentences which extend over more than one line include at least one coordinating or subordinating conjunction.

Le Passager du Transatlantique relies principally on human imagery and is limited to the surface of land or sea; contact with height or depth is marked by fear: "Babord prenez garde aux montagnes," or by some other pejorative context: "Avec la mesure d'une peine progressive / nous atteindrons quelque sommet un jour ou l'autre." The poet is bound to his human condition and to living in wakefulness; hence, the dream of "Chaufferie mélancholique" and death in "Alarme mal calculée" and "Bar pour bar fumoir pour fumoir" are both viewed as dangerous alternatives to his current state. Psychological substrata are limited to memory and ethnic consciousness; the range of the optic is physically circumscribed. In *Immortelle Maladie,* on the other hand, he is no longer traveling on the surface; rather he moves within natural cycles. Trading his restricted human viewpoint for one based in the elements, he finds the capacity for inserting himself into any point in the changing landscape and achieves poetic consciousness. The "nous" of *Le Passager du Transatlantique* is abandoned for the "je" of the self-conscious poet existing apart from other men. In compensation for this lack of companionship, the hostile physical environment of *Le Passager du Transatlantique* becomes humanized or personified.

Le Passager du Transatlantique is distinguished from later collections by simple syntax, positive valuation of physical movement,

---

[31] The divisions of both collections are untitled; they will be referred to by their first words.

and a specifically human point of view in which anything non-human is antagonistic. The latter characteristic is evident in the following lines from "Babord pour tous": "Mais nous crachons en l'air / et les hirondelles crachent sur nous." The continuity imposed on the poems by their titles contrasts with a diversity which shows the poet to be in a period of experimentation with a variety of styles, from the "poème-conversation" of "Babord pour tous" and the word-play of "Petit Hublot de mon cœur" to the extended metaphysical aphorisms of "Bar pour bar fumoir pour fumoir." This formal plurality is not immediately rejected; *Le Grand Jeu,* with its large number of texts, also displays different styles and techniques, but the majority of its contents is of a length and syntactic complexity more characteristic of Péret's later work.

Le Passager du Transatlantique has several points in common with Péret's later poetry. The folklore tone of texts such as "Petit Hublot de mon cœur" and "En arrière" reappears in the first poem of *Le Grand Jeu,* and occasionally throughout this collection. Its importance is evident in "Les Beautés du ciel et de la terre," a tale of "un grand monsieur aux cheveux sales" and his three accordions, "Mémoires de Benjamin Péret," which is built on incremental narration with many repeated elements and no pronouns, and the final texts in the 1928 collection, "Chanson de la sécheresse," with its refrain, "Va-t-il pleuvoir ciel" and repeated lines beginning "S'il pleut" and "S'il ne pleut pas." Repetition, though never so common in *Le Grand Jeu* and later volumes as in *Le Passager du Transatlantique,* continues to be an important technique. Although word-play never dominates a poetic work by Péret as it does his contributions to *152 Proverbes mis au goût du jour,* it is a constant factor, as for example in "Jésus disait à sa belle-sœur," from *Le Grand Jeu:*

> Nous avons fait le fumier
> pour les fumières
> L'évangile pour le crottin
> et le malin pour la mâtine.

Péret does not reject his Dadaist phase, but rather incorporates it into a Surrealist whole which includes traits which predate his involvement with Dada and appear at an early stage in his tales.

Rather than taking Dada as a model, he uses aspects of it as they appeal to him and rejects others; Dadaist revolt and rejection of traditional poetics become part of Péret's credo, while the denial of language and utter social and political nihilism do not. The process of expansion is evident in several realms. Folktale becomes myth, both in the Surrealist sense and as an attribute of primitive man; repetition becomes the regularity of the creative process, especially in *Histoire naturelle,* where elements, animals, vegetables, and minerals appears with scientific order; and the interplay between words becomes the material encounter of objects and phenomena. The physical situation of the poet is no longer the spatially limited, transient ship on which the transatlantic passenger travel; it has grown to encompass the universe.

B. THE SURREALIST VISION

Like the other future Surrealists, Péret was ready to break with Dada by the fall of 1922. If his poetic production of the Dadaist period is any indication, his adherence to the movement was always qualified by personal and ideological differences with its members.[32] Gershman indicates that the split between followers of Breton and Tzara began as early as 1921[33] and dates the definite break from the "Soirée du *Cœur à barbe*" of July 6, 1923.[34] Péret gives his reasons for leaving Tzara and his cohorts in a text in *Littérature* of October, 1922. The fourth among the eleven reasons enumerated is especially revealing in view of Péret's own contribution to the movement:

> La grande séduction qui se dégageait des idées apportées par Dada, fit qu'on se satisfit d'elles sans chercher mieux. De là vint, rapidement, une impossibilité de transformation et la mort de Dada.[35]

---

[32] As Bédouin states, "Péret, tout comme Breton, comme Aragon et comme Eluard, était loin d'adhérer sans réserve à Dada" (p. 27).

[33] Gershman, p. 142.

[34] *Ibid.,* p. 83.

[35] Benjamin Péret, "A travers mes yeux," *Littérature,* nouvelle série 5 (1 October 1922), 13.

The title of this text, "A travers mes yeux," indicates that Péret recognizes the importance of his new vision to his own and the group's future. Dissatisfaction with Dada is, for Péret, a corollary of his unwillingness to become self-satisfied. The poet is still characterized by his motion: "Demain, je serai encore prêt à sauter dans la voiture de mon voisin s'il se dispose à prendre une direction autre que la mienne."[36] This capacity for *disponibilité* means that the poet and his work can continue their existence to the extent that they are able to change. The works which follow *Le Passager du Transatlantique* are consistent with these principles in that they differ from the early collection and among themselves while they do not follow any linear evolution.

The works of Péret's early Surrealist period, however, share a unity of tone and vocabulary which sets them apart from the collections that precede and follow them. *Immortelle Maladie,* published in 1924, is Péret's first volume of poetry which appears within the new movement. In view of the unavoidable delays between writing and publication, it seems probable that *Immortelle Maladie* was written at the same time as the "Premier Manifeste du surréalisme," or even earlier. The document which defines and illustrates Surrealism was in a sense a collaborative work, and Péret undoubtedly contributed to the formulation of its principles. *Immortelle Maladie* is also contemporary with the opening issue of *La Révolution Surréaliste,* the first explicitly Surrealist review; the first three numbers were co-edited by Péret and Pierre Naville. From the fourth issue onward, Breton took charge of *La Révolution Surréaliste,* but Péret continued in close collaboration with the writing and editing of the review as with succeeding Surrealist publications.[37] Gershman notes that after the change in direction of *La Révolution Surréaliste,* the change in orientation, despite Breton's disclaimers, was patently in the direction of literature and away from the artistic and intellectual isolation of the earlier numbers.[38] Breton himself notes that the issues of *La Révolution Sur-*

---

[36] *Ibid.*

[37] According to Gershman (*A Bibliography of the Surrealist Revolution in France,* p. 52), Artaud was the editor of the third number of *La Révolution Surréaliste.*

[38] Gershman, p. 54.

réaliste for which Péret served as editor "ne comportent pas de poèmes, alors que les textes automatiques y foisonnent." [39]

In 1923 and 1924, Péret's production is still principally in the form of prose: six tales, including the long "Il était une boulangère" (published in 1925), are from this period, along with two book-length prose works, *Mort aux vaches et au champ d'honneur* (dated 1922-3) and *La Brebis galante* (dated 1924). This is also the "époque des sommeils," in which Péret played an important part: according to Breton, "Péret s'endort au cours des séances suivantes et tient des propos d'un caractère plutôt jovial." [40] *Immortelle Maladie,* appearing in the midst of this Surrealism in non-poetic forms, reaffirms Péret's allegiance to poetry. The close relationship between this volume and the 1926 collection *Dormir dormir dans les pierres* is evidence that the mutual concerns of the two volumes were of enduring importance for Péret as a poet despite the diffusion of his activity in the years that separate them. His optic on the world is that of a poet, and all other Surrealist practice is integrated into the ruling concept of poetry as active as well as literary endeavor.

The elemental vision of *Immortelle Maladie* and *Dormir dormir dans les pierres* is first expressed in images which equate human death with the insertion of man into natural cycles. The death of Dada was, for Péret, due to its inability to transform itself, but after human death in his poetry a new sequence of changes is opened. Historically this is true of Dada in its posthumous dispersion into such diverse areas as English poetry, advertising and the animated cartoon. In *Immortelle Maladie,* death is viewed as an inevitable form of change, a natural event, but fear of death and its concomitant loss of human identity are also acceptable. This revolutionary attitude toward death is, as Jean-Christophe Bailly notes, "gênant parce qu'il est l'irruption du sens dans l'univers ordonné des structures." [41] The Christian view of death, defined by Péret as separating man from nature by situating existence after death in another realm, [42] is countered in this collection with a

---

[39] Quoted in Courtot, p. 18.
[40] *Ibid.,* p. 17.
[41] Jean-Christophe Bailly, *Au-delà du langage* (Paris: Losfeld, 1971), p. 25.
[42] An example of this rejected attitude toward the relationship between life and death appears in "Bar pour bar fumoir pour fumoir": "Mais vous quand aurez-vous votre jour C'est tout simple mourez d'abord."

positive attempt to create a poetic myth which would make awareness of death a part of life; afterlife is significant in the incorporation
of the human body into nature.

"Sur la colline," the first text in *Immortelle Maladie,* presents
death as a physical integration into the earth. The landscape is
humanized: "Sur la colline qui n'était inspirée que par les lèvres
peintes." But the explicitly human is dead: "les yeux blancs s'ouvrent à la lumière de la fête / et la respiration va mourir de sa
belle mort." The turned, whitened eyes of the dead person open
upon a new stage in his corporeal existence, a "fête" which is
neither an afterlife in which he remains intact or is resurrected, nor
a horrible hell. Breathing, a purely physical function, ends in beauty,
while the mental process involved in vision becomes part of the
new state. The humanization of the landscape continues to be reas-
suring: "On dirait qu'une main / se pose sur l'autre versant de la
colline." Man is part of nature, not superior to it, as Breton suggests: "Je crois qu'il ne serait pas mauvais, pour commencer, de
convaincre l'homme qu'il n'est pas forcément, comme il s'en targue,
le *roi* de la création." [43] This suggestion, made in 1942, is one of
several instances in which Péret anticipates and executes the desires
of his close friend and leader before they are enunciated. Even the
sound of the wind, identified with human voices, is integrated into
the unalienated nature of "Sur la colline." Interaction between man
and nature as it takes place in the exchange of human life for the
natural personification is a self-sufficient cycle. The intervention of
God is superfluous: "C'était du ciel de Dieu que tombaient les
paroles absurdes." The presence of the dead in natural rather than
human company may make them inaccessible to living people, but
dreams and poetry are means of communicating with them.

In "Où est-il," the second text in *Immortelle Maladie,* the possibility of interchange between living and dead is set forth:

Où est-il
Parmi les étoiles accroupies
ou les minéraux inconnus . . .
Si je rêvais je pourrais répondre
Il descend du bec de la colombe

---

[43] André Breton, "Prolégomènes à un troisième manifeste du surréalisme
ou non," *Manifestes du surréalisme* (Paris: Pauvert, 1962), p. 348.

ou bien
Il monte les escaliers de neige qui conduisent aux roches soupirantes
les grands escaliers bénévoles
où vivent les poètes en caoutchouc.

The ability of the dead to exist in the high and the low, in vegetable
and mineral states is also attained by "les poètes en caoutchouc"
whose spiritual flexibility is conveyed by the image of rubber already
used in the *Le Passager du Transatlantique* text, "Emigrant des
mille milles." In "Courir sur un miroir," the fourth text of *Immortelle Maladie,* this poetic capacity is perceived as a duty to the
moribund: "Si je passais ils resteraient éternellement moribonds /
C'est pourquoi il faut que je défile devant eux / avec mon ombre."
This is an immediate need; its urgency is emphasized by reference
to the continual change in the world: "Mais le vent aura chassé
les êtres de leur élément naturel / Avant que je passe." The universality of death is finally summarized in the first line of the sixth
and last text: "Il s'agit de la pluie qui a mouillé les os les plus
rebelles." Again, an image of death is presented in interaction with
dream, and both are linked to natural forces:

La pluie des os atteindra un jour les oreilles les plus rebelles
et l'on saura que se prépare la mue des fruits
leur départ sur les ailes des monstres aux yeux de quartz
qui pleurent devant le soleil levant.

Night, with its capacity for creating harmony between animal (monsters), vegetable (fruits), and mineral (quartz), is the poetic place of
election in both *Immortelle Maladie* and *Dormir dormir dans les
pierres,* and its passage is deeply regretted.

The close alliance between the human and the non-human appears in "Le Doigt dans l'eau," the third *Immortelle Maladie* text,
as a synthesis of human growth with change effected upon the
earth. The naïve folksong tone of the first lines of this text recalls
the use of this simplicity in *Le Passager du Transatlantique*:

Le doigt dans l'eau
les chanteurs aimant chanter
ont l'air d'une fleur fanée
Fleur fanée cœur aimée
dit l'autre.

Already, man in the role of the singer with his finger in the water is within a natural element. When he comes into contact with his environment, he change it, and these changes are immediately evoked visually by coal dust and aurally by the sound of shovels:

> Mais toi poussière de charbon
> tu n'es pas aimée
> et tu t'envoles vers le soleil
>
> Nous grandissons dans le bruit des coups de pioche
> Que fait-on à la terre.

The ascending movement of coal dust is denied its usual positive connotations because it interferes with another natural process, the necessary giving of light by the sun. Human growth is similarly vitiated by the destruction wrought by human implements on the earth. The interplay of ascent and descent obliterates any progressive net gain in height, and the remainder of the poem takes place on a horizontal plane. In the world of emotional awakening already introduced by the words of the singer's companion, love has negative connotations. The last two divisions of the poem show the masculine "nous" as they are introduced to love by "la jeune fille aux oranges." While her fruit links her with nature, she is also affected by the birth of love and expresses her anxiety as she "aspire l'air à pleins poumons et pleure"; this reaction is approved by the poet: "il faut pleurer sans cesse." Finally, her future integration into the non-human is projected through the medium of love: "tu connaîtras l'amour des cordes de pendu / tu connaîtras l'amour et la caresse des plumes." The first of these images reappears in "J'existe sous le sceau des vignes," the third text of *Dormir dormir dans les pierres,* where it is also connected with love and is one half of a pair:

> C'est aussi la rencontre au moment où le flux devient reflux
> d'une corde à nœuds et d'un pendu
> Et la corde dit au pendu
> O toi échappé de mes nœuds que me veux-tu ...
> toi qui as fait la corde et les nœuds
> pourquoi m'as-tu quitté.

The hangman's rope, a concretization of human death, is analogically capable of love, another human phenomenon. Feathers also participate in the imagery of *Dormir dormir dans les pierres*; like the rope, they are humanized, as in the first text, "De la corne du sommeil," where reference is made to the "plumes de mes oreilles."

Like *Le Passager du Transatlantique, Immortelle Maladie* ends on a line of gratuity and lack of literary intent. Despite the presence of the poetic "je," the poet is not trying to produce a masterpiece. The final "pour moi je demande que le ciel s'en aille avec les nuages / avant que je devienne tout à fait imbécile" may be compared with the last line of "Bar pour bar fumoir pour fumoir": "Au surplus je ne vois pas pourquoi nous causons de tout cela." The threat of mental collapse, already broached in *Le Passager du Transatlantique* in the text "Chaufferie mélancholique," gives the poetic stance adopted in *Immortelle Maladie* a certain ambiguity. After delineating the means (namely death, poetry, dream and love) by which the poet enters into harmony with the non-human, Péret expresses a need to maintain his faculties in order not to become "imbécile." The exchange of forces between man and nature must take place on a basis of equality; man must not allow himself to become passively absorbed into the non-rational.

But Péret is not anti-human in either *Immortelle Maladie* or *Dormir dormir dans les pierres*; rather, he seeks a reinstatement of the human within the natural similar to that found in primitive myth. Throughout *Immortelle Maladie,* manifestations of lucidity stand in evidence of the poet's continued control. Every text contains either a reference to sight or mention of a light source, or both. [44] The poet's power lies in his capacity for experimentations with possibilities outside the bounds of rationality. The fourth and fifth texts are especially pertinent to this aspect of poetic activity, for they show the poet attempting to become closer to the elemental process in order to participate actively in the course of change. Before fulfilling his duty to the moribund in the fourth text, "Courir sur un miroir," the speaker presents his current desires: "Courir sur un miroir comme un aveugle / et chanter dans l'oreille des dieux." Interchanging sense perceptions by substituting touch for the sight

---

[44] Light sources appear in "Sur la colline," "Où est-il," "Le doigt dans l'eau," and "Il s'agit de la pluie"; they include "lumière," "étoiles," and "soleil." References to sight are found in "Sur la colline," "Courir sur un miroir," "Montrez-moi le savant," and "Il s'agit de la pluie"; among these are "nous verrons," "miroir," "montrez-moi," and "regards."

usually associated with a mirror is an action equal in audacity to direct communication with supernatural powers, and both assert mythic status. The necromancy which is present as an urgent need in the remainder of "Courir sur un miroir" is also described as an alternative chosen above another in the fifth text:

> Montrez-moi le savant amoureux de la femme-cyclope
> que j'en fasse mon égal
> après pourra venir l'ère des fleurs galantes
> des squelettes patriotiques
> et des catastrophes sans importance
> je m'en fous
> J'irai près des pyramides . . .
> et je danserai devant ces fameuses pyramides
> jusqu'à ce qu'elles disparaissent.

Once the poet has proved himself the equal of the highly rational scientist on the plane of mythical love, he will have passed a self-imposed test and the world can, as the ironic examples indicate, degenerate. Pyramids, monuments to the dead which perpetuate a past state, are diametrically opposed to the organic attitude toward human change advocated in the first text, "Sur la colline." By dancing to perform a ritual effacement of the pyramids he is an agent of destiny, for the pyramids, despite their endurance, are "destinées à disparaître." Having established himself in one of the closely-linked realms of love and death, the poet can perform magic in the other.

With the "soleil levant" of the final text comes the dispersion of the elements of these dark forces into the waking world: "Les poissons de chaleur s'envoleront / à l'équinoxe d'automne." Fish, inhabitants of marine depths, are released into the air at a time when day and night are equal, but night is about to dominate. The integration of elements of these depths into every part of life is expressed numerically: [45] "et s'arrêteront à toutes les villes enchantées par les nombres élevés / les fractions infinitésimales." The last line of this text before the final coda is a synthesis of lucidity and death which, by its use of female personae, includes the theme

---

[45] The importance of numbers for Péret is evident in several texts in *Le Grand Jeu,* most strikingly in "26 Points à préciser," which is composed of increasingly complicated formulae which define aspects of human existence.

of desire: "et les regards des femmes qu'enveloppent les fleuves débordantes." Death by drowning, an immediate means of human integration with an element, has already been evoked in the first text:

> Maintenant partons pour la maison des algues
> où nous verrons les éléments couverts par leur ombre
> s'avancer comme des criminels
> pour détruire le passager de demain
> ô mon amie ma chère peur.

Fear, like the open eyes of the drowning woman, is an expression of retained human consciousness within death itself.

The narrator of the prose text *Mort aux vaches et au champ d'honneur* (dated "Hiver, 1922-3") also maintains his lucidity through changes in his corporeal state. In Chapter One, "A pieds joints," he travels through natural states on a journey like that of Alice in Wonderland, and he "dies" twice within four pages. The first instance is triggered by the narrator's eating a bunch of grapes; immediately afterward, he feels endowed with superhuman strength and sets forth on a long, shadowy journey at the end of which he finds himself before a subterranean mirror. However,

> ... ce n'était pas mon image qui y était reflétée, mais une sorte de pluie lumineuse qui, sur la glace, occupait une surface deux fois moindre que mon image normale. Je me retournai machinalement, supposant que la pluie lumineuse tombait derrière moi.... Je tombai des heures durant. J'avais naturellement fait le sacrifice de ma vie, n'imaginant pas un instant que je puisse revenir de cette aventure. [46]

In the liquid state, he survives the fall and exists for some time, like natural moisture, under the earth. He regains human form only to lose it again; the narration of this event shares the dispassionate tone of the preceding passage:

> Je me sentais en danger de mort.... une explosion formidable se produisit et j'éprouvais immédiatement une sen-

---

[46] Benjamin Péret, *Mort aux vaches et au champ d'honneur* (Paris: Losfeld, 1967), p. 15.

sation de froid glacial. Un liquide vert s'échappa abondam-
ment de mes yeux — de la chlorophyle, sans doute! —
... je m'élevais dans l'atmosphère d'autant plus vite qu'il
coulait plus de liquide. Soudain je me sentis déboucher en
plein soleil.... J'étais dans un immense jardin. [47]

No break occurs in the narrator's consciousness, as he feels in
sequence the heat and fatigue of battle, the explosion and chill of
death, transformation into a liquid state, and arboreal growth. His
condition after death is obviously preferable to his previous incarnation as a combattant who clings to life in uncomfortable circumstances. In the first passage, death leads him into the corridors
of the marvelous, while in the second it situates him in an Edenic
garden. These two posthumous settings are aspects of the "fête"
referred to in "Sur la colline" as following death. As Péret states
in his essay "La Nature dévore le progrès et le dépasse," "la mort
n'est qu'une manière d'être temporaire de la vie, masquant un côté
de son prisme pour que la lumière se concentre, plus brillante, sur
les autre faces." [48] The natural process of change by which the human
body becomes part of the non-human is conveyed by the poet, whose
mode of consciousness, unlike that of other men, is analogous with
that of extra-human phenomena. The poetic optic is more effective
than ordinary vision; not only can the poet perceive everything
around himself when conventional vision is blocked, but he can
also see without physical eyes.

The title of *Dormir dormir dans les pierres* makes this 1926
collection continuous with *Immortelle Maladie*. The importance of
sleep is emphasized with the repeated infinitive; it is presented as
physical communion with nature as represented by rock, its most
impenetrable form. To sleep in the rocks is to carry the activity of
the first *Immortelle Maladie* text, "Sur la colline," one step further:
death on the hillside is replaced by an immediate but more temporary
integration into the natural surface. Alcohol, a third means of escape
from rational consciousness, is explicitly mentioned for the first time
in the third text of *Dormir dormir dans les pierres*, which alludes
to wine in its first line: "J'existe sous le sceau des vignes":

---

[47] *Ibid.,* pp. 18-19.
[48] Benjamin Péret, "La nature dévore le progrès et le dépasse," *Minotaure,*
10 (1937), 20-21.

cet alcool qui s'ouvre chaque jour comme un compas
dont les deux pointes marquent le la.

As a readily available means for disturbing waking thought patterns,
alcohol was used by Péret along with other Surrealists, but its extrinsic influence is less frequently relied upon than internal, subconscious stimuli or the inspiration of *le merveilleux quotidien.*

Immortelle Maladie places less emphasis on the poet as a group
member than does *Le Passager du Transatlantique,* but other human
figures are still present in the 1924 volume. [49] They are progres-
sively decorporalized, being reduced to their eyes in the last two
texts, which mention "la femme-cyclope," whose quasi-mythical
identity is a function of her eye, and "les regards de femmes"; the
gaze has metonymically taken the place of the human body. This
elimination of human presence is extended in *Dormir dormir dans
les pierres,* where human interlocutors are almost entirely absent
and a "toi" is more likely to be addressed to a flower or a feather
than to a man or woman. The speaker in these texts is a solitary
figure, alone in a landscape of desert rock, sea, and sky. Only the
third text, "J'existe sous le sceau des vignes," escapes this desolation;
it has a human partner for the speaker: "Esaü lève ta tête et montre
tes cornes semblables à une évasion." But Esau, with his animal-like
skin and deceitful activities, is only nominally human, and even he
is immediately returned to a non-human state:

> Esaü tu es le cornet et les lentilles
> et tu seras ainsi jusqu'à ce que les surfaces lisses
> sentent apparaître les premières rugosités.

A "maîtresse" for the poet appears in the first line of the fourth
text, but she is only a point of comparison and not an active element
of the poem: "Nue nue comme ma maîtresse / la lumière descend

---

[49] The following people are present before human presence is reduced to
eyes in the fourth and fifth texts: in "Sur la colline," "les hommes" and the
dead person on the hill, and later the companion to whom the poet says "par-
tons"; in "Où est-il," "il" and "les poètes"; in "Le Doigt dans l'eau," "les
chanteurs," "nous," and "la jeune fille aux oranges"; and in the first line of
the fourth text, "le savant."

le long de mes os." Human and natural incarnations are latent in one another, and a person can become part of the natural environment in the poetry as well as in *Mort aux vaches et au champ d'honneur*. Human identity can even be extended to encompass the whole visual scope of nature, as in these two passages from the second text, "Soleil route usé":

> Jetez les orties dans le gosier du nègre
> borgne comme seuls savent l'être les nègres
> et le nègre deviendra ortie
> ... ...
> le paysage n'est presque plus qu'une courte paille
> que tu tires
> C'est donc toi fille aux seins de soleil qui seras le paysage.

In the first of these examples, as in the prose text, the metamorphosis is preceded by ingestion, while in the second, it is the result of the operation of chance as integrated with the landscape itself in the form of a short straw.

Despite its length, *Dormir dormir dans les pierres* demonstrates greater unity than *Immortelle Maladie* through the repetition of images at the beginning and end of the collection:

> De la corne du sommeil aux yeux revulsés de soupirs
> il y a place pour une cornemuse bleue
> d'où jaillit le son fatal du réséda fleuri
> ... ...
> A quoi bon la corne gelée qui ne se renversera jamais sur mon
>   amour
> car il est autour de la corne
> comme les pierres autour de la maison.

This passage links *Dormir dormir dans les pierres* with *Immortelle Maladie* by denoting death as the combination of turned eyes and expulsion of breath. Sleep is represented by a horn which evokes the horn of oneiric plenty at the moment when it pours out its abundance in dreams. In the space between dream ("la corne du sommeil") and death ("les yeux revulsés de soupirs"), the poem occurs through an association of the horn of sleep ("corne") with the "muse" of dream. The color blue, which replaces the usual plaid of the bagpipe, is characteristic of Péret's chromatic usage.[50] It is significant that the instrument chosen, apart from its verbal ties with the preceding line, is one of popular rather than orchestral music; the poem as bagpipe does not belong to the realm of literary culture, and its status as an auditory phenomenon, along with its link to death, is reinforced by the "son fatal" mentioned in the third line. The connection of dream with music has been noted in the early text "Je rêve d'une musique indolente et fanée," but the music of *Dormir dormir dans les pierres* has an opposite character; it is energetic and highly-colored, not indolent and faded. Within the first text of *Dormir dormir dans les pierres,* sixty-one lines after the first passage quoted above, the same image returns in its integrity: "Souffle ô corne un azur sombre et verbal"; the sound of the horn has explicitly become language. When the horn appears for the last time in the final lines of the collection, the image includes love, the fourth link in the chain of dream, death and poetry, and love in turn is identified with the "pierres" of the title.

At this point, stone, a non-human aspect of the landscape, and human emotion of love are joined with "comme." Péret uses "comme" frequently to juxtapose two elements which, despite the force with which they are thrown together, retain separate identities that are other possible incarnations of phenomena beyond their present state. Whereas the metaphorical identification of two or more things, as for example in "A quoi bon": "comme l'eau reste vent et le vent éponge," multiplies their status in the poem's present, the indication of similarity through the use of "comme" makes them susceptible to future metamorphosis. In this case, the frustration felt by the poet at his failure to dream of love is resolved by another, even stronger identification in which love appears as the frame of his sleep-horn, an image which is equated with the identity of stones as the structural armature of a house.

As the title of this collection indicates, stones are a dominant element in the landscape of these texts, and they appear at least once in every poem. Aside from the general term "pierre," each text has its own set of minerals; shiny or crystalline substances oc-

---

[50] As Claude Courtot points out, "que dire de ce *bleu* soutenu, plus mâle et plus riche que l'azur mallarméen, qui est comme un vaste lit ouaté sur lequel tous les objects scintillent dans un équilibre vibrant?" (p. 191).

cur most frequently. [51] Despite the vegetable imagery in its first line, "J'existe sous le sceau des vignes" is particularly rich in mineral forms; they include glass, aluminum, iron, and slate. In the fourth and fifth poems, coal appears; as a product of subterranean change, it is remarkably capable of further transformation. Coal thus serves as a metaphor for hidden truth, as in the reference in the fifth text, "A quoi bon," to "les lignes de la main et le charbon qu'elles cachent." The apparent solidity of these elements does not prevent them from becoming involved in the processes of change within the texts, as for example in the fourth, "Nue nue comme ma maîtresse":

> car le charbon chante aujourd'hui
> le charbon chante comme un liquide d'amour
> un liquide aux mouvements de volume
> un liquide de désespoir.

Coal and liquid interact in this sequence; the bulk and darkness of coal give the liquid the qualities of "volume" and "désepoir," while the movement of liquid leads to the attribution of song to the coal.

Wind is also an omnipresent element in the landscape of *Dormir dormir dans les pierres* and appears in every text. As a metaphor for change, wind, already of major importance in *Le Passager du Transatlantique,* is now directly associated with other forms of climatic turbulence, which include hurricane, storm, squall, and tempest; in all of these, moving air is combined with water to create transformations both in and out of the air-water system. "De la corne du sommeil," the first text, contains a sequence on wind in the tenth of its thirteen divisions which is exemplary in this respect:

> Assise flamberge assis vents
> la mer se décolore et le rouge domine
> le rouge de mon cœur est le vent des îles
> le vent qui m'enveloppe comme un insecte
> le vent qui me salue de loin
> le vent qui écoute le bruit de ses pas décroître sur mon ombre
> si pâle qu'on dirait un poisson volant.

---

[51] Mirrors and glass appear in "Sur la colline," "Où est-il," "Le doigt dans l'eau," and "Il s'agit de la pluie"; quartz, salt, and crystal are mentioned in all of these except "Le doigt dans l'eau."

Wind, sea, the color red, and the poet interact in analogical chains between the invocation "assise flamberge," which creates a pause in the turbulence preceding this passage, and the flying fish which act as a point of exit. The presence of wind is responsible for a series of apparent paradoxes which it resolves through a process of interaction. The statement "la mer se décolore et le rouge domine" is clarified in the next line by the identification of the sea with human blood, which is in turn made possible by the equilibration of this liquid with the island wind. The wind-blood-sea element is both near and far in the two lines that follow, present at once as chrysalid and as distant response. The sound of the wind, with reference to the third line, becomes that of steps which are equated with human heartbeats. A further transformation of color is found in the pale shadow: compared with a flying fish, it presents a final synthesis of wind and water in which animal life is included. Similar associations appear in the poem "As de pique" from *Le Grand Jeu*: "le vent le cœur humain la colonne de mercure." Interior and exterior landscapes are thus equated through metaphors of movement based on the incessant wind.

The creation of new phenomena through the metaphorical fusion of two existing disparate elements is one of the most common poetic devices in all of Péret's Surrealist work, and its operation is easily observed in *Dormir dormir dans les pierres*. As Breton notes, "Le compartiment étroit qui s'oppose à toute nouvelle entrée en relation des éléments significateurs figés aujourd'hui dans les mots accroît sans cesse la zone d'opacité qui aliène l'homme de la nature et de lui-même. C'est ici que Benjamin Péret intervient en libérateur." [52] The freedom of interaction which characterizes the phenomenal world must be reproduced in a verbal system that purports to deal with this world. The dialectic of objects and concepts first appears in "De la corne du sommeil" in the form of a hypothesis: "Si la justice naît de la rencontre des raisins et d'une corbeille / les tuiles carresseront les sages noyés dans le désert." In the following division, it is even clearer: "Si l'amour naît de la projection d'une groseille dans le bec d'un cygne / j'aime." Each of these two pairs is composed of a fruit and a cone-shaped receptacle, and their similarity could not be accidental in view of the Surrealist equation

---

[52] Breton, *Anthologie de l'humour noir,* pp. 384-85.

of love with justice. Poetic synthesis may be incomplete or fail to produce the expected result; Péret does not find any two elements automatically compatible:

A quoi bon mon torpilleur et mon cauchemar se confondent
dans une goutte d'eau qui tombe perpétuellement sous mon crâne
et jamais ne fera un lac ni un ruisseau
car c'est l'inverse que je vois.

Péret's creation is a new world which liberates every aspect of reality from the limits placed upon it by ordinary speech.

Transformation of an image through the intervention of a catalyst is another common structure of change in *Dormir dormir dans les pierres*. A variety of catalytic elements are often present, and they create a network of possibilities, as in these two examples from "De la corne du sommeil":

Telle plume qui pâlit sera verte demain
si l'ouragan lui dévoile son destin
Et telle plume qui disparaît comme un ABCD
se retrouve au printemps sur la tête des cieux
... ...
car il part et revient comme une feuille
car il est bleu
car il est rouge
suivant que ton regard se fixe ou s'égare comme un drapeau.

An example of catalytic creation which fails to operate is explained in the second text, "Soleil route usé":

Tous les tentacules n'arriveront jamais à transformer le
ciel en mains
car le ciel s'ouvre comme une huître
et les mains ne savent que se fermer sur les poutres des mers.

Tentacles, despite their linking properties, cannot change the open form of the sky into the closed form of hands; this negative illustration shows that when the process functions, it is for an intrinsic poetic reason. Openness is maintained when a plurality of possible directions for change is indicated.

The greatest agent for change in *Dormir dormir dans les pierres* is sleep itself, and its importance is often made explicit, as in the third poem, "J'existe sous le sceau des vignes":

Car ici tout dort
et le sommeil de l'air est propice à la naissance des montagnes
la plus légère brise suffit pour qu'elles apparaissent dans le
    creux de ma main
accompagnées de tous leurs attributs.

Dream becomes an element in a new process: "à quoi bon mon torpilleur et mon cauchemar se confondent." In the nocturnal atmosphere, chance shows its power in unresolved encounters which are in turn related to the internal operations of the poet as a physical creature:

> car mon sang ce soir
> ce soir comme toujours
> n'est ni moins ni plus beau que le plus brutal hasard
> celui qui provoque le rencontre dans l'escalier de bouteilles
> d'une orange et d'un porte-monnaie.

In "Nue nue comme ma maîtresse," these encounters are elevated to their purest state according to an absolute simile recalling Lautréamont which links them through "comme" with beauty itself: "belle comme un trou dans une vitre / belle comme la rencontre imprévue d'une cataracte et d'une bouteille." The final lines of this text emphasize the intrinsic exchange between juxtaposed objects which smile at one another:

> comme sourient les nuages aux miracles
> comme sourient les liquides aux enfants
> comme sourient les traits aux points.

The accumulation of "comme" leads to an ectasy of analogy. An ultimate synthesis by melting is proposed in the fifth text, "A quoi bon," making this separation futile and closing the space of greeting:

> A quoi bon
> les saluts des interstices qui séparent la chair des arbres
> si les arbres s'effondrent dans l'océan des talons
> comme s'effondrent mes yeux au passage de midi.

Dream and drink are no longer necessary for the perception of change through identification or analogy, for this vision is equally possible in the bright light of noon.

The multidimensional dream-world of *Dormir dormir dans les pierres* fuses planes in space as well as objects. Images of depth outnumber those of height, which are limited to sky, stars, sun, and moon. The low, dark or hidden is often linked with the elevated, bright, or open, as the following examples show. The easiest way to move from height to depth is along an inclined surface; examples of this junction are "la rencontre dans l'escalier," ("J'existe sous le sceau des vignes") and "la nuit roule perpétuellement sur la pente du poison" ("A quoi bon"). Vertical movement of solid objects is another possibility, as in "la chute des feuilles" ("Nue nue comme ma maîtresse") and "une longue barre de cuivre se dressera comme une flamme" ("Soleil route usé"). The movement of water in its various forms takes place on many planes: "vous qui descendez et montez comme le dégel" ("Nue nue"); "elle s'évapore trop vite" ("A quoi bon"). Solid elements which are characterized by their height or depth may insert themselves into other dimensions: "que le charbon est beau sur les routes tournesol" ("Nue nue"); "les germes des astres dans le sillage des végétations obscures" ("Nue nue"); or this insertion may be attempted and fail: "les canaux dont les berges tentent vainement de saluer les nuages" ("Soleil route usé"). Finally, images can combine the high and the low, presenting them as a single unit, as in "le soleil des caves" ("J'existe sous le sceau des vignes") and "les corbeaux ont des lueurs d'église et se noient tous les soirs dans les égouts de dieu" ("Soleil route usé"). Confusion of dimensions occurs in the space of mirror reflections which are either evident, like "les gares aux gestes de miroir," or occult, like the "miroir que nul ne découvrit" in the first text, "De la corne du sommeil." Although the mirror emphasizes the speaker's solitude, it can be the site of a rare appearance of human flesh, which serves as a mirror, reversing the customary order of reflection and reflector: "reflet de la peau si douce qu'on voudrait s'y mirer ("De la corne du sommeil"); "vous dont la nudité reflète des miroirs" ("Nue nue"). Physical laws and the geometrical dimensions of the world are no longer sacrosanct; the givens are gainsaid, resulting in the voiding of the entire body of conclusions.

Although human life is nearly absent in the landscape of these poems, plant life is abundant and is not limited to desert flora. The *réséda* or marguerite, originally a desert flower, is the central image of the first three divisions of the thirteen-part "De la corne du sommeil." This humble flower is elevated to quasi-mythical status when it is associated with human life, the sky, various forms of water, and the wind. Other flowers are equally diverse in their implications: the water-lily is presented as the vegetable aspect of the early morning ("qui nous conduit au petit jour / porteur de nénuphars et semeur de colliers") and the acacia is humanized in the phrase "les malheurs des acacias." Grass, thistles, seeds, and grain also appear, but fruits are present in greater number, including cherries, gooseberries, oranges and grapes. These types of vegetable life are especially susceptible to humanization because they are edible. They are given anthropomorphic associations in the poetry: cherries become red blood cells, gooseberries are half of the synthesis which gives rise to love, an orange is similarly associated with a coinpurse, and the grapevine is the seal of the poet's existence in the third text, "J'existe sous le sceau des vignes." Trees and leaves also appear; the single species designated is the willow, a tree which connects air, water and earth.

The quadruple thematic network of dream, death, love, and poetry in *Immortelle Maladie* and *Dormir dormir dans les pierres* persists throughout Péret's work. The superimposition of these four visions in shifting proportion defines his optic. Death, which is specifically characteristic of these collections, is an important element of *Le Grand Jeu* as part of the eschatological game in which the borders of life, death, and non-human forms of existence are in a continual state of flux. [53] Titles such as "Les Morts et leurs enfants," "Le pirate me dévore," "Cou tordu," and "Les ossements s'agitent" attest to this continuing concern with death although not all these texts refer to the dead or dying other than in their titles. Occasional lines recall *Immortelle Maladie,* as for example in "Cou tordu": "et son appel ressuscitera la grande muraille des têtes coupées," but more often the physiological aspects of the disintegrating human body are evoked. Two texts, "Par le trou de la serrure" and "Preuve formelle," are detailed treatments of the subject of death and its

---

[53] Two other works by Surrealists in the year 1924 reflect a preoccupation with death. Paul Eluard's *Mourir de ne pas mourir* resembles *Immortelle Maladie* in that its title juxtaposes continuity with death. Robert Desnos' *La Liberté ou l'amour!,* which was not published until 1927, begins with the following note: "Robert Desnos / Né à Paris le 4 juillet 1900 / Décédé à Paris le 13 décembre 1924 / jour où il écrit ces lignes."

redefinition. The marvelous as a sequel to death, a suggestion presented in the first text of *Immortelle Maladie,* appears in "Par le trou de la serrure." In the earlier poem, dead eyes open, while in the later one, a dead head rises:

> Lève la tête et fais le mort
> Quand tu t'en iras les pieds devant
> les barreaux de la cage auront des ailes légères.

Also comparable with "Sur la colline" is the equation of breathing with life, and its ambiguous appearance:

> Les grands arbres seront morts
> et les seins suspendus à leurs branches
> se soulèveront régulièrement pour signifier leur sommeil.

Death is finally, as in the earlier collection, communion with animal and vegetable states, "comme on meurt blessé au coin d'un bois / et surveillé par les grands papillons blancs chemises des herbes": "Preuve formelle" bears a close resemblance to the fifth text of *Immortelle Maladie;* whereas a poet who has proved himself through a trial in mythical love can make pyramids vanish, in "Preuve formelle," the passage of a test gives access to super-human powers:

> Sais-tu mourir sans la permission du nageur
> si tu réponds oui
> tu es l'homme annoncé par la loi.

The poet's capacity to pass between the worlds of the everyday and the mythical is guaranteed by his status as "le savant démoniaque qui changera le monde en filet de sang."

Other interlocking themes of *Immortelle Maladie* and *Dormir dormir dans les pierres* are also common in the later texts. Several works are specifically devoted to the exploration and definition of love as *l'amour sublime;* they include *Je sublime* (1936), *Un point c'est tout* (1946), and the long poem "A garder précieusement" (1948). The *Anthologie de l'amour sublime* (1956) is an extensive collection of passages from other authors which illustrate Péret's theory of love; the theory itself is explicated in the introduction to this volume, entitled "Le Noyau de la comète." Dream is increasingly integrated with other facets of the human subconscious, especially with primitive thought, in *Air mexicain* (1952) and *Dernier Malheur dernière chance* (1945). In essay form, it is discussed in "La parole est à Péret" (1942), which defines the poet in relation to early and modern society, and in "Le Déshonneur des poètes" (1945).

Poetry becomes increasingly important in Péret's works after the publication of *Dormir dormis dans les pierres*; it is equated with Surrealist expression in general and replaces prose almost entirely as a means for verbal creation. Once Péret's optic has been defined in the early stages of Surrealism, it never changes. Unlike Louis Aragon, Paul Eluard, and Robert Desnos, Péret never converts from Surrealism to militant realism. No personal or philosophical differences mar his lifelong friendship with André Breton as they truncated the Surrealist experiences of Philippe Soupault, Pierre Naville, and Antonin Artaud. Péret is the single example of unswerving fidelity to the optic of Surrealism as suggested by Breton, and his work represents the most precise delineation of the Surrealist vision.

II

DESIRE AS THE FORCE OF CHANGE

Desire is, for Péret, the motivating force which causes change in the human and natural world, the outreaching of the human spirit to overcome the distance between its wishes and the shape of the world. He explores three facets of this working of desire: first, he presents desire in its most recognizable form as eros; he then expands its definition to show desire as having shaped man's perception of the world; finally, as a consequence of this view of his environment, he exteriorizes desire in social and political areas. Moreover, these three aspects of desire are closely interconnected in Péret's Surrealism, and they all participate in his poetry of change.

For Péret, desire as *l'amour sublime* is both myth and morality; its implications encompass the functioning of desire as world-view and as ideology. *L'amour sublime* is aggressive and defensive; it strikes out against anything which impedes its fulfillment and it shields the true sublime lovers from time and death, the classic enemies of love. As part of the world of movement and transformation, *l'amour sublime* is a continual striving and an ongoing process of sublimation, which, in alchemical terms, implies perpetual change until the ultimate purity is attained. Should this final state of sublimity be reached, change is still present in the image of fire, which is the change and exchange of elements for one another. Thus Péret describes desire as "souverain phénix qui s'engendre indéfiniment de sa propre fin." [1]

---

[1] Benjamin Péret, "La pensée est UNE et indivisible," *VVV*, 4 (1944), 12.

The expression of desire in the work of the poet is the image. Although dream and various emotional states are important intermediaries between the desire and its execution, "l'image est . . . la voie *directe* entre le désir et sa formulation." [2] Poetry, the vehicle for images, is intrinsic to *l'amour sublime* and shares with it the possibility of filling the void left in modern man by the failure of science to satisfy human expectations. Like the poetic image, love arrives in a *coup de foudre,* instantaneous, unmistakeable, and compelling. The filter of experience is the poetic image, "le lieu géométrique de l'amour et de la révolte," [3] as, for example, in the title of the collection "Un point c'est tout." The poet, the image-maker, is broadly defined as anyone capable of seeing "dans la vie quotidienne un outil négligeable s'il n'est pas au service d'une existence visant à l'élévation de l'homme." [4] This attitude endows the poet with gifts for *l'amour sublime* and for its image in poetry when his desire is so great and so sublimated that it makes him want to execute the Rimbaldian command, "changer la vie." As the Marxist critic Frederic Jameson states, "whoever speaks of Surrealism as a meditation on the figures of Desire is also at the same moment describing a technique for the release of the subjectivity from a single, limited desire; . . . and for the satisfaction through such release of all desire, of Desire as a force." [5] The attainment of a state analogous with the final product of alchemical sublimation is the great victory of *l'amour sublime.* Once the conciliation between mind, body, and heart is accomplished, all obstacles to human happiness vanish and the individual trimphs over his natural adversaries, for "l'amour sublime représente d'abord une révolte de l'individu contre la religion et la société, l'une épaulant l'autre." [6] Through its force of desire and its expression in the image, *l'amour sublime* reconciles the Rimbaldian doctrine with the Marxist "transformer le monde"; as Breton puts it, " 'transformer le monde,' a

---

2 Jean-Christophe Bailly, *Au-delà du langage* (Paris: Losfeld, 1971), p. 51.
3 Benjamin Péret, "Le Noyau de la comète," *Anthologie de l'amour sublime,* p. 70.
4 *Ibid.*
5 Frederic Jameson, *Marxism and Form* (Princeton: Princeton University Press, 1971), p. 102.
6 "Le Noyau de la comète," p. 21.

dit Marx: 'changer la vie' a dit Rimbaud: ces deux mots l'ordre n'en font qu'un." [7]

Desire acts upon the external world, and the changes it brings about in its environment facilitate its own fulfillment, which was previously impeded:

> l'amour sublime doit donc livrer un combat tout à fait inégal à la société qui l'écrase. C'est pour quoi ses cris se confondent si souvent avec les gémissements du désespoir. L'amour sublime ne saurait en effet admettre la moindre restriction: *tout ou rien*. [8]

The process of subversion is aided by the Surrealist liberation of erotic desire from service to socially condoned goals. Even the course of time is changed; a series of equidistant markers no longer suffices to account for the lapse between desire and fulfillment, absence and presence. *L'amour sublime* is an aggressive answer to every constriction, even those which are normally accepted as inevitable. In this capacity, it has both destructive and constructive aspects; it is at once "a literary weapon designed to defend the individual at his most intimate from a society become oppressively addicted to routine" and "an illusion capable of both revivifying and liberating." [9] The alchemical metaphor on which the terminology of *l'amour sublime* is based finds an expanded counterpart in the realm of the macrocosmic action of desire. Péret's work in this area includes three long poems, *Dernier malheur dernière chance* (1945), *Toute une vie* (1950), and *Air mexicain* (1952).

A.   "L'Amour sublime": The Heart of Desire

The essay entitled "Le Noyau de la comète," which introduces Péret's *Anthologie de l'amour sublime* (1956), explains and illustrates Péret's theory of love. He is unequivocal in stating the fundamental relationship of l'*amour sublime* to the human and the poetic:

---

[7] André Breton, "Discours au Congrès des Ecrivains," *Manifestes du surréalisme*, p. 285.

[8] "Le Noyau de la comète," p. 24.

[9] Herbert Gershman, *The Surrealist Revolution in France*, p. 5.

> De tout temps, l'amour, même considéré sous son aspect
> le plus élémentaire, a été l'axe de la vie humaine. Il le de-
> meure, qu'il soit source d'exaltation et de lyrisme ou su-
> blimé au plus haut degré jusquà perdre tout contact direct
> avec l'homme pour acquérir une signification cosmique ou
> prendre une valeur mystique. [10]

Love, like everything else in Péret's world, is capable of taking
many forms, but in whatever aspect it appears, it is basic to human
life; it is a *primum materium* for both poetry and the multiform
manifestations of sublimation, for even indirectly it has cosmic and
mystical meaning. As J. H. Matthews notes, "in Péret the marvelous is the image of the universe of desire." [11]

L'amour sublime can be defined in comparison with two kindred
theories of love: Breton's *amour fou,* as delineated in his book of
the same name (1937), and Stendhal's *amour-passion,* which is the
subject of *De l'amour* (1822). Although Péret delves into several
other expressions of love, such as those of Baudelaire and of the
theoreticians of *l'amour courtois,* Breton and Stendhal are the most
relevant. Of Breton, Péret states that "plus que tout autre, André
Breton a reconnu dans l'amour le centre explosif de la vie humaine,
qui a le pouvoir de l'illuminer ou de l'enténébrer, le point de départ et d'arrivée de tout désir, en un mot, l'unique justification de
la vie." [12] Stendhal is the focus for much of the discussion in "Le
Noyau de la comète," and he is praised for having isolated "de
tout ce qui lui faisait ombre une forme de rapports amoureux qu'il
estime supérieure à toute autre." [13] Despite his acknowledged importance as a precursor, Stendhal is not without flaws: "il veut
conférer à son essai un caractère documentaire, voire scientifique,"
and "entend donc n'exposer que des phénomènes vérifiables par
tous." [14] His pseudoscientific emphasis on the physiological aspect
of love lost the author his Romantic audience and restricted his influence. The greatest weakness in *De l'amour,* and that which Péret
seeks to correct in his own work, is that although "c'est l'amour
en 1820, il ne s'interroge jamais sur la nature de cette passion." [15]

---

[10] "Le Noyau de la comète," p. 7.
[11] J. H. Matthews, *Vingt poèmes/Péret's Score* (Paris: Minard, 1965), p. 5.
[12] "Le Noyau de la comète," p. 67.
[13] *Ibid.,* p. 8.
[14] *Ibid.,* p. 11.
[15] *Ibid.,* p. 12.

The differences between *l'amour fou* and *l'amour sublime* are more subtle, as there can be no doubt that the two Surrealists influenced one another in this area as in many others. Their theories are similar in several respects: exclusivity once the real object of love is found, the importance of change and receptivity in the search, and the liberating power of the female force or *anima* in opposition to the over-masculine world. Péret includes three selections from Breton's works in his anthology.[16] Yet the love described by Breton is one in which he can never fully participate; he describes an ideal which is by definition unattainable because it would negate his human essence, which is incapable of sublimity. The following statement by Breton shows the difference between his attitude and that of Péret:

> A se maintenir dans les très hautes sphères où le situent des poèmes tels que . . . presque tout le receuil *Je sublime* de Péret, cet amour porté à l'incandescence tendrait vite à se désincarner.[17]

Claude Courtot emphasizes the degree of faith in so extreme a theory as the basic difference between Breton and Péret: "Breton reste sur la terre . . . bien décidé à saisir, au premier passage, la chevelure de feu qui l'emportera définitivement. Péret, lui, est déjà au noyau de la comète."[18] For Péret, accession to *l'amour sublime* is the final affirmation of man, his divinization, and he sees manifestations of its potential existence in everyday human life; as Mary Ann Caws remarks, he "sees his *amour sublime* as the *reachable* summit of desire."[19] For Breton, on the other hand, the quest endows man with sacred madness, but it is doomed to failure. Although Péret acknowledges that the way to *l'amour sublime* is difficult and that it requires intense devotion, the goal is potentially within the bounds of man's life on earth; like all the appearances of the marvelous, "il revient en quelque sorte à ses sources pour découvrir sa véritable issue et s'inscrire dans les limites de l'existence humaine."[20]

---

[16] Exerpts from *L'Air de l'eau, L'Amour fou* and *Arcane 17* appear in the *Anthologie de l'amour sublime,* pp. 352-58.

[17] André Breton, *Entretiens 1913-1952,* p. 141.

[18] Claude Courtot, *Introduction à la lecture de Benjamin Péret,* p. 88.

[19] Mary Ann Caws, "Péret's *amour sublime* — just another *amour fou?*" *French Review,* 40 (1966), 208.

[20] "Le Noyau de la comète," p. 20.

The distinctive feature of Péret's *amour sublime* is its incorporation of the concept of sublimation. Sublimation is, first, the process of change in which desires manifest themselves in forms
different from those in which they were conceived; by extension,
sublimation is a stimulus to further change, as desire and the marvelous become concrete aspects of human existence. *L'amour sublime,* "à la fois charnel et spirituel,"[21] fuses body and spirit in the
most important of these changes: "le désir se voit chargé d'opérer
cette fusion qui est sa justification dernière." Finally, desire becomes "une voie de transmutation aboutissant à l'accord de la chair
et de l'esprit."[22] Thus in Péret's usage, the process of sublimation
goes much further than the basic definition given it by Breton in
his introduction to Péret's "Trois Cerises et une sardine" in the
Anthologie de l'humour noir. While for Breton, sublimation is simply "l'ascension du subtil en fonction de sa séparation d'avec
l'épais,"[23] for Péret it is the basis for *l'amour sublime,* which "im-
plique le plus haut degré de l'élévation, le point-limite où s'opère
la conjonction de toutes les sublimations, quelque voie qu'elles aient
empruntées, le lieu géométrique où viennent se fondre en un dia-
mant l'esprit, la chair et le cœur."[24] The vocabulary of alchemy
is evident in this sentence in images of height, conjunction and
coalescence, as well as in the word *fondre.* Like the product of
alchemical sublimation, *l'amour sublime* has a concrete existence
resembling that of a magnetic field, affecting everything it touches.

The *Anthologie de l'amour sublime* bases its conclusions on historical examples, most notably those of Baudelaire's love for Madame Sabatier and of Héloïse and Abélard. Creative works are presented in chronological order from Appolonios of Rhodes to Léo
Ferré; each selection illustrates in its own way the quest and attainment of the state of *l'amour sublime.* With this mass of evidence
at hand, Péret detects two varieties of woman capable of respond-
ing to *l'amour sublime*: "la femme-enfant et la sorcière, la première
figurant l'expression optimiste de l'amour, la seconde sa face pessi-
miste."[25] They are complementary figures who incarnate light and

---

[21] *Ibid.,* p. 19.
[22] *Ibid.,* p. 20.
[23] André Breton, *Anthologie de l'humour noir,* p. 384.
[24] "Le Noyau de la comète," p. 9.
[25] *Ibid.,* p. 27. In *Surréalisme et sexualité* (Paris: Gallimard, 1971), Xavière
Gauthier criticizes this division of women into two kinds: "Pour Péret, tout

darkness, future and present, salvation and perdition. Both motivate revolt by accusing present conditions: the child-woman exists in radical contrast with the status quo, while the sorceress represents the negative, desperate aspects of things as they are. Whichever variety of partner is elected, the sublime lovers recognize one another immediately in a *coup de foudre*; their union, unless interfered with by society, will last as long as they live. The chosen woman fills needs which are basically subconscious: "le corps de la femme est l'incarnation du rêve de l'homme. Une femme est belle dans la mesure où elle incarne le plus complètement les secrètes aspirations de l'homme." [26] In order to find one another, prospective lovers must enter a state analogous with that of the Surrealist quest for *le merveilleux quotidien*: "c'est à tâtons qu'ils doivent se chercher, dans un état de vacance qui multiplie les aléas de leur quête." [27] Within the context of sublime love, sexual freedom is the rule, but this freedom is not to be confused with license, which is the reverse of sublimation and thus inimical to *l'amour sublime*. Promiscuity and prostitution are outlawed in the quest, but all forms of sexual expression are sanctioned for those who participate in sublime love. Surrealism gives heterosexual "perversions" high ideological value, viewing "la liberté de pratiquer ces perversions comme une condition essentielle de la mise en question des bases mêmes de la société et du principe de rendement." [28]

L'amour sublime is a major theme in Péret's poetry and tales, and it shares with revolt and myth the distinction of having entire works centered about it. Two important collections, *Je sublime* (1936) and *Un point c'est tout* (1946), are given thematic unity by the concept of *l'amour sublime,* and the long poem "A garder précieusement" (1948) expresses its continuing importance. In contrast with these works, *Les Rouilles encagées* (1929) shows heterosexual relations in their more debased aspects, but they are nonetheless

---

est très simple; la gent féminine se divise exactement en deux types: l'horrible sorcière et la femme-enfant.... Vouloir que la femme reste enfant, c'est vouloir qu'elle reste *dépendante*" (p. 109). On the other hand, it can be said that Péret's two types of women do not include all women, but rather those who are susceptible of becoming the object of his *amour sublime*; in addition, Péret makes very clear the subjective male nature of his account of women.

[26] "Le Noyau de la comète," p. 70.

[27] *Ibid.,* p. 24.

[28] Gauthier, p. 195.

closely linked with poetry and rebellion. In the tales collected in
Le Gigot: sa vie et son œuvre (1950), love and lovers are not
always positive elements: the grotesque couple of Pope Pius VII
and the wife of General Boulanger exemplifies the use of humor
when love is placed in an incongruous context ("Il était une boulangère," 1924), whereas the sympathetic couples in "Une Vie
pleine d'intérêt" (1922) and "Pulchérie veut une auto" (1924) show
the power of love, in the proper hands, to overcome obstacles because of its link with the marvelous. In many other works, span-
ning the length of Péret's career from "Passerelle du commandant"
in *Passager du Transatlantique* to *Histoire naturelle* (1958), human
desire in erotic form is present as part of the variety of experience
upon which Péret draws in the writing of a text.

The sixteen texts of *Je sublime,* written between January and
March of 1935, form the single collection of Péret's poetry which
is most intrinsically connected in title and content with the theory
expounded in "Le Noyau de la comète." The title links the dual
aspects of metamorphosis through sublimation in love because of
its grammatical ambiguity: when *sublime* is taken as an adjective,
"je sublime" denotes the self at the point of mind-body union
where, according to the essay, love is able to "diviniser l'être humain." [29] When *sublime* is understood as the first person singular
of the verb *sublimer,* the title appears as an expression of the
subject's power to transform external phenomena and the shape of
his own desires. The titles of the poems in *Je sublime* are remarkable for their brevity; eleven use only one word, and only one
text, "Le Carré de l'hypoténuse," uses the phrase-length title which
is generally characteristic of Péret's works. The biographical context
in which these texts can be situated is vague; six mention a woman
named Rosa who is neither of Péret's wives and who appears in
neither Bédouin's nor Courtot's account of his life. Her reality is
beyond question, but Péret's natural unwillingness to discuss his
personal affairs prohibits positive identification.

The dominant imagery of the collection is of upward movement
or flight in conflict with various obstacles created by the precarious-
ness of human happiness within a hostile societal context. Five texts

---

[29] "Le Noyau de la comète," p. 20.

begin with images which are based on birds,[30] and every text
contains at least one reference to airborne movement. This element
is stated or reinforced early in ten texts by verbs denoting flight
or ascension,[31] such as "batte de l'aile" or "se jette vers le ciel," or
raising up, as with the verbs "s'élève" and "se dresser." In contrast,
the six remaining texts present the speaker as "meurtri par les
grandes plaques du temps" or surrounded by blackness, in a state
of exhaustion, or needing shelter. Like the comet of the title of
Péret's introduction to the *Anthologie de l'amour sublime,* the world
of *Je sublime* is in constant movement, and motion is the product
of a variety of brief actions. In the poetry of this collection, it is
the end product, the core of the image which persists in the cumulative result. Poetry is thus like the alchemical process of sublimation, in which the intermediate steps are important primarily
as they contribute to the ultimate goal. The following sequence
from "Nébuleuse" illustrates the subordination of transient to permanent images:

> Quand la nuit de beurre sortant de la baratte
> noie les taupes des gares dont les yeux barissent
> et s'agrandissent comme une station de métro qui s'approche
> et se recouvrent de ton image
> qui tourne dans ma tête comme un héliotrope affolé par le mal
>   de mer.

The gyroscopic stability of the woman's image is superior to the
images of passage which finally take on its appearance: "se recou-
vrent de ton image." It is likewise the durable center of the comet
which is emphasized in the essay's title, not the part burnt off in
its passage. Hence, a second interplay, one between the transience
of this movement and its permanent core, is closely connected with
the juxtaposition of upward movement and physical restraint in *Je
sublime.* This interaction is also related to Breton's definition of
beauty in *L'Amour fou* as "l'explosante-fixe," which is, moreover,

---

[30] "Egaré" ("mésange turquoise"), "Homard" ("aigrettes"), "Je ne dors pas"
("vol de corbeaux"), "Clin d'œil" ("perroquets") and "Déraper" ("alouette").

[31] "Egaré" ("batte de l'aile"), "Homard" ("jaillissement"), "Clin d'œil"
("vols ... traversent"), "A quand" ("éclater," "jaillir"), "Aujourd'hui" ("surgis-
se"), "Le Carré de l'hypoténuse" ("s'élève"), "Je" ("se dresse"), "Déraper"
("se jette vers la culotte de gendarme du ciel"), "Ecoute" ("hérissé") and "Je
ne dors pas" ("vol ... t'entoure").

necessary for the presence of beauty: "il ne peut, selon moi, y avoir beauté — beauté convulsive — qu'au prix de l'affirmation du rapport réciproque qui lie l'objet considéré dans son mouvement et dans son repos."[32]

The imagery of "Allo" illustrates Breton's definition: it is built on a sequence of accumulated phrases which are metaphorical equivalents of the woman; each begins with the possessive *mon* and is composed of a permanent element in conflict with forces of change. That which is apparently stable, in the various forms of a castle, an eiderdown quilt or a tomb, is juxtaposed with a force which sets it in motion. In the case of the castle, the force is a flood of Rhine wine, while the eiderdown, being "de paradisiers," threatens to take flight, and the tomb explodes. While most of these images are presented in one line or less, the final image of "Allo" is more extensively developed as an ultimate elaboration of the preceding duality in eschatological terms:

mon revolver de corail dont la bouche m'attire comme l'œil d'un
    puits
scintillant
glacé comme le miroir où tu contemples la fuite des oiseaux-mouches
de ton regard
perdu dans une exposition de blanc encadrée de momies
je t'aime.

The mouth of the revolver, a site of transience for the bullet and, potentially, for human life, is described as being both shimmering and glazed in a fusion of dynamism and stasis which is an image of the movement from life to death. The mirror performs an analogous function in contrast with its reflected images. The object of love is first identified with the frenzied activity of hummingbirds, but this displacement is immediately lost as it is absorbed into a vision of death characterized by mummies. The woman's capacity for synthesizing these two elements is acknowledged by the poet with the final line, "je t'aime."

The texts which make up *Je sublime* are remarkable for their use of color, which not only recalls the color-symbolism of alchemy but which also forms a self-contained network of relationship in the

---

[32] André Breton, *L'Amour fou* (Paris: Gallimard, 1937), p. 13.

collection. Transience has chromatic analogues in two types of color images, that of shimmering or changing color and that of red or burning. The former category includes a wide variety of mineral elements such as opal, mica, mirror or crystal glass and the aerian phenomena of the rainbow and the aurora borealis. These images are manifestations of the irisation of the world transformed by love. Fire is the primary representative of the red or burning category of images; they also include concrete objects such as red eggs and the bloodstone. The latter, along with the multicolor mineral elements mentioned above, achieve the position of synthesis in uniting the transience implied by their color with physical hardness. The burning, purifying flame, apart from its obvious link with alchemy, is a primary image of change in the Heraclitean world, [33] and it is used by Péret as the title for *Feu central* (1947), the collective volume which includes *Je sublime*.

In her study of *Feu central*, Marie-Odile Banquaert identified fire and desire: "le feu érotique est aussi le feu central." [34] For Banquaert, this fire is part of a mythic attempt by Péret to liberate an imprisoned world made static by the death of God. However, further investigation of the use of color in *Je sublime* shows that Banquaert's explication, in which fire is a positive force opposed to the negative darkness, is insufficient. Certainly, in the first text, "Egaré," as Banquaert suggests, "la nuit doit être remontée," [35] and a bird, the turquoise titmouse, is the vehicle. But night is never entirely negative for Péret, to whom dreams are so important, and images incorporating the color black are positive in *Je sublime*: the "iris noirs" and "écume noire" of "Allo" are examples. The text "Je ne dors pas" begins by describing a woman entirely in terms of black:

> Dis-moi reflet de cobalt
> pourquoi le vol de corbeaux qui t'entoure
> comme le charbon étreint le feu qui l'a fait en avalant des
> piments.

---

[33] Phillip Wheelwright, *Heraclitus* (Princeton: Princeton University Press, 1959), p. 59. Fragment 104 develops this idea: "Le Tout est transmuté en feu et le feu en toutes choses" Yves Battistini, "Héraclite," *Trois Contemporains* (Paris: Gallimard, 1955), p. 36.

[34] Marie-Odile Banquaert, "Le Mythe de l'amour sublime dans *Feu central* de Benjamin Péret," *Cahiers Dada Surréalisme,* 1 (1966), 69.

[35] *Ibid.,* 67.

Likewise, *L'Amour fou* begins with black but positive imagery in the description of those who have provided metaphysical keys for Breton: "le propre de ces personnages est de m'apparaître vêtus de noir." [36] As movement appears directly linked with a concrete, static core, so light is complemented by dark: "je me plais à figurer toutes les lumières dont a joui le spectateur convergeant dans ce point d'ombre." [37] Marc Angenot recognizes the positive aspect of black and night in Surrealist love imagery; he defines the "soleil noir" which, aside from its alchemical status, is used by many Surrealist poets, as "l'expression par synecdoque de ce monde parallèle dont les surréalistes sont en quête." [38] Thus the use of the color black in the context of love poetry "marque la femme aimée qui semble un transfuge du monde de la nuit." [39]

In *Je sublime*, red and black are joined in the image of volcanic lava which appears in "Je ne dors pas" and "Déraper." For Banquaert, this image reproduces blood in the turmoil of love or revolt, but the obvious sexual connotations of the vulcano in the context of *Je sublime* are not to be ignored. The volcano is a metaphor for the generative force of desire; through eruption and transformation, it brings new land masses to light. Another black and red image appears in "Ah": "Hérissées de plumes de corbeaux à tête d'évêques." The images of red and black cannot be fixed in categories; they interact in a process of change similar to combustion, and it is the metamorphosis inherent in their action which is important in the poetry.

Banquaert also fixes the recurrent use of the color blue in these texts as denoting "la couleur primaire vers laquelle regressent toutes les autres." [40] But blue objects are no more static than any others in *Je sublime*; the turquoise titmouse of "Egaré" has an active counterpart in the "fontaine de turquoises" of "Ah," and in "Le Carré de l'hypoténuse" blue appears as one of the multiple colors of the sun. The "cascade bleue" of "Allo" along with the "perroquets" and the "timbres poste bleus et verts" of "Clin d'œil" are

---

[36] Breton, *L'Amour fou,* p. 7.
[37] *Ibid.,* p. 8.
[38] Marc Angenot, "Le Surréalisme noir," *Les Lettres Romanes,* 26 (1972), 190.
[39] *Ibid.,* 192.
[40] Banquaert, 65.

other examples of the mobility of the color blue in these texts. As with the parakeets and the postage stamps, the "verre d'œil" in "Parlemoi" exists in an intermediate chromatic state between blue and green; it is described as "parfois bleu comme une étoile filante réfléchie par une œuf / parfois vert comme une source suintant d'une horloge." Again, the capacity for change and interaction prevails over any fixed attributes of these colors. This principle persists in Péret's other collection of love poetry, *Un point c'est tout* (1946), as the following examples illustrate:

> qui bondit comme un tigre poursuivi
> du vert au blanc
> > ("Deux mots")
> et le soleil pareil à une bouteille de vin rouge
> s'est fait nègre
> > ("On sonne")
> qui mousse tellement que les bulles obscurcissent le soleil
> le verdissent comme un vieil entrecôte
> le bleuissent comme une vigne au printemps
> > ("Tout à l'heure")
> pleine de l'embrun de tes yeux semblables à deux oranges
> > ("Sais-tu")
> Je t'aime comme le grain de blé aime le soleil se levant en
> haut de sa tête de merle
> > ("Où es-tu").

The longer text "A garder précieusement" (1948) presents an extreme example of this chromatic indeterminacy, as black and white are synthesized in "l'obscure voie lactée que hantent les étincelles noires et velues des puits de mine."

Un point c'est tout introduces the image of the earthquake to the lexicon expressing change as a continual state. The vocabulary of disaster which appears frequently in *Je sublime* is never entirely negative, and the same ambivalence applies to the earthquake in the later collection. Earth in movement may give rise to new phenomena, as in "Tout à l'heure":

> Par la faille qui s'est ouverte par le dernier tremblement de
> terre
> s'échappent des oiseaux en forme de pipe
> les chats bondissants parce que leur queue s'envole
> et de grands jets de champagne.

In "Un Matin," on the other hand, the movement of the earth and the accompanying sound are among several symptoms of the fact that "le monde est tout dépeigné" by the absence of the woman. The upward movement which characterizes many of the texts in *Je sublime* is replaced by images of tension and fragility. Apparent progress upward is either deceiving, as in "Pour ne rien dire": "croître de son ombre en se nourissant de soi-même," or inconsequential, as in "On sonne": "un saut de puce comme une brouette dansant sur les genoux des pavés."

In all these texts, the poet and the object of his love are present, and most are addressed to her in the second person. Only "Egaré" and "Source" in *Je sublime* omit the "tu" and the latter text repeats her name, while only "Tout à l'heure" in *Un point c'est tout* is not directed toward a second person. The interaction between the speaker and the woman to whom he speaks is entirely one-sided and the effect upon him is often violent but, like the images discussed above, this violence is never unambiguously negative or positive. In "Homard," for example, she has influence over him in both elements of sets of apparent opposites:

> ton souffle de pensées sauvages
> se reflétant du plafond sur mes pieds
> me traversent de part en part
> me suivent et me précèdent
> m'endorment et m'éveillent
> me jettent par la fenêtre pour me faire monter par l'ascenseur
> et réciproquement.

This reciprocity is expressed on the level of perception in "Clin d'œil," where Rosa is the means by which he comes into sensory contact with the world: "Aujourd'hui je regarde par tes cheveux . . . et je pense par tes seins d'explosion." Caws points out the syntactical difference between this text and Breton's "L'Union libre," which repeats the construction "ma femme à": "it is as if there were a certain comfortable distance . . . between the elements of Breton's universe, between the poet and the woman, the woman and her qualities. Péret's poetry leaves none . . . since she is literally part of that which in most poems she would only resemble." [41] Thus the

---

[41] Caws, 211.

woman is actually identified with the "avion en flammes" and the "château inondé de vin du Rhin" in "Allo" and these incarnations stand in a primary relationship with the poet, for each is preceded by *mon*. The woman is equally powerful in her absence: "Attendre" in *Je sublime* and "Un Matin" in *Un point c'est tout* show the poet prey to great difficulties without her. In "Attendre", they are expressed in the first lines: "Meurtri par les grandes plaques du temps / l'homme s'avance comme les veines du marbre qui veulent se ménager des yeux," and in "Un Matin" by the final lines: "car tu n'es plus là que je ne suis pas là sans toi / et le monde en est tout dépeigné." Her influence even extends into the future:

> Demain fera éclater les orages d'éclipses de lune
> ou jaillir des éclairs de sodium
> selon que tu le regarderas comme un wagon à bestiaux
> ... ...
> ou que tu l'appelleras comme un fantôme.
>
> ("A quand")

The poet is permeated so completely by the transforming powers of *l'amour sublime* that he, as speaker, seems threatened with the extinction of his ontological uniqueness. As Mary Ann Caws notes, "Surrealism wages war on the principle of *identity* and values love for its destruction of egoism." [42] Hence, the final lines of the poem "Ecoute" from *Je sublime* suggest that the destruction of the ego is wished for rather than feared. After an image of absorption of the self into the woman, "si tu m'abritais comme un hanneton dans un placard," the text concludes:

> et nous grimperions comme un escalier dans un tour
> pour nous voir disparaître
> au loin
> comme une table emportée par l'inondation.

She is equally essential to the speaker's being in a poem such as "On sonne" in *Un point c'est tout*: "Je voudrais être / car sans toi je suis à peine l'interstice entre les pavés des prochaines barricades."

---

[42] *Ibid.*

Between *Je sublime* and *Un point c'est tout,* the long text entitled *Dernier malheur dernière chance* (1945) shows the basic nature of love and desire by their appearance in a context where their pertinence is not immediately apparent. This text is concerned with the collapse of the myth of Western European moral superiority at the advent of World War II and with the need for the creation of a new myth. The image with which the poem concludes links it to "Le Noyau de la comète" in its evocation of desire:

Le flot continu des haleines emmelées sans prunelles et sans
    voix
plongeant parfois dans des gouffres interdits aux étoiles
...se dissolvant dans une cataracte
qui imite une comète déployant ses mille queues
fondues en un premier baiser.

The revival of the world is predicated on the freedom of desire, and Péret optimistically presents this "dernière chance" as being taken. Earlier in the fourth and final section of this text, the natural elements are newly infused with the power of desire, and this power is expressed in human terms: "des rochers qui se tendent les grottes de leur face / pour un baiser de premier âge." Desire in the form of love is finally, in this text, a liberating force, and it acts in opposition both to the circumstances which have led to war and to the threat of total annihilation and stasis which could be its aftermath. In *Je sublime,* the final lines also oppose love to repression and place it on the side of "liberté liberté chérie."

A much earlier text, *Les Rouilles encagées* (1929) makes this same equation, but in a different sense. The sexual activity in the prose and poetry of this work is continual and polymorphous but it is not presented as an expression of love; it has been called "un des rares écrits franchement pornographiques produits par les surréalistes." [43] Those who participate in the action of this text are members of several generations of a degenerate aristocratic family with which Péret links himself by using the name Satyremont, which appears in the text belonging to one of the characters. In "Le Noyau de la comète," he clarifies the value of sexual license: "la license sexuelle sans horizon ne peut que dimineur l'être humain

---

[43] Gauthier, p. 29n.

tout autant que les tabous les plus strictes." [44] The apparent contradiction between this statement and the revolutionary intent which
informs the depiction of lewd behavior in the 1929 text can be
resolved by the recognition that "Satyremont" relates events of the
past in an explicitly fictional and implicitly satirical context. His
protagonists are fancifully-named aristocrats whose behavior relates
to a social order which is entirely divorced from normal human
society. Within the fantasy, the primary object of ridicule is the
Church, and many of the intercalated poems parody its ritual. The
sexualization of liturgy is presented as a reaction to the emphasis
of the church on chastity, as in the example of the town where
inhabitants sing out the following protest at noon and midnight:
"Qu'est-ce qui m'a foutu un bougre de sale Dieu (une ordure de
vierge) incapable de jouir comme une trompette du jugement dernier?" [45]

In addition to this equation of sexual activity with revolt, *Les
Rouilles encagées* and *Je sublime* share a number of images. The
phallus is frequently referred to in the 1929 text as a "pine," and
several of Yves Tanguy's illustrations depict feathers or wings; [46]
references to birds and flight are an important element of the imagery in *Je sublime*. The vocabulary of catastrophe is used frequently in both *Les Rouilles encagées* and *Je sublime* and with the
same ambivalence. Floods of semen wreak destruction, but their
composition implies the perpetuation of human life. Objects participate in the universal orgy; these objects include mirrors, watches,
and the host. Most important, poetry plays a major role in *Les
Rouilles encagées*: poems make up much of its content and they
are spoken of within the prose section. After a genealogical recital
which is a litany of obscene names, Péret mentions "le poète Machevit de l'Enculade, dont les plus beaux vers nous sont parvenus
tatouées sur les fesses de sa famille." [47] The first poem in *Les Rouilles encagées* is also presented anatomically by means of "un membre

---

[44] "Le Noyau de la comète," p. 64.
[45] Benjamin Péret, *Les Rouilles encagées* (Paris: Losfeld, 1969), p. 14. As
is made clear by the title page, the title of this book is *Les Couilles enragées*;
the c and r have apparently been reversed so as to make the book saleable.
[46] Gauthier says of these illustrations that they are "aussi vulgaires et mala-
droites que celles des toilettes publiques" (p. 292).
[47] *Les Rouilles encagées,* p. 19.

gros comme l'obélisque sur lequel les veines dessinaient tout un poème hiéroglyphique." [48] A family superstition forbids their being read until the Marquis Braguetin de Satyremont courageously undertakes this task. These poems appear at intervals throughout the middle part of the text, and the evocation of the physical attitude of the family literary historian is humorously appropriate to their content. The poems have become concrete, humanized objects by virtue of their location, and for the same reason they are simultaneously debased. Surrounding them is a mysterious aura which leads to their being unread for generations, but this mystique is similarly counterbalanced by the association of these poems with rotting human flesh. A text thus inscribed would be altered over the course of time, subject to natural changes rather than being fixed in the artificial eternity of printed matter. The question of intentionality with regard to the obscene content of these texts is also raised; distortion of the skin on which the text is written might be held responsible for material changes, and this abdication of final influence over the poetic product is further suggested by the parodic nature of a number of these poems. Machevit's aleatory skin-poetry is as crude as the human flesh which inspires it and to which it returns; the parody of the Lord's Prayer which precedes the account of the final orgy is typical, beginning "Notre pine qui êtes au con." The only text by a Surrealist which approaches *Les Rouilles encagées* in ferocity and verve is René Crevel's *Le Clavecin de Diderot,* but its essay form and explicit Marxist base are vastly more conventional than anything in Péret's work. *Les Rouilles encagées* stands as a unique textual example of what it calls "leur vit roide lancé vers Dieu." [49]

"A garder précieusement" (1948) stands apart from Péret's other love poetry because of its effacement of the tensions which characterize his earlier works. The poem begins with an expression of continuity, "Ainsi va la vie," and proceeds to a resolution of the image of desire with its real incarnation in the last lines:

Femme au lit de barricade bruissante de poings dressés [50]

---

[48] *Ibid.,* p. 10.

[49] *Ibid.,* p. 14.

[50] Even in the calm of this text, images such as this link erotic desire with desire as it is expressed in revolt.

Femme aux mains de rayons de soleil et d'éclairs foudroyants
femme
toi.

Images of reciprocity and complementarity dominate the text, which
illustrates the woman's capacity to make even the most negative
images positive: "Le souffle de la dormeuse gonfle les voiles de la
barque / et les naufragés reprennent espoir." Even the apparent
death of the sun, which Banquaert's article emphasizes, is reversible:

> On sait qu'à midi le soleil soupirant
> se suicidera d'un nuage tourbillonant entre des cils
> pour renaître sur la passerelle tendue.

A succession of obstacles is raised only to be overcome by the force
of the balance which exists between man and woman:

> L'orange tranchée en parties égales
> laisse circuler une foule de somnambules
> dans le col ouvert entre la caresse d'acier
> qui dresse un doigt vaincu d'avance
> ... ...
> femme aux yeux de mangues mures
> qui dissolvent en se dissolvant
> les champs de mines qui nous entourent.

In both cases, the natural symmetry of the fruit appears as an agent
against unnatural death by slitting the throat with a knife or by
the explosion of a mine. The fruit is humanized in the first example
by its association with sleepwalkers and in the second by the identification of ripe mangoes with the woman's eyes. Forces of death
are overcome by human action in harmony with nature; this principle persists throughout Péret's poetic work after its definition in
Immortelle Maladie.

Images which characterize the two earlier collections of love
poetry reappear in "A garder précieusement," but in a modified
form. The earthquake is now the movement of the bed during
lovemaking: "inutile d'écouter le murmure indistinct des chevelures
/ roulant sur de blancs tremblements de terre"; the positive aspect
of lava is emphasized: "et les torrents de lave s'élevant des housses
poussièreuses / qu'elles régénèrent et vivifient." Despite the satisfaction of desire which gives rise to these images, the poet is not

content to remain lulled by this calm; speaking of eyes, he says "je les veux grands ouverts et distillant les soifs insatiables des forêts pétrifiées." Activity, triggered by the sound of the alarm clock, continues. The memory of the night is turned into the most treasured of relics, a poem, as the title indicates.

Between the moral depths of *Les Rouilles encagées* and the ecstatic height of "A garder précieusement" there is a remarkable consistency in Péret's imagery. The principles stated in the essay "Le Noyau de la comète" are so flexible that they can be applied to love as a manifestation of revolt or as the calming experience which neutralizes external obstacles. The combative force of desire is present in both extreme cases, as love is shown to be a way to counteract a world which is by definition hostile in its societal component. Whether sublime or debased, love is an exploration of the marvelous potential which lies both within its own context and in the world as transformed by desire. There are many other examples of love poetry in Péret's work; another text among the later poetry, "Aller et retour," [51] is much like "A garder précieusement" in its expression of harmony, while "Violette Nozières" (1933) is Péret's contribution to the collective Surrealist exhaltation of the woman who acts against social norms. The female form appears as an object of desire in heterogeneous contexts, and the collection *De derrière les fagots* (1936) includes a complement of stray breasts and limbs. As in the case of *Je ne mange pas de ce pain-là,* which has discursive analogues in the essays "La parole est à Péret" and "Le Déshonneur des poètes," the love poetry can be paired with "Le Noyau de la comète," but the implications of this essay, like those of the two texts on the position of the poet in society, go beyond any thematic pigeonhole. Love, like revolt, is an essential expression of desire in Péret's world-view, "the most decisive and thoroughgoing individual human experience, comprising the most delerious and overpowering moments of one's life ... violently opposed to the last shred of Christian morality and to every other conceivable social contraint." [52] As an expression of desire, love is a means to change which appears

---

[51] "Aller et retour" is included under the title "Autres Poésies" in the *Œuvres complètes,* II, p. 287.

[52] Franklin Rosemont, "An Introduction to Benjamin Péret," *Radical America,* 4 (1970), 7.

in all realms, not merely in the human. For the sublime lover, the shape of the world is that of his desire.

B. The Natural Movement of History

Despite the broad implications of *l'amour sublime* in the realm of revolt, the desire described in Péret's love poetry is basically limited to the couple sharing it. However, the poet's optic goes much further, to the perception of the workings of desire on a universal scale. Péret seems to gain an awareness of this extension of desire when he travels to South America for the second time (1941-1945). The impact of world events and the alien surroundings in which he finds himself lead to an expansion of the concept of desire; it is found to be applicable to areas far wider than the experience of the couple in *l'amour sublime*.

Péret wrote two long poems which relate to his Mexican experience and which can be described as historical. *Dernier Malheur dernière chance* (1946), dated 1942, was written in Mexico, and *Air mexicain* (1952) is concerned with Mexican history, although it was written in 1949, after Péret's return to Paris. A third text which is also historical in orientation and belongs to this period is *Toute une vie* (1949), a celebration of Péret's lifelong friendship with André Breton. The first two poems treat a historical and societal macrocosm, but *Toute une vie* evokes the circles in which Péret and Breton moved, and the events which had immediate effects upon them.

In this decade, Breton wrote longer texts than he had in the past, and these, like Péret's longer poems, are concerned with history. However, *Fata morgana,* the product of Breton's 1940-41 winter in Marseilles, and *Les Etats généraux,* which was written in New York in 1943, are different from Péret's texts in that they draw largely upon the mysticism of the European past and its applications in the present. Breton's last major poem, *Ode à Fourier* (1947), is also a long text, but its orientation is again strongly European despite its use of North American motifs. Both men wrote more expansively than before in their respective exiles when they confronted events which were enormous in duration and geographical scope. The major distinction in approaches is that Breton recasts the methods of the past, while, Péret seeks an entirely new vision through poetry itself as an expression of desire or through a world-view that is new to Western thought.

Air mexicain and *Dernier Malheur dernière chance* differ in their outlooks on world events; the former is diachronic, treating the change in a nation over the course of many centuries, while the latter is synchronic, being limited to a brief point in time when the choice is offered between the death of the world and its rebirth. Despite obvious references to events contemporary with its composition, *Dernier Malheur dernière chance* is not a political text; it adheres to the principle of avoidance of explicitly political poetry as an attempt to influence events which is defined in the 1945 essay "Le Déshonneur des poètes." In *Dernier Malheur dernière chance,* the world situation during World War II is described in new terms which are those of an eschatology of desire. No specific battle is cited and the presence of guns participates in a metaphorical structure which does not depend on outside references for its coherence. The great combat of clouds and fire which ends the text is closer to the Book of Revelations of John than to any explicitly historical text. *Dernier Malheur dernière chance* fulfills Lautréamont's requirements for poetry in relation to political reality:

> La poésie doit avoir pour but la vérité pratique. Elle énonce les rapports qui existent entre les premiers principes et les vérités secondaires de la vie. Chaque chose reste à sa place ... elle ne se mêle pas aux événements de la politique ... elle découvre les lois qui font vivre la politique théorique. [53]

Although *Air mexicain* names historical figures such as Juarez and Zapata and refers to past events, it is equally independent of political or propagandistic intent. Antagonistic figures, whether they are the conquistadors, the "humeurs de porridge" or the "barbares à face de dollar," derive their pejorative appearance from their relationship with the mythological and ethical stance of the native Mexican as it is translated by Péret. Being diachronic in orientation,

---

[53] Comte de Lautréamont, *Œuvres complètes,* ed. Marguerite Bonnet (Paris: Garnier, 1969), p. 284. A different interpretation of this statement appears in Eluard's "La poésie doit avoir pour but la vérité pratique" [Paul Eluard, *Poèmes politiques, Poèmes pour tous* (Paris: Editeurs français réunis, 1959), p. 148].

Air mexicain is largely concerned with past events; opposition to participants in these actions, like that expressed toward such figures as Foch in *Je ne mange pas de ce pain-là,* influences the attitude of the reader toward their place in history, rather than having an immediate effect on his current behavior. In *Dernier Malheur dernière chance,* Péret avoids the danger of falling into polemic by casting current events into mythological and eschatological terms which, far from being timid circumlocutions, elevate the importance of the contemporary poetic moment to that of a great turning point in the course of history. For Péret, poetry is a truer way of recounting events and translating reality than any other, and he defends himself in "Le Déshonneur des poètes" against those who reject the approach of poetry "comme si elle n'était pas la réalité elle-même, son essence et son exaltation." [54]

Dernier Malheur dernière chance and *Air mexicain* are alike in that they are longer than most of Péret's poems, but they differ in form. [55] The earlier of the two texts is divided by roman numerals into four parts which are approximately symmetrical; the second and third are some thirty lines shorter than the first and fourth sections. The individual lines of poetry are short phrases which accumulate to make up the long sentences of the text. In contrast, *Air mexicain* is not divided by numerals; the poem is separated into seven divisions of unequal length by white spaces. The individual lines of *Air mexicain* are longer than those of *Dernier Malheur dernière chance,* and often comprise complete sentences. In keeping with the mythological orientation of the text, formulaic diction similar to that used in liturgy appears frequently; when successions of phrases are used in consecutive lines, they are characterized by the repetition of the initial clause.

Despite its synchronic approach to history, *Dernier Malheur dernière chance* is built on a basic linear image, the connection of two separate places by a bridge. This image, which is extensively developed in the early part of the text, is carried through to the conclusion in the form of metaphors from nature such as clouds, fire, sand cliffs, and in the final linking of two disparate elements in

---

[54] Benjamin Péret, "Le Déshonneur des poètes," *Le Déshonneur des poètes, précédé de La parole est à Péret* (Paris: Pauvert, 1965), p. 77.

[55] *Dernier Malheur dernière chance* is considerably longer; it has 431 lines while *Air mexicain* has 131.

a kiss. In contrast with these images of conjunction across a horizontal plane, the threat of being swallowed up by depths is presented first in the form of a quarry and finally in that of a fall from
the height of clouds. The crossing of the abyss is undertaken simultaneously by a variety of participants in the text, and the account
of their attempts is situated beyond any ordinary temporal context.
Air mexicain, on the other hand, is circular in form; it begins and
ends with the contemporary Mexican and describes events from the
beginning of time as it was conceived by the early Mexican to the
present. This construction is closely related to the view of time
which is best known through the Aztecs; time is, for them, cyclical
rather than linear, yet events occur at a given point in time and
are not repeated. The Western linear concept of time is destroyed
by the multiplicity of synchronic events in *Dernier Malheur dernière
chance,* but the cyclical view of the Aztecs is also changed by the
poetic rendition of their history in *Air mexicain.*

As Claude Courtot remarks, the notion of time vanishes alto-
gether, and "on ne peut plus dès lors parler de temps mais de
rhythme." [56] However, the contrast can be made in general terms
between the linear form of *Dernier Malheur dernière chance,* both
in its superstructure and in its dominant image, and the circularity
of *Air mexicain,* which begins and ends in the present and is characterized by images derived from the mythology of the solar disc.
In "Le Noyau de la comète," Péret refers to the form of historical
time as that of a "mouvement héliocoïdal," [57] a combination of
circular and linear forms in the spiral. The tendency in both long
poems is to go beyond the time patterns of cultures into a more
flexible account of chronology. History is perceived as participating
in the natural movement of desire, combining the circle of primitive
time with the line of Western man's temporal outlook. In *Air
mexicain,* the fusion of human and natural history is accomplished
within the scope of native mythology, which personifies natural
forces as gods, while in *Dernier Malheur dernière chance,* the deci-
sion of man's fate is presented in the form of a conflict within
nature. Man is present in the latter text, but he abdicates his voli-
tional status at the end of the first section:

---

[56] Courtot, p. 92.
[57] "Le Noyau de la comète," p. 7.

> Le héros du drame embarque sur un radeau d'air pâle
> s'éloigne comme la dernière ombre
> exsangue
> que le soufre a dépouillée d'une peau trop rugueuse.

Dernier Malheur dernière chance begins with the voice of the poet, who proclaims his own insufficiency before his subject matter in terms of linear images:

> Il m'aurait fallu les quatre mains de signaux optiques
> avec les sept doigts de palme odorante de la chouette plate
> pour voler à ras de terre comme le bois de campêche
> qui a perdu son âme de chants liturgiques.

The historical situation is introduced as the space of four years and simultaneously the dominant image of the poem appears: "entre deux serments olympiques le passage d'un pont." The bridge is situated in time by the allusion to the suspended Olympic Games, then described as it exists in space with an attention to detail which emphasizes the importance of this image in the poem:

> La sortie du pont est fermée par le fond d'une carrière
> habitée de cendres que le vent assemble en légendes menaçantes
> On y a sculpté le commencement grondant du monde
> ... ...
> sans savoir que la fin
> égale à la dernière goutte d'eau
> s'y mélange.

The beginning of the world, which takes the elongated form of the sculpture, is ambivalently presented with the circular drop-form of the end of the world, and this uncertainty is highlighted by the "légendes menaçantes" formed by the ashes in the quarry. Water is used as a metaphor for the end of the world both here and at the end of the text, where the apocalypse is presented as a conflict between fire and rain clouds.

The leading image of the bridge reappears in the first section with the same connotations of uncertainty in the line "qu'une rue passante devient un pont prêt à s'écrouler," where the street was originally intended for "un troupeau qu'on mène à l'abattoir." In this negative context, the action of the human will in the slaughtering of the sheep is metamorphosed into a participation in the "dernier malheur"; again, the individual event is subsumed beneath the lager workings of eschatology. The next time the image of the bridge appears, its connotations are more hopeful: "quel pont ne franchirait l'abîme pétrifiant des paupières d'un tenace élan de ses racines / que retiendrait peut-être l'assouvissement d'un désir plus vaste que tous les horizons." Desire is associated with the passage over the bridge in a manner which is repeated in the final section of *Dernier Malheur dernière chance*. The extent of the desire is that of human will for the continuation of the world; desire is the positive, hopeful shape of history at this early point in the poem.

The quarry at the end of the bridge is developed as an image as the site of a second battle between the forces of life and death:

> Rien de plus assourdissant qu'une carrière abandonnée
> où les végétaux impatients se battent pour effacer les bas-reliefs
> tonitruants
> admirés des seules bêtes hystériques de la nuit.

Quarried rock, contaminated by human activity, is finally contrasted with mineral elements which, because they still belong to nature, are capable of enacting the revival of life through desire.

Man appears in this situation as a participant in

> un drame
> dont le héros bicéphale d'une tête dévore son fils
> giclant comme une aorte tranchée par un courant d'air
> et sur l'autre lisse des moustaches à flamme de chalumeau.

This horrible scene is repeated with other protagonists in the second section in the form of "une étoile au moins double / l'une morte à la tâche que lui avait imposée l'autre." In each image, a doubled element, head or star, destroys part of itself through a miscarriage of desire, which is perverted as a death instinct. Man's self-destructive tendencies are restated in the early part of the poem by the presentation of the hero as a "forçat camouflé de tôle on-dulée" and as a "couteau fardé de plusieurs sangs séchés comme des sabots au coin du feu." The designation of the human actor as hero characterizes this vision of man in rebellion against the Western concept of heroic human will; the activity of man is more likely to lead to his own imprisonment and death than to the recuperation of a threatened world. Human desire has been distorted by the social enforcement of repression.

Man is, nonetheless, capable of love, and "guette son héroine qui s'échappe par la sève." She will reappear near the end of the text as a Beatrice figure: "que la provocante démarche de l'amante obscure / . . . la conduise en une promenade de zéros hallucinant le un / . . . vers l'aimant de terre promise tyran de son un." For the moment, however, she disappears with her male human companion, and their absence is presented as a positive factor; after he has left, it is as if

> le soufre a dépouillé d'une peau trop rugueuse
> pour des mains si légères
> que le chant de la bouilloire amoureuse des tropiques
> s'effaçait comme midi
> balaie son minuit crépitant de siècles sans mémoire.

Thus the first section ends on a hopeful note for the macrocosm, but there is a distinctly negative attitude toward the effectiveness of human participation in great events. Péret's pessimism is understandable since the major human event contemporary with this text was World War II; Péret was not, however, a pessimist as a general rule, and the final movement of the poem is more than corrective of this initial negativity as regards the place of man in the world.

The second section of *Dernier Malheur dernière chance* moves from images of cold and desolation through a depiction of the evil effects of Western civilization on the world to a final appeal for freedom. Circular images such as the rose, the sun, and a "casserole" are associated with negative elements such as the cold, smoke, and a duenna, while the turbine is "déjà prête à tous les excès et même à simuler la fin d'une époque." In opposition to the tropical heat evoked in the final lines of the first section, the cold here is negative because it produces stasis:

> Mais le froid insiste épidémie de cuirs mal tannés
> et s'entête dans une attitude de musée des armures
> où tout se raidit jusqu'à la poussière.

The old civilization is presented through the figure of the "idole de vieux mensonges"; it is characterized by its repression of the small and by a fearful frog-like swelling in which it is fed by "l'encens de toutes les églises à feu de joie." The old ways, having reached their nadir, led to the war, and this war is sanctioned by the Church. Péret's hostility to the collusion of Church and State is expressed with regard to the First World War in "Le Cardinal Mercier est mort" from the collection *Je ne mange pas de ce pain-là,* and elsewhere in this collection. In "Le Déshonneur des poètes," he points out that Church and warmaking State are linked by all those who were parties to the war:

> Churchill ne prononce presque aucun discours sans s'assurer de sa protection; Roosevelt en fait autant, de Gaulle se place sous l'égide de la croix de Lorraine, Hitler invoque chaque jour la Providence et les métropolites de toute espèce remercient, du matin au soir, le Seigneur du bienfait stalinien. Loin d'être de leur part une manifestation insolite, leur attitude consacre un mouvement général de regression en même temps qu'elle montre leur panique. [58]

The combination of aggression and regression is given voice by the "poussière" which appears to represent duped mankind before the old idol. In *Dernier Malheur dernière chance,* this figure seeks aggression on all sides:

> effacez les visages tâches solaires trop endormies
> semez les barbes pour nourrir les somptueuses machines inutiles
> ... ...
> Que le ciel de collines abruptes se recourbe en un arc
> lançant de lourdes flèches qui barrent les mers des paumes
>   de la main.

The call for freedom is not made by men, but by the air and the stars which reflect liberated human desire in wishing "ni dieu ni maître." Their freeing power is shown in that it "détruit les chaînes de vampires / des sous-sols pavés d'or au corps supplicié." Revolt is first accomplished by elemental rather than human activity; this order also governs the final redemption of the world. Desire is extended to the non-human as the powers of poetry are expanded, recalling the beginning of the fourth section of *Les Chants de*

---

[58] "Le Déshonneur des poètes," p. 77.

Maldoror: "c'est un homme ou une pierre ou un arbre qui va commencer le quatrième chant." [59]

Despite this initial liberation, darkness and hunger are still
present in the third section, which begins "Toujours plus noire
jusqu'à la faim." Intimations that something is about to happen
appear almost at once with images of apertures, but these are not
positive:

> La nuit de charbon sans feu ni lieu
> trop mûre
> s'ouvre pour offrir un fruit sombre de volcan sournois
> ... ...
> et la faim tenace qui ouvre ses cratères d'argile
> plus molle qu'une vie prénatale
> ... ...
> Entre ses dents de ventre sourd aux cris rageurs de l'hématite
> qu'use un mal rapporté d'un séjour entre les eaux grises des
>   vieillards
> une menace d'an mil.

The combination of darkness and cold, which are associated with
stasis, cannot hold in a natural environment based on change. Forward movement is implied in the line "c'est un lourd sommeil de
marche forcée dans une veine de houille." The death's head of a
pirate flag is torn to reveal a ray of light, and suddenly an end is
in sight: "enfin au tournant herissé de piques de belladone toujours
cruelle / apparaît tête nue le débarcadère du rendez-vous." But
the validity of this vision is immediately called into question because it is associated with "un académicien," "la table d'un conseil,"
and "le drapeau à aigle rouge." The end is not to be reached by
these traditional means; in "La Société des nations" (*Je ne mange
pas de ce pain-là*) there is a similar rejection of attempts to save
the world while maintaining its present structure.

The agent of salvation is first presented as coming from beneath the earth in the form of "une énergie bégayante de larmes /
coulant d'un visage aussi vite apparu que perdu." This awakening
of the dynamic force of desire is responded to by "des rochers qui
se tendent les grottes de leur face / pour un baiser de premier âge."
The union of two sides over a chasm is accomplished by the rock

---

[59] Lautréamont, p. 163.

faces themselves rather than by the erection of a bridge; natural movement again proves more effective than human endeavor. The chain reaction initiated by the tearful energy continues as the kiss moves "dans un cliquetis de métaux encore vagues / les ruines de plantes à bajoues d'eunuque." This return to life is a form of revolt which is marked by "poings d'émeute dressés vers la cendre du ciel"; desire is designated as being valid when it unites erotic passion with rebellion against old institutions. The final battle between fire and clouds is heralded by the cry "Aux nuage aux nuages"; the significance of this line is reinforced by its typographical appearance, set off by white space from the lines that precede and follow. Fire is first "l'incendie sournoise migration d'insectes à bannières étincelantes d'été," but once it consents to take the generative position of "une place de grand-père" it acquires completely human form as "le chef apache" in order to meet the advancing clouds. Their combat, "le duel à la loyale," is initiated by the cloud leader "dressé sur ses ergots / mâle protégeant un troupeau promis au vainqueur." In the epic struggle, the fire begins to gain ground when "ses désirs éclatent"; hence, the use of the theme of desire continues in this last section. A final cry ends the battle: "Aux nuages Sus aux nuages / géôliers des nerfs qui allument des brasiers"; the arrival of lightning and rain ends the sterile tension of the second and third sections.

Three long imperative sentences which begin with *que* indicate a reordering of the world returned to life. The last one introduces an intriguing image:

> Que la provoquante démarche de l'amante obscure
> ... ...
> la conduise en une promenade de zéros hallucinant le un
> emporté par la tempête des zéros et des uns
> vers l'aimant de terre promise tyran de son un.

The transition from nothingness to being is made by woman through the natural attraction of the magnet and the lines that follow express an insensate flood of sexuality: "le flot continu des haleines emmêlées sans prunelles et sans voix / plongeant parfois dans des gouffres interdits aux étoiles." Progress is made in a positive direction during this "temps de ruines sucé par un temps de mésanges," and the flood of joined breath is "un torrent paré de tous les joyaux inventés par des bouches jamais rassassiées." This primal form of desire will crystallize into a kiss as the appearance of a rainbow signals the final breaking of stasis as described in the last four lines:

> qui sentent sourdre en elle la lave brûlante des châteaux
> se dissolvant dans une cataracte
> qui imite une comète déployant ses mille queues
> fondues en un premier baiser.

Dernier Malheur dernière chance thus unites in the concept of desire two major ideas which are expressed in two such disparate collections as *Je ne mange pas de ce pain-là* and *Je sublime*. The desire that motivates love and revolt leads to their synthesis in a vision of the world at a point of crisis. The transformations enacted by this desire are part of an entirely poetic approach to the historical world. The positive conclusion of this text is a manifestation of what Emmanuel Berl calls "l'aspect 'foi' du surréalisme," [60] for the recuperation of the world is accepted by Péret as having occurred despite all evidence to the contrary.

Air mexicain is the product of a sustained interest in Central and South American civilizations; although Péret may have acquired this interest in part from the rediscovery of primitive culture in the wake of Apollinaire, he was also influenced by his own contact with these cultures on the occasion of his visit to Brazil in 1929 with his wife, a native Brazilian. This interest was heightened when he lived in Mexico during World War II, and photographs show him on several visits to ancient Mexican landmarks. [61] Victor Serge refers to one aspect of his activity in Mexico by naming him among those who, "boycotted because asphyxiating orders of silence were imposed on non-mystical themes, accumulated their manuscripts." [62] Péret's extended stay in Mexico led to a strong sympathy with the people of this country, and the product of this intercultural understanding includes the *Anthologie des mythes, légendes et contes populaires d'Amérique* (1960), the long poem *Air mexicain*

---

[60] Emmanuel Berl, "Hommage à Benjamin Péret," *Arts,* 442 (1959), 3.

[61] Photographs of Péret at several Mexican sites are reproduced by Courtot (pp. 43 and 44) and Bédouin (among the illustrations following p. 96).

[62] Victor Serge, "Letter from Mexico," *Horizon,* 15 (1947), 67.

(1952), and several articles.[63] The continuing influence of this Mexican experience on Péret is shown by his writing *Air mexicain* some eighteen months after his return to Paris and by his compiling the anthology ten years later.

Air mexicain begins in the present tense with a description of the modern Mexican, the heir to a magnificent civilization who is now suppressed by the forces of alien cultures. The continuity expressed in this presentation is confirmed by anthropological studies:

> A perusal of the nineteenth and twentieth century travel books on Spanish America ... reveals the same story: every author believes that the pre-Columbian mind is manifest everywhere in the people's behavior and that the ancient patterns have never been erased.[64]

The person who appears in Péret's text is not named, but his identity is revealed in the line "il écoute et n'entend couler que le torrent de sa sueur d'or avalée par le nord noir," which alludes to the modern exploitation of Mexican labor and natural resources. He is a combination of the extremes of negation and affirmation:

Le feu vêtu de deuil jaillit par tous ses pores
La poussière de sperme et de sang voile sa face tatouée de lave
... ...
Son geste de cœur brandi à bout de bras s'achève en 52 ans dans un brasier d'allégresse
... Il respire et dort comme une mine cachant sous ses douleurs inouïes ses joyaux de catastrophe.

The accumulation of apparent opposites such as the colors red and black in the image of fire and mourning, death and life in the juxtaposition of the heart torn from the body with the joyful flames, and pain and joy in the final image, illustrates the paradoxical state in which this man exists. He is identified with geological forces, the volcano and the mine, and thus he is in possession of inalien-

---

[63] For a list of Péret's books and articles on South American subjects, see Appendix.

[64] Francisco Guerra, *The Pre-Columbian Mind* (London: Seminar Press, 1971), p. 269.

able strength, but at the same time he is prey to the hazard of a nature with which he is intrinsically linked.

Péret uses terms derived from Aztec mythology in order to give an accurate translation of the modern Mexican's attitude toward his ontological status; an example is the fifty-two-year cycle which is their equivalent of the century. In his earthly existence, the Mexican is insecure at best, as Jacques Soustelle explains: "the glyph *ollin* ... which shares the centre of the Aztec calendar with the sun-god's visage, has the double sense of 'movement' and 'earthquake.' "[65] For the descendant of the Aztecs, the world is in a state of flux, and it has ended four times in the past.[66] Death, in compensation, is not eternal oblivion but the passage of man into another state through reincarnation. Hence, the description which begins *Air mexicain* applies equally to the Mexican man at the beginning of another time, as the state of continual flux in which he exists leads to the repetition of beings and events throughout history.

Each of the poetic lines in the first section of *Air mexicain* is a declarative sentence and the last three, which repeat the third person present tense in their first two words with the verbs "écoute," "chante," and "respire," give a general account of the subject's being. In contrast, the second section is built on a series of subordinate clauses and repetitions of prepositions. The cumulative effect of these sequences is to describe the creation of the world from a point of total oblivion: "Quand l'aile chatoyante de l'aube se perdait dans les gouffres du crépuscule habité de gestes mous / quand les larmes du sol éclataient en gerbes infernales d'années sans nuits." Ordering is later expressed in the series of optative imperatives which comprises eleven sentences, each of which begins with "que." Other series follow: "Nul ne savait ... / Nul ne savait"; "vers les étendues ... / vers le délire"; "Et de tendre ... / et de reconnaître." The formulaic dignity of this mode of speech reinforces its

---

[65] Jacques Soustelle, *Daily Life Among the Aztecs* (London: Weidenfeld and Nicholson, 1961), p. 96.

[66] This uncertainty is also expressed as a Surrealist attitude by Paul Eluard in "Physique de la poésie," *Œuvres complètes* (Paris: Gallimard, 1968), I, p. 936: "Quelle est, à ma taille, la taille du monde? Autant prendre la taille de l'eau. — les rapports entre les choses, à peine établis, s'effacent pour en laisser d'autres, aussi fugitifs."

concern with the apprehension by man of the mythic significance of his created environment. Human images such as "chatoyante," "gestes mous," and "larmes" are used in reference to inanimate phenomena and show that the psychological mechanism of projection greatly influences this primitive comprehension of the world. The Aztec idea that fire, especially that of the sun, must be fed and perpetuated by human blood, is already present before the creation of man: "les cierges s'allumaient de toutes leurs griffes à futur sang fidèle." These lights show man the way to "la route des grands miroirs," another mythological allusion; yet life is not yet present and the earth is described as "une caverne qui attend la vie." Another reference to ancient Mexican mythology appears in the description of the sea as proceeding from the god Tlaloc, "rosée qui ne s'était pas fait reconnaître." With the dawn of the new year, man appears: "les hommes jaillissent de l'ombre comprimée à l'ouest du rayon vert une graine à la main comme un fantôme aux yeux." Men arrive in a world which has already been formed, but the details of their existence within it are their own creation.

Shape is given to human life in a series of imperative clauses, the first of which is a synthesis of the mythological and the quotidian: "il est temps disaient-ils que la terre secoue sa chevelure vivante selon le rhythme des airs du jour en pyjama." These men are aware of their creative power over their surroundings both in their extensive use of specifically human terms such as "le jour en pyjama" and in their reference to "les géants tapis sous la terre les eaux le feu et nos gestes qui les créent comme un plat succulent." Although the sterility of white has been replaced by the fecundity of green, which symbolizes the revival of plant life, these men live in fear of catastrophe. Soustelle's statement that the Aztecs had "no real confidence in the future" [67] can be compared with Péret's description of "l'horreur du toit qui s'écroule et s'émiette sans mot dire." It is this fear which leads the early men of *Air mexicain* to the formulation of a religion; they reach to the sky and "recognize the place from which dawn emerges. At this point, the original god of pre-Columbian civilization, "le chef de la dualité," is named; he is appropriate to Péret's world of multiple identity. They already foresee the raising of a pyramid "que carressera le soleil

---

[67] Soustelle, p. 101.

arrêté pour ronronner au-dessus de nous," and the debasement which this act expresses is presented through the voice of these men in the last line of the section: "aussi lui dresserons-nous sa montagne pareille à un chien jappant au retour de son maître." The combination of self-assured power and willing subservience is another paradox in the series which constitutes Mexican man in the past and in the present.

The third section is marked by a more rapid succession of events and by the coalescence of poetry with recorded history. Some time has passed: "la terre a oublié depuis des milliers de brasiers reconnaissants qu'elle naquît semblable à un squelette jadis honoré d'assauts de curés crochus." A modicum of stability has been maintained over this time, and the appearance of something new though the fusion of two existing elements is suggested in the depiction of "l'éclair du quetzal fuyant vers son complément." The "éclair" becomes the great god-king of the Toltecs, Quetzalcoatl, who appears as a plumed serpent in Mexican iconography but who is also presented as a historical ruler of the Toltecs: "the god of settled, civilized people of the high plateau, the inventor of the arts, of writing and the calendar, Quetzalcoatl was the expression of everything that makes life kinder and more lovely." [68] In the context of the poem, his appearance is another example of the fusion of apparently paradoxical opposites, and he is thus a fitting god for men who exist in states which are contradictory in Western terms. Quetzalcoatl's advent is accompanied by a more positive view of natural order: "Rien . . . n'empêchera que l'herbe grandisse / . . . rien n'empêchera plus que l'homme aux yeux fourmillant de mirages entrevus ne la contemple comme son amante."

Yet soon, in the macrocosmic temporal view of this text, man's conception of "les voix obscures" leads to human sacrifice as a means of perpetuating the idyll: "le puits de son regard intérieur appelait sa vierge ravie de porter aux dieux la prière haletante de la tribu et lui promettait un remède de miracle aux calamités d'une saison de haines imméritées." At the outset, life is willingly given as propitiation to the gods, but ritual suicide risks becoming ritual murder. The arrival of the people who actually constitute the Aztec group is presented ominously as the appearance of "vagues d'être"

---

[68] *Ibid.*, p. 115.

from "le Nord en deuil perpétuel," and they raise new monuments to new gods. [69] A modern student of the Aztecs finds their religion fundamentally different from that of their predecessors and characterizes the new dogma in a manner which closely resembles Péret's treatment of the subject: "considérant la volonté comme la seule force magique possible, les hommes de cette époque semblent vouloir se différencier avec orgueil du monde animal et végétal auquel ils s'étaient jusque-là étroitement liés." [70] The worship of Quetzalcoatl, though no longer the official religion, continues:

> de l'œil qui éveille pour mieux endormir était descendu le
> serpent à plumes blanc et barbu offrant comme jadis
> aux sommets des monts d'adoration à la lumière et à
> l'ombre valsant toute la vie les couleurs vivantes créées
> par leur souffle d'or et d'argent alterné.

The complication of this single line, with its pairs of waking and sleeping, serpent and feathers, white and bearded, light and shadow, and gold and silver, indicates the complexity which the ritual had attained. But the confidence in continuity expressed in this line is belied by the appearance of the omen of the god to Mohoctezuma in the form of a smoking mirror with a voice, presumable that of Quetzalcoatl, which presages disaster while describing the immediate past in terms of four Aztec ages.

This brief section is cast in liturgical terms; first it describes the four incarnations of the deity and then it lists his gifts to those who worship him. For the Aztec, time was in the fifth cycle; it had already passed through four periods, each of which ended in catastrophe. The latest or contemporary cycle is referred to by the god in more negative terms than the rest because it is the time of his absence from the world of men:

---

[69] The actual origin of the new peoples is uncertain, but Péret's indication of direction is verified by Laurette Séjourné in *La Pensée des anciens mexicains* (Paris: Maspero, 1966): "A partir du XIe siècle, des tribus nomades commencent à arriver au centre du Mexique où, depuis les commencements de notre ère, régnait une très haute civilisation. Le lieu d'origine de ces tribus ... on le situe généralement au nord du pays" (p. 25). It is very likely that Péret was acquainted with Séjourné, who was married to his friend Victor Serge.

[70] Séjourné, p. 26.

mais à la cinquième j'abandonnerai l'œuf éclos l'an passé
des têtes sourdes comme des champignons larmoyants
et m'envolerai chez l'aigle qui tombe en avalanche.

The decline and fall of the Mexican people is foreordained and inescapable, and the physical existence of the individual is threatened: "à l'œil s'entr'ouvrant il ne restera plus que la coquille de ton corps." Quetzalcoatl leaves for the east, and the gods are no longer physical presences for men; Cortez is apparently mistaken for the returning Quetzalcoatl, who is presented iconographically as being white-skinned and bearded. Laurette Séjourné finds the omens and uncertainties of the time to be symptoms of a civilization on the verge of collapse; she notes that "tant de signes avertisseurs ne pouvaient surgir que dans un monde qui a perdu son équilibre." [71]

The longing and joy as responses to absence and return are twin motifs in the fifth section. While the gods are gone, they still participate in a process of change: "les dieux sont allés hiverner au cœur des hommes et attendent en muant." The arrival of the conquistadors is integrated with natural order in an evolutionary manner for the native whose point of view is that of the text:

> Ils arrivent du berceau des hérons d'aurore et marchent pendant que les années se nouent d'elles-mêmes en deux bottes d'asperges décapitées
> L'oiseau sorcier né tout armé de la vierge à la jupe de serpents repousse d'une étincelle ses quatre cents ennemis excités par les souffles des ténèbres tenaces renaissant comme l'œil s'ouvre et se ferme de leur cadavre toujours prêt à le harceler.

Cortez and his men are welcomed as "les vrai chefs du jour et de la nuit aztèques," and Cortez is designated "le héros." But the exultation which initially greets their arrival is followed by increasing doubt and confusion; the positive assurance, "nul doute que le grand serpent à plumes las d'une migration sans espoir ne revienne vers son peuple," is contradicted by negative evidence: "non pourtant l'abjecte croix qui supprime lance des feux de supplice et l'hostie variolée pourrit celui qu'elle touche." The values of the newcomers conflict with those of the natives, especially as

---

[71] *Ibid.,* p. 47.

the conquistadors "exigent l'or qui ne vaut pas les plumes du matin et du soir et torturent au nom d'un monarque angenouillé devant deux baguettes entrecroisées." Religious repression and imperialist greed, two evils which Péret combatted throughout his poetic and political career, are the arms of the conquistadors against the Mexicans. The desire for unity with the world through the gods of the Aztecs is frustrated. This section, which recounts the breaking of old cultural patterns by the Christians, is in formal contrast with the preceding section in that the repetitions which marked Quetzalcoatl's song have entirely disappeared; the confusion of the speaker when he is confronted with the phenomenon of conquest is echoed in the confusion of textual structure.

In the following section, the Mexican, now dominated for several generations, expresses his desire for freedom in a return to formulaic style. Old customs were based on fear of catastrophe, and the fact that they are no longer observed makes the Mexican fear for the future. The ways of the new rulers are in conflict with the order of nature as he understands it:

> Les étrangers n'ont allumé que des bûchers pour ceux que
> le soleil enchante de vols pouffant de rire qui saluent
> la grenouille s'épuisant à les nourrir et craignent que
> ne s'éveille le géant qui ronfle sous les montagnes l'abri-
> tant des grands vents qui balaient la terre pour que
> Tlaloc s'y repose.

Their religion, unlike that of the conquistadors, is based on harmony with nature; the liberation of the Mexican political unit would therefore coincide with the freeing of nature from its bondage to those whose way of life is in conflict with natural order. The "air de liberté" which he sings is therefore cast in terms drawn from his physical environment; the world around him would be improved, according to the words of the song, by the departure of the aliens. The song enumerates these potential ameliorations of water, snow, paths, springs, maize, and gold; even "l'air sera plus clair si n'y retentissent que des voix sans espion et sans contrainte." But as the poem is not divorced from historical reality, this liberation does not take place: even as they sing, "ceux qui hument du porridge écoutent." The treasures of ancient Mexican civilization continue to be depredated by "le Nord stérilisant" despite the efforts of a

Juarez who "disperse les vols noirs dégoulinant le latin." The most
positive moment of the text is marked by images of upward movement and light: "une voix d'alouette éblouie s'élève du sol baillon-
né" and "les forêts de têtes penchées se redressent et s'illuminent."
The liberation of Mexico is achieved in the text through the metamorphosis of "les huttes de misère séchée" into the human form
which they once had. Zapata, who fought as a guerilla during and
after the 1910 revolution, is named as champion of these reincar-
nated men in that he "fait lever la moisson à jamais mûre des
chants déshérités." Again, the reunion of Mexican man with his
old status is depicted in metaphors drawn from nature, in this case
the lark and the harvest.

If this positive climax marked the end of the text, *Air mexicain*
would not reflect the truth, which is the ultimate goal of the text.
Péret, as a recent resident of Mexico, is aware that another set of
conquerors now threatens the freedom of the embattled nation. The
end of *Air mexicain* presents a radical contrast with the positive
conclusion of *Dernier Malheur dernière chance,* but brevity and a
reference to the future suggest that the story is not over:

> Hélas rien qu'un épars Demain la foudre
> Les Voilà qui reviennent les ombres barbares à face de
>   dollar numéroté. Regardez-les ronger les pierres qui por-
>   tent la honte au front ronger la terre qui les voudrait
>   dissoudre ronger les hommes jusqu'au cœur qu'elles
>   empestent.

Repetition of the verb *ronger* establishes a distinction between this
conquest and that of the Spaniards, who had military splendor and
dignity in their favor. Natural elements suffer from the new inva-
sion as much as men and they are equally antagonistic toward the
villains as they wish to bring them shame and "dissolve" them.
The use of the imperative draws the reader into Péret's condemnation of North American activities, but the text remains lyrical
rather than polemical to the end. As its title indicates, it is an air,
a song rather than a story, and its ground is in history as a whole
weighing on every event at every moment.

Péret translates the cultural heritage and experience of the Mexican in terms of the present residue of the past rather than in the
linear form of narrative history. Beginning and ending in the pre-

sent, the text creates an impression of the great consistency of
Mexican history in its cycles. The arrangement of space-time in clus-
ters is reproduced by the division of the text into lines of poetry
which comprise complete thoughts and events, often of great complexity. In the context of the poem the past exists only insofar as
it impinges upon the present, and change over time is presented
as it effects the ontological status of Mexican man. Through the
circular lens of the past which is described in the text, the present
is seen with greater clarity.

The fundamental desire of the persona of *Air mexican* is the
union of man with nature. To this end he worships aspects of nature in humanized, understandable form and, in the series of invasions, combats those whose ethos separates human behavior from
its environmental context. Desire as the impulsion toward unity is
also a primary goal of the Surrealist movement:

> Tout porte à croire qu'il existe un certain point de l'esprit
> d'où la vie et la mort, le réel et l'imaginaire, le passé et
> le futur, le communicable et l'incommunicable, le haut
> et le bas cessent d'être perçus contradictoirement." [72]

The generalization of the desire to reach this point is the founda-
tion of all Surrealist activity. Thus there is common ground between the worldview of the native Mexican and that of the Surrealist poet. Their histories are mutually informed by their striving
for a world in which the dualities established by Western philosophy since the Greeks are abandoned for a vision of unity.

The history recounted in *Toute une vie* (1950) is that of the
Surrealist movement through the person of André Breton. This text
was composed before *Air mexican* (it is dated "Ile de Sein, 15-23
juillet 1949"), but it is oriented toward Péret's Parisian present
rather than the Mexican past. The entire poem is cast in the second
person and addressed to Breton;[73] it is an affirmation of Péret's
unswerving fidelity to Breton and to Surrealism, and its tone is
therefore the opposite of the anguish expressed in *Dernier Malheur*

---

[72] André Breton, "Second Manifeste du surréalisme," *Manifestes du surréalisme* (Paris: Pauvert, 1962), p. 154.

[73] "Toute une vie" was originally published as part of *André Breton, essais
et témoignages,* ed. Marc Eigeldinger (Neuchâtel: A la Baconnière, 1950). For
further discussion of the text, see Mary Ann Caws, *The Inner Theater of
Recent French Poetry* (Princeton: Princeton University Press, 1975), pp. 80-83.

dernière chance and *Air mexicain*. The joyful humor of this text is evident from the first line: "les sinistres glapissements tricolores crevaient comme des poissons en sueur," but it is serious in intent and might be included among what it calls "les chants en poings dressés des éternels rebelles avides de vent toujours neuf."

Toute une vie moves chronologically from the formative years of the First World War to the writer's present in 1949. The text can be divided into three parts: a description of the pre-Surrealist world, an account of the circumstances and content of Breton's early ideas and activities, and an affirmation of the persistence of this spirit in the present. Occasional historical references give the text a narrative quality which is belied by the entirely lyric use of elements of Surrealist doctrine. The bond between Péret and Breton as expressed in this text is so strong that many of the statements can be attributed to either man, but Péret accredits Breton with major events: "Lâchez tout disais-tu" and "Tu lançais le Manifeste du surréalisme."

Breton's early opposition to the status quo is attributed by Péret to the influence of Jacques Vaché on one who was already aware of himself as existing apart from the world into which he came:

> et déjà la voix d'un cheveu blond emporté par le vent qui s'élève
>   des tikis
> t'avait fait traverser d'un seul élan les rues en danse de
>   Saint-Guy
> où Vaché allait disparaître comme une giboulée dans un salon.

The major weapon in these early days is humor: "rien qu'une avalanche de rires dévalant des montagnes phystiques et bien peignées." Vaché's *umour* was directed against all of contemporary society but Péret, perhaps alluding to Lautréamont's domestic scenes, uses the family to represent the degradation of the old values. His attention then turns to the historical situation of art; in this context art is no more than an ironic description of something belonging to the past:

> l'art un coup de bouteille de champagne sur la tête
> s'écroulait dans une boue de décorations et de barbes arrachées
>   comme des affiches de mobilisation.

Into this atmosphere of degeneration comes "un air frais de premier lilas de l'année" which brings with it "le mot liberté." The advent of *l'esprit nouveau,* proclaimed by Apollinaire in 1917, is presented by Péret as a natural occurrence in the course of time, an aggressive element of change with which Breton was in harmony. Those who cannot live in this new air are represented in retreat through a humorous succession of descriptive clauses:

> pendant que les bêtes à tuer du talon
> geste de sacré-cœur
> regard de portez armes
> nez de pensum
> face de circulez
> sourire de compte en banque
> grognement de ministre
> demi-cervelle de soumis
> courbure de vendu
> gueule de faux témoin
> rentraient la truffe dans la base bien pensante. [74]

These are the animals which, in a natural process, have failed to evolve and are thus unadapted to the new environment. In contrast, there are those like Tzara who can survive; "le rat des Carpathes" is accused of misusing the new freedom, calling for "liberté en pensant Pour les flics et mon monocle." This duplicity is condemned along with vulgar sensationalism, and Péret's pejorative account of these aspects of the Dadaist movement is presented as paralleling that of Breton, whose own ideals were higher:

Lâchez tout disais-tu pour voguer sans nord et sans étoile à
   travers les tempêtes ...
Lâchez tout Maintenant la proie qui comble et plus tard son ombre...
Lâchez tout La poussière du jour déjà hier ne doit pas obscurcir
   le soleil de demain
Lâchez tout.

"Lâchez tout" was the title of Breton's definitive farewell to Dada; the following extract shows the fidelity with which Péret translates the spirit of the document into poetry:

---

[74] The use of such a series of images is often associated with the poetry of Jacques Prévert. For a discussion of Péret's influence on Prévert, see Courtot, pp. 120-25.

> Lâchez tout. Lâchez Dada. Lachez votre femme. Lachez
> votre maîtresse. Lâchez vos espérances et vos craintes.
> Semez vos enfants au coin d'un bois. Lâchez la proie pour
> l'ombre. Lâchez au besoin une vie aisée, ce qu'on vous
> donne pour une situation d'avenir. Partez sur les routes.[75]

For Péret, Breton was proceeding correctly in conjunction with the course of history which calls for the liberation of desire from material goals. Others, who are less adept, cling passively to old ways; rather than hearing "l'heure du réveil sonnée par les alouettes," they hide "pour répudier les seismes de leurs rêves." Again in this passage, the change in the atmosphere of the times is presented in terms of a natural phenomenon, the song of a lark, and the unwillingness of others to abandon themselves to the new movement is contrasted with Breton's "Lâchez tout."

The sharing of memories held in common by the author and his subject begins the second section, and the intimacy of this shared past is emphasized in the opening words, "Souviens-toi." The exciting beginnings of Surrealism are recalled with references to the play *S'il vous plaît* (1921) and to the "Cadavre" (1924) written upon the death of the author Anatole France, who is here named "Anatole Crasse." This portion of the poem refers to the time before the actual constitution of the Surrealist movement, and its advances are indicated as not yet having occurred:

> L'écriture automatique allait multiplier les merveilles que
>   l'œil ouvert dissipait
> L'orchidée du savon allait fleurir comme une lampe qui
>   fredonnerait des chants nègres.

After a further account of the historical situation in which the marvelous force of desire is taking an increasingly stronger part, the poetic depiction of Breton's doctrine appears in flamboyant terms:

> Le temps était aux aurores boréales invisibles dans les salles
>   d'attente du dictionnaire
> tu lançais le Manifeste du surréalisme
> comme une bombe explosant en vol de paradisiers faisant
>   le vide dans la basse-cour.

---

[75] André Breton, "Lâchez tout," *Littérature,* nouvelle série 2 (April 1922).

Péret immediately ascertains that this new development is for the good of poetry: "les hirondelles des mots qui ouvrent les persiennes du matin / s'envolaient à tire-d'ailes." In this passage and the preceding lines, the words "aurores boréales," "bombe," "paradisiers," and "s'envolaient" translate the freeing of desire in Surrealist poetry. This liberation is contrasted with the conservatism of those who oppose the new poetry; they are represented by

> quelque digne vieillard à trogne d'élégie
> qui soupirait en ajustant son monocle
> La poésie perd ses tripes et ces voyous marchent dessus
> sans imaginer que son perroquet empaillé couvait toutes les
> mites qui paradaient sous son crâne.

In addition, this comic scene is a serious objection to the inbred, closed world of traditional poetry in contrast with the Surrealist openness to the inspiration of chance.

The three main tenets of Surrealist doctrine in the *Manifeste du surréalisme* are explicated in the following lines: "le rêve libéré du cachot" is followed by "liberté liberté couleur d'homme" and "consubstantiel à l'homme / l'amour." Although each principle is illustrated in turn, all three are interdependent: dream is presented as coming into the street "pour la révolution surréaliste / armé de son seul regard à arracher les serrures," while freedom contributes to the proliferation of dreams in waking life because it acts against that which vilifies existence by perverting desires. The strongest expression of this interconnection is made with regard to the link between love and liberty: "car toute liberté exsude fouet et chiourme si l'amour a des devoirs qu'il ne se connaît pas." At the end of this section, this link is reinforced: "tant que l'homme sa compagne à la main n'aura pas exploré tes forêts que n'habite aucun monstre / . . . la liberté ne sera qu'un demain on rasera gratis." Péret shares Breton's position on the necessary association of love with freedom in the liberated context of desire. The end of *Dernier Malheur dernière chance,* in which the freeing of the world is accomplished through a kiss, also expresses this idea. On the subject of love, Péret's other orientation in this section of *Toute une vie* is toward the renewal of the theme, which he himself develops in such collections as *Je sublime* and which Breton explores in *L'Amour fou* (1937) and *L'Air de l'eau* (1934), among other works. In oppo-

sition to the apparent futility of talking yet again about love because "tout était dit de l'amour depuis les onomatopées jusqu'aux
formules qui les condensent," [76] Péret supports Breton's continued
exploration of the theme of love: "plus de conscience toujours plus
de conscience de l'amour." Breton's last book-length work, *Arcane
17* (1945), speaks at length about love, which is, as Péret con-
firms, a subject for ceaseless Surrealist speculation.

Breton's ideas are affirmed in the present by the third section
of *Toute une vie,* but the problems which Surrealism faced at the
outset have not yet been resolved. For Péret, the main preoccupation is truth:

> Il serait inutile de parler de la vérité si l'on ne lui avait tant
>   craché au visage
> que son regard en étoile polaire obstinée à marquer le la
> s'est aujourd'hui effacé comme une ville rasée par les barbares
>   que déjà la brousse envahit.

This thirst for truth is the greatest bond between Breton and Péret,
and it leads to the strongest statement of their unity: "c'est cela
André qui nous rassemble en grains d'un même épi." Their friendship is expressed with a metaphor drawn from nature, but unlike
the important images of this type earlier in the text, this one is
characterized by its persistence and its capacity for growth. Truth
itself is part of the extra-human order, "sauvage," while freedom
is identified with the natural change brought about by an avalanche.
Desire is released in a force that destroys the old to create a new
order. The final image of *Toute une vie* is yet another expression
of the unity of Surrealist aims with the movement that is beyond
the scope of human manipulation: "ceux qui crient de tous leurs
poumons ensevelissant les pompei / lâchez tout." The revolutionary
fervor of the Surrealists is finally shown to be capable of repro-
ducing the volcanic action of Mount Etna, which destroys the old
civilization. Here as in *Je sublime,* the image of the volcano translates the liberated force of desire. Breton's battle cry is the basis
for the victory in geological terms as it has been the structuring

---

[76] This statement can be compared with the following from "Le Noyau de
la comète": "Tout a-t-il donc été dit de l'amour? Assurément non. Il ne pourrait
en être ainsi qu'au cas où, l'humanité n'étant plus susceptible d'évolution, les
rapports entre les êtres devraient rester à jamais figés" (p. 7).

force for the Surrealist revolution. For the Surrealist movement, as for Marx, "le point de départ ... se situe dans les entrailles du sol." [77]

Toute une vie ends in the future; thus Péret predicts that Breton's influence will extend into generations to come and that his work will be carried on. Although basically historical in its orientation, the text begins and ends, like *Air mexicain,* at a moment of crisis which is combined with confidence in its resolution; the poem is a perception of a cyclic structure in the course of change across time. In all three long poems of the forties, Péret expresses desire for change, as well as delineating the transforming power of desire itself.

C. The Politics of the Marvelous

In *Dernier Malheur dernière chance, Air mexicain,* and *Toute une vie,* Péret brings the force of desire to bear on the general shape of history, whether it is his own or that of a culture with which he closely identifies. Within the context of his life as a French citizen, he finds much to be corrected by the liberation of desire. The sublimation of erotic impulses in the form of revolt is a primary element of his theory of *l'amour sublime.* This aspect of desire is the subject of a major collection of poetry, *Je ne mange pas de ce pain-là* (1934), and is further explicated in the essays "La Parole est à Péret" (1943) and "Le Déshonneur des poètes" (1945).

Political change is primary among Péret's goals, and expressions of revolt against the established status quo characterize all his work. The poetry-love-dream-death network explored in *Immortelle Maladie* and *Dormir dormir dans les pierres* has a negative counterpart in the repressive alliance of Church, police and State or, more generally, of established religion, physical repression, and its ideological counterpart. These negative forces, like the liberating powers, are intrinsically linked, and mention of one inevitably summons up another. They support ideological stasis and use murder and degradation to this end; these major transgressions are reinforced by the unattractiveness of the representatives of these powers.

---

[77] Georges Bataille, "La Vieille Taupe et le préfixe *sur* dans les mots *surhomme* et *surréaliste,*" *Tel Quel,* 34 (1968), 8.

Although Péret makes general condemnations of the powers of
repression, as for example in his introduction to the *Anthologie des
mythes, légendes et contes populaires d'Amérique,* specific targets
do not escape mention. *Je ne mange pas de ce pain-là* names the
villains and makes pointed accusations which label them as evil.[78]
But this work is not alone in this specificity; for example, in "Il
était une boulangère" (1924) Pope Pius VII and the wife of General Boulanger are principal characters and their comportment is
alternately undignified and obscene. An episode in the same work
reveals Poincaré as a dentist who advertises the free extraction of
a tooth but who, as the unlikely couple is warned, will also remove
the remaining teeth and charge dearly for the operation. In "Au
125 du boulevard Saint Germain" (1922), the king of Greece appears as a ludicrous secondary character, and Poincaré is again the
target of Péret's humor: "Au loin on pouvait apercevoir le Prési-
dent de la République, revêtu d'un scaphandre et accompagné du
roi de Grèce, qui semblait si jeune qu'on avait envie de lui ap-
prendre à lire." But individual attacks are moderated by the whim-
sical humor of the context. The most aggressive defamation occurs
at the end of "Il était une boulangère," where the heroine's transformation into a bird is a revelation of her true character and the
narrator adopts a paternal tone in speaking to the Pope:

> Mais malheureux, que fais-tu là? La Boulangère n'est pas
> morte. Cette pie-grièche qui pousse des cris assourdissants,
> perchée sur un bras du crucifix, c'est elle, qui te souhaite
> l'éternelle félicité. Tu as tout ce qu'il te faut pour être
> heureux, pape: le Vatican et la Boulangère! que veux-tu
> que je fasse de toi maintenant? Rien . . . alors, adieu.

The rare texts in *Le Grand Jeu* which refer to named individuals
are also mild when compared with those in *Je ne mange pas de ce
pain-là.* The worst said of Louis-Philippe, for example, is that he
"vit de pillules et de buvards / mange sa mère / et perd l'heure
en marchant." *Je ne mange pas de ce pain-là* is not so easy on its
victims; this characterization can be compared with that of another
historical ruler, Louis XVI, in *Je ne mange pas de ce pain-là*: "Pue

---

[78] Gershman says of *Je ne mange pas de ce pain-là* that "it is clear, on
reading the above, where Aragon found his inspiration for *Front rouge,* especially
as that sort of violence is exceptional in his work" (p. 52).

pue pue / Qu'est-ce qui pue / C'est Louis XVI l'œuf mal couvé."
In *Le Grand Jeu,* the Pope is guilty of being the lover of a dancer
in a bloody dress; in *Je ne mange pas de ce pain-là,* the text "Le
Pouvoir temporel du pape" describes him as born of "des vierges
putains qui soulagèrent leur ventre / dans la tinette du bénitier."
Paul Claudel is ridiculous but not distasteful in "Un Oiseau a fienté
sur mon veston salaud," also from *Le Grand Jeu,* for he owes his
ambassadorial post to simultaneous bites of a bear and a telephone.
Another text from *Le Grand Jeu,* "Le Dernier Don Juan de la
nuit," is closer to the tone of *Je ne mange pas de ce pain-là:*

> Le quarante-deuxième pose son urine sur le canapé
> Dansez voltigez les biroutes
> Dépêche-toi j'ai envie de dormir
>   EDMOND ROSTAND

The single literary figure treated in *Je ne mange pas de ce pain-là*
is subjected to more personal criticism; Péret's characterization of
him shows him to be a pederast, a hypocritical Communist, and a
secret chauvinist. In contrast, the earlier treatment of Rostand
lacks the extension of the later works and does not draw political
conclusions; Rostand's transgression is allowed to remain in the
realm of literary boredom, while Gide is condemned for serious
moral wrongs.

Péret acquired considerable notoriety from the 1945 publication of a brief essay entitled "Le Déshonneur des poètes." [79] This
text begins by defending the poet and poetry, then continues with
an outspoken criticism of Resistance poets, specifically those whose
works were collected under the title *L'Honneur des poètes.* Although
Georges Hugnet took this essay to be a rejection of political activism on the part of the poet, [80] a closer examination of the text

---

[79] "Le Déshonneur des poètes," pp. 71-89.

[80] The negative reaction to "Le Déshonneur des poètes" was led by Georges
Hugnet, whose attitude is clear in the following quotation from an article on
Eluard in *Arts,* 891 (1965), 5: "Il a fallu, les saletés se reproduisant comme le
reste, que ce tire-au-flanc, ce pousse-au-crime, ce parasite embusqué le plus
loin possible, le nommé Benjamin Péret, se chargeât de publier, à Mexico, en
1945, l'abject *Déshonneur des poètes.*" In response to this attack, several of
Péret's friends visited Hugnet and, according to his wife, physically threatened
him. The events are recounted in detail from the friends' point of view in *De
la part de Péret* (Paris: Association des Amis de Benjamin Péret, 1963).

shows this interpretation to be erroneous. "Le Déshonneur des poètes" does not reject thematically political texts, but rather those publications in poetic form which purport to be political acts. As Claude Courtot remarks: "le poème devient . . . un geste à *imiter, une démonstration d'envol, un moyen: il a cessé d'être une fin.*"[81] According to Péret, the poet must be a revolutionary on all fronts:

> celui de la poésie par les moyens propres à celle-ci et sur le terrain de l'action sociale sans jamais confondre les deux champs d'action sous peine de rétablir la confusion qu'il s'agit de dissiper et, par suite, de cesser d'être poète, c'est-à-dire révolutionnaire.
> ... ...
> En tout cas, la poésie n'a pas à intervenir dans le débat autrement que par son action propre, par sa signification culturelle même. [82]

Within this context, he finds Louis Masson, Pierre Emmanuel, Louis Aragon, and Paul Eluard guilty not only of perverting poetry in the cause of propaganda, but also (in the cases of Eluard and Aragon) of repudiating their erstwhile radicalism and embracing Church and State. The denunciation of Eluard, "qui de tous les auteurs de cette brochure, seul fut poète," [83] is especially bitter as the two men had been close friends and collaborators. Péret quotes Eluard's "Liberté" extensively, albeit slightly inaccurately, as an illustration of the depths to which his close friend has fallen. As late as 1936, Eluard seems to agree with Péret on the independence of poetry: "la poésie, malheureuse de plaire quand elle se satisfait d'elle-même, *s'applique,* depuis toujours, malgré les persécutions de toutes sortes, à refuser de servir un ordre qui n'est pas le sien." [84] Like the other Resistance poets, Eluard was guilty of exhalting an ill-defined liberty while at the same time invoking Church and State, the two principal obstacles to freedom. Unlike the texts of these poets, *Je ne mange pas de ce pain-là* is unyielding in its blasphemy of established religious and political order and has no direct propagandistic goal; its targets are for the most part dead and gone.

---

[81] Courtot, p. 108.
[82] "Le Déshonneur des poètes," pp. 76 and 87.
[83] *Ibid.,* p. 85.
[84] Paul Eluard, "L'Evidence poétique," *Œuvres complètes,* I, 513.

In a study of *Je ne mange pas de ce pain-là,* J. H. Matthews remarks that "la répugnance physique se relie au dégoût moral" because "chez Péret l'opposition n'est pas poétique parce que morale; elle est à la fois poétique et morale." [85] The translation of moral disapproval into terms of physical debasement and degeneration dominates the collection. In this sense, it is analogous with Georges Bataille's definition of "les formes mentales révolutionnaires" in an article which attempts to denigrate the Surrealist effort in the area of social change. Bataille says of true revolutionary action that "c'est l'agitation humaine, avec *toute* la vulgarité des petits et des gros besoins, avec son dégoût criant de la police qui la refoule, c'est l'agitation de *tous* les hommes." [86]

Eleven of the twenty-eight texts in *Je ne mange pas de ce pain-là* are concerned with the death of an individual and the rotting of his body, and seven others center on the carnage and base activities associated with war. While the remaining ten texts have no given basis for aggressive description of physical degradation, they do acquire negative implications by their situation in a contaminated context. Five concern religion, an obvious target for Péret, of whom one of the best-known pictures shows him "insultant un prêtre." [87] Three poems, "6 février," "6 décembre," and "La Peste tricolore," are based on the political strife of 1934, in which left and right are equally subject to vilification. An abstract topic like the financial insecurities surrounding the Depression is easy prey in "La Baisse du franc" and "La Stabilisation du franc" because of its link with capitalism. Even the Tour de France is not too trivial a topic; in "Le Tour de France cycliste" it is an accessible concretization of nationalism and participates in the modern mythology of the French state. All these attacks are in accord with Péret's statement of one aspect of the poet's role: "c'est à lui de prononcer les paroles toujours sacrilèges et les blasphèmes permanents." [88]

---

[85] J. H. Matthews, "Invective et merveilleux dans *Je ne mange pas de ce pain-là* de Benjamin Péret," *Kentucky Romance Quarterly,* 18 (1971), 412 and 414.

[86] Bataille, 16.

[87] The photograph is reproduced in Jehan Mayoux, "Benjamin Péret, ou la fourchette coupante," *Le Surréalisme Même,* 3 (1957), 57.

[88] "Le Déshonneur des poètes," p. 75.

The texts in *Je ne mange pas de ce pain-là* span ten years in Péret's poetic life: they indicate a tendency in all his work rather than a transient phase. The formal similarity of nine texts which range in original date of publication from 1926 to 1936 illustrates this continuity. [89] They begin with the circumstances of an individual's birth, then proceed through his early career and entrance into public life and conclude with a general characterization of his person and, if he has died, of the implications of his death. Three of these texts, "Le Cardinal Mercier est mort," "Mort de la mère Cognacq," and "La Mort héroïque du Lieutenant Condamine de la Tour," date from 1926; "Pour que Monsieur Thiers ne crève pas tout à fait" originally appeared in 1930, and four texts, "Briand crevé," "La Peste tricolore," "Le Pouvoir temporel du pape," and "Jeanne d'Arc," were first published in *Je ne mange pas de ce pain-là*. The formal continuity in these violent texts creates a pattern which correlates on a larger scale with the Surrealist use of regular syntax; changing the content rather than the position of structural slots is a technique which creates an ironic, mock-epic effect in *Je ne mange pas de ce pain-là*. Another example of this juxtaposition of formal syntax with unexpected images appears in "La Société des Nations": "Or en ce temps-là les pissotières marchant au pas cadencé / se retrouvaient à Genève." The biographical detail in some of these texts is almost obsessive: Foch's childhood is treated with reference to ages six, eight, ten, and fifteen. But in every text the atmosphere of disgust has a moral base; the unat-

---

[89] The following exerpts serve as examples:

"Issu de la sueur des mains sales
le cardinal Mercier grandissait . . .
Un jour dieu comme une vieille tâche d'huile
apparût à ses yeux" ("Le Cardinal Mercier est mort")

"Enfin ce sperme mal bouilli jaillit du bordel maternel
Un rameau d'olivier dans le cul . . .
Voilà Monsieur Briand" ("Briand crevé")

"Un jour d'une mare de purin une bulle monta
et creva
de l'odeur le père reconnut
ce sera un fameux assassin" ("L'Assassin Foch")

"Issu d'un vomissement dans un pot de chambre bleu
Chiappe la vieille chique sucée et resucée . . .
Enfin un jour . . .
on découvrit Chiappe entre deux trognons de choux pourris
et l'on fit de lui le chef des assassins" ("6 février").

tractive descriptions of the persons in question reflect inner qualities. Thiers, speaking of his victims' blood, says "ça vaut mieux
que l'eau / et ça coute moins cher." Cardinal Mercier wishes for
war as if it were Advent; Madame Cognacq abets Indochinese massacres of "familles nombreuses / qui pour chaque enfant / reçevait
une pelle à feu"; Briant is associated with "le sang des 1 500 000
morts"; Condamine de la Tour "cherche des massacres"; Foch is
a "fameux assassin"; Chiappe is ready to accept anything that will
keep him in power; the Pope is morally accountable for Italian
Fascism; Joan of Arc is responsible for the religious infestation of
French life.

The same fundamentally moral tone pervades the collection as
a whole. Péret's attacks, violent though they are, are not indiscriminate. The greatest villains are the perpetrators of war or civilian
murder and those who feign peaceful intentions to further bloodthirsty aims. Writing between the two World Wars, in a decade
when repercussions of the first were increasingly drowned out be
noise of the approach of the second, he had ample subject matter.
As Breton notes,

> Au cours des trois années qui précèdent la nouvelle guerre,
> le surréalisme réaffirme sa volonté de non-composition avec
> tout le système de valeurs que met en avant la société bour-
> geoise. Cette volonté s'exprime avec le maximum d'intran-
> sigeance et d'audace dans le receuil de Benjamin Péret: *Je
> ne mange pas de ce pain-là.* [90]

Yet the poems in this collection are not limited to current bel-
licosity: "Pour que Monsieur Thiers ne crève pas tout à fait,"
"Jeanne d'Arc," and "Premier Empire" concern conflicts in the
more or less distant past and the venom is not diluted by the passage of time: "le poète lutte contre toute oppression," [91] past as
well as present. He is at once firmly rooted in his time, with its
Foch and Chiappe, and possessed of a vision which penetrates beyond
time into a past marked by the evils which continue in the present.
The past is dead or dying, and the villains presented in *Je ne mange
pas de ce pain-là* are placed in contrast with the future, which
belongs to revolutionary Surrealist liberation. The two living sub-

---

[90] André Breton, *Entretiens,* p. 193.
[91] "Le Déshonneur des poètes," p. 75.

jects, Gide and the Pope, are identified with a literature and a religion of this decaying past. The inclusion of texts relating to anterior events creates a context for the present and elevates poems which have temporal delimitations, like "6 février" and "6 décembre," beyond topicality and into the realm of human history.

Texts which are principally concerned with religious matters also decry war-mongering nationalism; one element is not present without the other. In the realm of militant activism, Péret enunciates this position in a document protesting the French passivity with regard to the Spanish Civil War. Although "Au feu" (1931) is signed by many Surrealists, Péret's name appears first and it seems probable that he composed the text:

> Détruire par tous les moyens la religion, effacer jusqu'aux vestiges de ces monuments de ténèbres où se sont prosternés les hommes, anéantir les symboles qu'un prétexte artistique chercherait vainement à sauver de la grande fureur populaire, disperser la prêtraille.... Tout ce qui n'est pas la violence quand il s'agit de la religion ... est assimilable à la pactisation avec cette innombrable vermine du christianisme qui doit être exterminée. [92]

In *Je ne mange pas de ce pain-là,* Joan of Arc is an obvious representative of the alliance between religious and military fervor, but André Gide's presence in this context is less expected and his participation in bigotry and chauvinism is presented as a revelation:

> Tel une tomate agitée par le vent
> Monsieur le camarade Gide fait un foutu drapeau rouge
> dont aucune salade ne voudrait
> un drapeau rouge qui cache une croix
> trempée dans le vitriol
> et bien française comme pas un chien de concierge
> qui se mord la queue en entendant la *Marseillaise.*
>   ("La Conversion de Gide")

Tearing aside the communist disguise, Péret reveals the Christian essence of Gide as shown by his conversion.

---

[92] "Au feu," in Maurice Nadeau, *Histoire du surréalisme* (Paris: Seuil, 1964), p. 328.

Conversely, those poems which have political repression as their
principal topic usually condemn religion as well. Revolt against the
forces of social stasis, those which impede the liberation of desire,
is simultaneous on both fronts, as in "Macia désossé":

> Mais la Catalogne qui rôtit
> les curés et les nonnes
> après les avoir mariés
> comme Carrier
> fera
> des notes de musique avec tes os.

Péret's condemnation of political phenomena such as the Big Four
pact and the League of Nations includes attacks on the religious
identities of the participants:

> Je suis italien dit le troisième
> Heureusement que j'ai le pape comme nouille
> ("Le Pacte des Quatre")

> Et la pissotière anglaise était pleine de débris de bibles.
> ("La Société des Nations")

The instability of the French franc is repeatedly equated with the
imminent failure of the church in "La Baisse du franc"; the franc
is referred to as "curé," "effigie," "général des jésuites," "hostie,"
and finally "dieu pauvre franc usé." Capitalist worship of money
is made analogous with worship of God in order that both may
be rejected. God Himself, a "betterave sans sucre" in the same text,
is considered wanting by those who assemble in His name at the
"Congrès eucharistique de Chicago":

> Ah qui nous donnera un dieu rafraîchi comme un crâne sortant de
> chez le coiffeur
> un dieu plus sale et plus nu que la boue
> Le nôtre lavé par les rivières
> n'est plus qu'un absurde et livide galet.

At times the intimate association of Church and State is explicit,
as in "6 février," which shows priests "tirant sur leurs frères flics."
More often, this association serves as a basis for imagery which
connects the two elements: "Les nonnes garderont les tranchées
pour le plaisir des rengagées" ("La Loi Paul Boncour").

The Manichean world of *Je ne mange pas de ce pain-là* does not allow for compromise; it is constructed about a series of dualities which are mutually exclusive. The most prevalent of these is the alternation between life and death, which is equated with another binary set, that of the speaker and the group with which he identifies in contrast with those against whom he speaks. The we-they duplet coincides with that of living and dead and with another set, repression and liberation. In the temporal realm, this distinction is to some extent reproduced by the difference between past and present, but Péret is sufficiently aware of current evils to place some of his villains in the living present and to project the triumph of liberation and of the *nous* of the text into the future. Within the realm of the dead, the dominant binary set is that of ingestion and excretion, with the latter term prevailing. In a wider context, the hate which permeates *Je ne mange pas de ce pain-là* and the love of *Je sublime* are equally representative of the strength of desire in all of its forms.

Within the scope of the verbal revenge wrought by the texts of this collection, the theme of popular reprisals recurs. The subjects of the texts are usually dead; Gide and the Pope are the only two important living figures. The fact that the others are dead gives Péret a qualified pleasure: "Mais maintenant que tu es crevé / si le monde a moins d'ulcères / les hosties gardent leur goût de cadavre" ("Le Cardinal Mercier est mort"). Péret is as bloodthirsty as those he condemns when the identities of the victims change. While they stand accused of mass murder, his aggression is directed toward an individual. He certainly approves the taste of the sea monsters in "Nungesser und Coli sind verreckt": "Quant à nous nous aurons des banquiers soufflés / des généraux couverts de vomissures / et de sombres bourriques de tous les pays." "La Loi Paul Boncour" ends in a vision of revolution in which senators, priests, and generals are the representative groups destroyed,[93] while the "chœur des ouvriers trahis" in "Briand crevé" has the final word: "Dommage qu'il soit mort trop tôt / notre guillotine n'aurait jamais si bien fonctionné / Heureusement qu'il nous reste des banquiers des généraux des députés des évêques." Vengeance is also possible

---

[93] In the letter "Aux communistes" (April 29, 1927) signed by Péret among many others, is the exclamation "A bas la loi Paul Boncour!" (Nadeau, p. 273).

in the cases of those already dead, as in "Peau de tigre," where maggots devour the corpse of Clemenceau and his bones serve as revolutionary whistles. All these expressions of popular reaction appear at the ends of texts; with the removal of the repressive figure, revolutionary change is again possible.

Three texts stand apart from the rest of *Je ne mange pas de ce pain-là* because of their distinctive form and tone. Although they were not originally published together, "Hymne des anciens combattants patriotes," "Epitaphe pour un monument aux morts de la guerre," and "Petite Chanson des mutilés" [94] appear consecutively in the final version and form a veteran's trilogy. Unlike the other poems in the collection, these three are quite regular in form: "Hymne des anciens combattants patriotes" is composed of six four-line stanzas and a two-line coda; "Epitaphe pour un monument aux morts de la guerre" repeats a single rhythmic refrain five times in the first section and at every other line in the second; "Petite Chanson des mutilés" has two refrains. Péret, himself a veteran, [95] expresses compassion along with contempt for those who have willingly sacrificed themselves to the chimera of military glory:

> les grenades me pètent au nez
> et les citrons éclatent dans ma main
> Et pourtant je suis un ancien combattant
>   ("Hymne des anciens combattants patriotes")

> nous sommes crevés
> le doigt dans le trou du cul
> Priez pour nous
>   ("Epitaphe pour un monument aux morts de la guerre")

> Prète moi ton bras
> pour remplacer ma jambe
> les rats me l'ont mangé
> à Verdun (bis).
>   ("Petite Chanson des mutilés")

---

[94] "Hymne des anciens combattants patriotes" and "Epitaphe pour un monument aux morts de la guerre" were published in *La Révolution Surréaliste,* 12 (1929), while "Petite Chanson des mutilés" appears for the first time in *Je ne mange pas de ce pain-là.*

[95] Péret was a *cuirassier* from 1917 to 1919. A more detailed account of his military career is given by Courtot, p. 12.

Like the fallen cyclist in "Le Tour de France cycliste," they are
held at least partially accountable for their own misfortunes, but
they also represent a populace betrayed by its leaders. In the final
text, "6 décembre," these leaders are named Blum and Thorez, [96]
and the volume ends on a pessimistic note: "Encore une fois nous
sommes trahis." Péret's refusal to place himself among these victims
is evident in his treatment of them in *Je ne mange pas de ce pain-là*
as well as in his choice of its title for his epitaph.

The vocabulary of this collection is consistently scatological and
occasionally obscene as Péret exposes the negative side of *le merveilleux quotidien.* The use of this lexicon is often effective in its
aggression on accepted ideas as it creates an atmosphere of disgust:

> Les perles de ma femme sont des yeux des fédérés
> et mes couilles de papier mâché
> je les dégueule tous les matins
> Si j'ai des renvois de nougât
> c'est parce que Gallifet me gratte les fesses.
> ("Pour que Monsieur Thiers ne crève pas tout à fait")

Péret explores the resources of slang vocabulary as well as those of
standard usage in his invective and vilification, and he rarely repeats
himself from text to text. The words which appear most frequently
in this context are general pejorative terms such as "sale" and
"pourri," but fourteen synonyms are found for excrement and nine
for places reserved for excretory functions. In the complementary
realm of corporeal imagery, the "ventre" or "panse" predominates,
along with "gidouille," a term associated with Alfred Jarry. The
word "crever," rather than the standard "mourir," is often used to
note death; its German equivalent is used in the title of "Nungesser und Coli sind verreckt." Like "crever" and several of the synonyms for excrement, much of the vocabulary of *Je ne mange pas
de ce pain-là* associates the persons described with animals. Twenty
species appear in these poems as a repertoire of distasteful types:
rats, flies, maggots, and toads appear often. Obscenity is less common; although sexual references appear, they are limited to parts
of the body and words associated with sodomy and prostitution.

---

[96] At the time "6 décembre" was composed, Blum and Thorez were the
leaders of the French Socialist and Communist parties, respectively.

Vocabulary relating to the sense of smell appears more frequently, and the constant evocation of rot and stink adds to the physical disgust created by these texts. Marxist thought and alchemical theory are united by their use of this imagery: for Marx, "dans l'histoire comme dans la nature la pourriture est le laboratoire de la vie," [97] while for the alchemist, "our whole mystery is based on putrefaction; for it can come to naught, unless it is putrefied." [98]

A typical poem in *Je ne mange pas de ce pain-là* has a subject to which the entire length of the text adheres with a consistency that is unusual, but not unique, in Péret's work. An example of this technique is "Le Tour de France cycliste," in which sixteen of twenty-eight lines contain some explicit reference to the bicycle race. "La Guerre Italo-Abyssine" is based on a stable symbolic system in which noodles stand for Italy and black bread for Abyssinia, while in "Jeanne d'Arc," the English and French soldiers are "poux" and Joan herself is a "punaise." Matthews remarks that Péret is most effective when the poem has "dépassé les bornes rationelles," [99] but the texts in this collection begin beyond these borders. References to extrinsic boundaries are replaced by a coherence based on an internally ordered syntax of images. The historical nature of the characters and events which appear in these texts or their existence as it is placed within the bounds of rationality is less important than their status as representatives of the antagonistic forces for the revolutionary poet. Objective reality is relevant only insofar as it is reconstituted as part of an intra-textual causal system; for example, in "Louis XIV s'en va à la guillotine," Louis is identified as an ill-hatched egg and shown with his head falling off, two elements derived from his egg-like rotundity and his beheading. But the rotten egg of empire is not presented as the victim of the guillotine; Péret reveals another cause for his decapitation: "sa tête tombe dans le panier / sa tête pourrie / parce qu'il fait froid le 21 janvier." He has lost his head to rot, usually a function of heat rather than cold; hence he is shown to be in a state of discord with natural processes. Again in "Nungesser und Coli sind verreckt," the death of the aviators is a consequence of their nature: "mais ils étaient déjà pourris."

---

[97] Quoted as the epigraph to Bataille, 5.
[98] Edward Kelly, "The Theater of Terrestrial Astronomy," *Io*, 4 (1967), 55.
[99] Matthews, 413.

Péret does not comment on history or react to the conduct of individuals; rather, he reveals its true course by acting poetically upon the historical presentations of events. As he states in "La Parole est à Péret," poetry is for him "la source de toute connaissance et cette connaissance sous son aspect le plus immaculé." [100] In *Je ne mange pas de ce pain-là,* the act of knowing appears in its most aggressive incarnation. Paul Eluard's definition of the epistemological value of Surrealism reflects this poetic militancy in speaking of "le surréalisme qui est un instrument de connaissance et par cela même un instrument aussi bien de conquête que de défense." [101] In the "parce que" of "Louis XVI s'en va à la guillotine" and the declarative statement "mais ils étaient déjà pourris" of "Nungesser und Coli sind verreckt," a causality is revealed by the poet, the only human being capable of finding it. The same explanatory technique occurs frequently in *Je ne mange pas de ce pain-là* and shares the action of revelation with descriptive processes. Sometimes the two are combined, as in "Le Congrès eucharistique de Chicago": "C'est que dieu constipé depuis vingt siècles n'a plus de boueux messie pour féconder les terrestres latrines."

For Péret, the marvelous is not necessarily physically attractive or benificent: "le merveilleux est partout, dissimulé aux regards du vulgaire mais prêt à éclater comme une bombe à retardement." [102] In *Je ne mange pas de ce pain-là,* the marvelous springs forth from such unexpected sources as latrines, piles of excrement, tombs, and overfed bellies. Although Péret's ideological stance is transparent, he explicitly denies that reason operates within the poetry itself: "Petit franc petit franc qu'as-tu fait de tes os / Qu'en aurais-tu fait sinon le *poker dice* qui projette ces mots sur le papier" ("La Baisse du franc"). The operation of chance in the world is reproduced by the automatism of the poem, which becomes an autonomous agent of revolt:

> Crève encore pourri dont les pissenlits ne veulent pas
> crève
> que ta poussière noie les écrits
> de ceux qui diront du mal de ce poème.
>
> ("Macia désossé")

---

[100] "La parole est à Péret," *Le Déshonneur des poètes,* p. 35.
[101] Eluard, "Physique de la poésie," 989.
[102] "La parole est à Péret," p. 35.

It is the poem, not the poet, which is subject to criticism; the revelation of causality or description is the product of the interaction between poetry itself and inherent qualities of the poem's subject. Paul Eluard's insert to *De derrière les fagots* was written in 1933 after most of the poems in *Je ne mange pas de ce pain-là* had appeared, and he seems to be speaking of them at the beginning of this text:

> Une des principales propriétés de la poésie est d'inspirer aux cafards une grimace qui les démasque et qui permet de les juger. La poésie de Benjamin Péret favorise comme nulle autre cette réaction aussi fatale qu'utile. [103]

When the poet speaks in the first person, it is usually as a member of a group, as in "Mort de la mère Cognacq": "Dansons dansons en rond," and "Peau de tigre": "Faisons erreur mes amis." The poetic stance of one speaking for a group is also recommended in "Le Déshonneur des poètes"; poetry should be "le produit d'une exaltation collective réelle et profonde que traduisent leurs paroles," [104] not an attempt to excite the masses to this state. More often (in nine texts) Péret addresses the poem directly to its subject in the second person or presents the person or persons as speaking for themselves (nineteen texts). Again, it is the inherent qualities of the subject which prevail over poetic manipulation of it. The plurality of voices relates this collection to *Le Passager du Transatlantique* and distinguishes both from the bulk of Péret's poetry. Dialogue, which dominated *Le Passager du Transatlantique,* has entirely disappeared except as it occurs between persons within the poem; Péret as poet does not speak to his subject. As the collection's title indicates, he refuses to interact with the enemy.

The vocabulary of elimination and alimentary imagery appear frequently in *Je ne mange pas de ce pain-là,* as the title suggests. Péret's desire not to partake of the menu is understandable; the list of things eaten is limited to sacramental objects, human flesh, vermin, excrement, and a hammer. The host and holy water are reduced to the level of simple foods and further degraded by their juxtaposition with the other items on this list. Eating is often associated with

---

[103] This *prière d'insérer* is found in Eluard's *Œuvres complètes,* II, 846.
[104] "Le Déshonneur des poètes," p. 80.

degradation: a king devours breasts and feet in "Jeanne d'Arc" and a cat swallows the scatological incarnation of "l'assasin Foch." Sometimes it is a form of revenge: Gide is forced to eat the Communist hammer, and maggots consume the corpse in "Peau de tigre." Frequently, those who eat are not humans but rather sea monsters, rates, mites, or maggots which represent the power of nature over human flesh. Although more ordinary comestibles appear throughout *Je ne mange pas de ce pain-là,* they are never presented as being eaten; they serve either as elements in analogical descriptions of the subject of the poems, as do the noodles in "Pacte des quatre" and "La Guerre Italo-Abyssine," the tomato in "La Conversion de Gide," and the "betterave sans sucre" in "La Baisse du franc," or as images of the subjects' action. Moreover, these foods may form an associational chain within the poem: Gide as tomato immediately calls forth the word "salade," the macaroni in "Pacte des quatre" echoes an earlier mention of noodles and the Chicago beefsteak has its accompanying "frites" in "Le Congrès eucharistique de Chicago." Consistent with the emphasis on rotting matter in this collection, edible items appear in the process of decomposition as "légumes avariés," "trognons de chou pourris," or "poisson pourri." One food that is never mentioned is the bread of the title, which designates, as is general French usage, anything eaten. The "pain noir" of "La Guerre Italo-Abyssine" is not French bread, and its color makes it a metaphorical equivalent of the black Abyssinians. As in the colloquial expression "je ne mange pas de ce pain-là," eating in the imagery of the collection represents mental as well as physical assimilation of an external element to the self, allowing alimentary imagery to take on expanded significance. An example of this extension is the phrase "elle mangea les poux" in "Jeanne d'Arc": since the vermin have been established as French soldiers, Joan's eating them becomes a metaphor for her attempts to achieve masculine military prowess.

Like *Immortelle Maladie, Je ne mange pas de ce pain-là* manifests a belief that death is not complete removal from the living world. The vocabulary of the text, especially in its emphasis on rot and putrefaction, indicates that the dead (or, in the cases of Gide and the Pope, the rotten living) are still in the process of reincorporation into physical nature. From this degenerating animal matter, in combination with the vast quantity of manure that is markedly present, something new and alive will grow; this is the suggestion of "6 décembre," which mentions "des assistants dont on ferait un si bon engrais." The moral analogue to this physical process is the development of a new order from the remains of the past after it has undergone the necessary changes of degeneration. Although the shock value of the invective has its own justification, it is noteworthy that the material that pollutes also fertilizes. Political change is thus integrated into a natural context in this collection as the death of the past encourages growth in the future. The unleashed strength of desire leads to the perpetuation of life and the subversion of forces which lead to death and stasis.

The poetry of *Je ne mange pas de ce pain-là* does not attempt to influence the course of events or to inspire the reader with revolutionary zeal. The emotions expressed are those which, according to Péret, already exist within his prospective audience. Change occurs in these texts on several levels: the identities of the subjects are in a state of turmoil; they themselves change from living to dead matter, and thence into new constituents of life. Prospectively, life itself is changing with the death of these obstacles to freedom and, externally, the nature of persons and institutions is changed from its conventional form. The poet himself, however, does not change; his style and attitude are constant during the ten years spanned by the texts collected in *Je ne mange pas de ce pain-là,* and they are reflected in earlier and later works.

From the erotic desire of *l'amour sublime* to the generalized desire for unity in the long poems of the forties, the structure of change is the same, informed by human emotions and the active will to carry then to their ends. Desire, which has its source in the deepest and most private aspects of human life, is projected into man's view of every part of his existence: "le désir ... loin de perdre de vue l'être de chair qui lui a donné naissance, tend donc en définitive à sexualiser l'univers." [105] Vague longings for change are crystallized in the dynamic force of desire, which is, paradoxically, constantly realized in erotic love, in history or in revolt, and yet remains perpetually unfulfilled.

---

[105] "Le Noyau de la comète," p. 22.

III

REINVENTING THE WORLD

Within Péret's Surrealism, new creations come into being and are explored through the ongoing process of change; the eternal state of becoming is the definitive mode of existence for all things in Péret's works. This change is brought about through the limitless power of the verbal expression of imagination. As Breton asks, "Qu'est-ce qui me retient de brouiller l'ordre des mots, d'attenter de cette manière à l'existence toute apparente des choses?"[1] His response is copiously illustrated in Péret's Surrealism: "Il n'est rien, selon moi, d'inadmissible."[2] From the primordial beginnings of the world to the present, change is the expression of the moving force of desire. In the change which dominates Péret's works, desire as expressed in the dream is one key to the sequences of events and things which appear in poetry and prose. Yet the goal of continuing transformation and metamorphosis is a perfection which is never attained because of the inherent mutability of all things. Hence, Péret's utopian state is defined by dynamism rather than by stasis.

Among Péret's works, *Air mexicain* and *Dernier Malheur dernière chance* have been shown to suggest the possibility of an investigation of the earliest states in which existence can be defined. In *Air mexicain,* pre-human time is evoked by the Aztec speaker: "quand l'aile chatoyante de l'aube se perdait dans les gouffres de crépuscule habité de gestes mous." However, this primordial state

---

[1] André Breton, "Introduction au discours sur le peu de réalité," *Point du jour* (Paris: Gallimard, 1970), p. 23.

[2] *Ibid.,* p. 26.

is not devoid of created phenomena; even human artifacts such as candles are already present. *Dernier Malheur dernière chance* evokes another early state which follows destruction and is the basis for a process of re-creation. Both works reveal the assumption that the basic components of the world were not created by some divine force; rather, they exist independently. A similar principle is stated by Heraclitus: "Ce monde, uniformément constitué, n'a été créé par aucun dieu, ni par aucun homme. Mais il a toujours existé, il existe et existera toujours" (fragment 33). This basis is maintained in *Histoire naturelle* (1958): the elements can engender creatures or man can act upon them to bring new things into being. Creative change is intrinsic both to elements and to man's existence in the elemental world. Only an imagination as infinitely renewed as that of Péret himself can answer the challenge of the possible in a "feu d'artifice inoubliable et perpétuel." [3] He is able to describe (and thus to create) this state because he is "at the center of the world . . . striving to resuscitate that mythical time when being and reality were one." [4]

The time of Genesis is identified with the present through the intrinsic nature of change in Péret's prose tales. Once again, it is Breton who provides the formula: "nous en sommes encore à lire les toutes premières pages de la Genèse." [5] Péret's tales, most of which were published in *Le Gigot, sa vie et son œuvre* (1957; for tales not included in this collection, see Appendix), reveal a utopia in which, in Freudian terms, the reality principle is continually conquered by the pleasure principle. Two of the aspects of the Wonderland revealed by Péret's tales are the abundance of food and the prevalence of play as a basic mode of activity. Like his poetry, Péret's prose texts are remarkably consistent. From "Au 125 du boulevard Saint Germain" (1922) to *Histoire naturelle,* change is depicted as the exuberant center of all existence. The dominance of change makes everything potentially possible and the fulfillment of every wish within every person's grasp.

---

[3] André Pieyre de Mandiargues, "Benjamin Péret," *Deuxième Belvédère* (Paris: Grasset, 1962), p. 83.

[4] Gershman, p. 121.

[5] Breton, "Introduction au discours sur le peu de réalité," p. 25.

A. GENESIS AS CHANGE

Péret's world of constant change is based in a primordial reality which is elaborated and metamorphosed to bring other phenomena into being. In *Histoire naturelle,* he sets forth a detailed explanation of this initial state and uses the classical model of four elements and three kingdoms as his referential base. It is the interaction and manipulation of earth, air, fire, and water which leads to the creation of everything else, and once the three kingdoms have been constituted, their relationships provide the rationale for fundamental processes. Péret's account of the creation of the world goes beyond that of Genesis in its attempt to rebuild human perception of the world on bases other than those of Judeo-Christian thought. *Histoire naturelle* is Péret's last publication in prose and appears only a year before his death, but this work is essential to a comprehension of Péret's world; it also serves as a basic text for the study of his contribution to Surrealism in poetry and prose. It provides an answer to the question posed by Louis Aragon in *Le Paysan de Paris*:

> Je me dis qu'après tout, réserves faites du langage, on pouvait se demander s'il n'existait point un sentiment mythique particulier, aujourd'hui efficace, qui se restreignît à ce qui fut jadis la nature. Y a-t-il des mythes naturels modernes? [6]

The style of *Histoire naturelle* combines straightforward declarative sentences and textbook or manual explanations with the elaborate narration of Péret's tales. When the elements themselves are discussed the reasoned elaboration of the text is reinforced by parodic scientific jargon, as in the following example:

> Dans un récipient contenant de l'air sous une pression de trois atmosphères et soumis à une très basse température, la terre fournit l'aiguille à tricoter. En augmentant la pression et en diminuant la température, on a le merle, le berceau, le petit pois et l'horrible motocyclette.

---

[6] Louis Aragon, *Le Paysan de Paris* (Paris: Gallimard, 1966), p. 158.

This humorous deadpan technique mixes a serious tone with incongruous nouns filling slots where other nouns are expected. While many examples of startling creative combination are found in the primitive myths and legends collected in Péret's *Anthologie des mythes, légendes et contes populaires d'Amérique,* they are presented in terms of cosmogony rather than in those of modern experimental science. Numbered lists of products add to the impression of scientific accuracy and recall Péret's predilection for toying with combinations of numbers in poems in *Le Grand Jeu,* especially the texts "26 Points à préciser" and "Mystère de ma naissance." The stylistic consistency of the first section of *Histoire naturelle,* composed of the treatises on the four elements, and its contrast with the following chapters on the three kingdoms may be attributed to the thirteen years which elapsed between their composition: the four earlier chapters were completed in Mexico in 1945, and the last two in Paris in 1958, while "Le Règne minéral" is dated "Ile de Sein, 1950." Nonetheless, the continuity between the parts is so strong that the link between the first four chapters and the last three is made with a subordinate clause:

> Lorsque l'eau, l'air, la terre et le feu furent lassés de danser en rond autour d'une glaciale flamme de vide, ils soufflèrent dessus, l'éteignirent, et, rompus de fatigue, s'assirent serrés les uns contre les autres car s'ils avaient dansé si longtemps un ballet d'ours en cage, c'était tout simplement pour se réchauffer.

The initial clause, beginning with *lorsque,* indicates that the events described in the opening of "Le Règne minéral" take place immediately after those with which the descriptions of the elements concluded. In the last three chapters, the elements speak and interact physically in order to produce, by willful or accidental combination, the components of the animal, vegetable, and mineral kingdoms. These chapters, unlike the preceding four, bear a close resemblance to Péret's earliest prose.

In the 1945 section on the elements, the agent who effects metamorphosis is outside the text; he functions both as the narrator who acts through his theory and as the reader in a potential future. This potential agent is referred to as "on," a designation which leaves his identity entirely open and as free to participate in the process of change as the elements in the narrative. Péret's use of this pronoun recalls Breton's prediction in the *Premier Manifeste* of a prose in which characters "se comportent avec la même aisance envers les verbes actifs que le pronom impersonnel *il* envers des mots comme: *pleut, y a, faut,* etc." [7] The creators in the three kingdoms are, in contrast, present in the text: for the mineral kingdom, they are the elements in conjunction; in the vegetable kingdom, these creative participants are joined by a blade of grass; in the animal kingdom, the major generative power is attributed to an agave plant. Their creations are described as history, not as instructions as in the sections on the elements; hence, their activites cannot be repeated as such although the creative work of the human and non-human world remains open-ended throughout Péret's work. As it takes place, the metamorphosis of one thing into another entails the effacement of the original nature of the material in question. In this sense, the events described in *Histoire naturelle* parallel those of Max Ernst's process of *frottage,* the products of which were also called *Histoire naturelle*:

> J'insiste sur le fait que les dessins ainsi obtenus perdent de plus en plus, à travers une série de suggestions et de transmutations qui s'offrent spontanément . . . le caractère de la matière interrogée (le bois par example) pour prendre l'aspect d'images d'une précision inespérée. [8]

Thus the detail with which Péret describes the results of various producations is analogous to the change emergence of precise images from the undistinguished material of *frottage.*

Histoire naturelle is a myth in Lévi-Strauss' sense; it is the work of a *bricoleur.* [9] The "materials" used in this construction are as diverse as any in Péret's work; they include the elemental, the

---

[7] Breton, "Premier Manifeste du surréalisme," p. 46.

[8] Max Ernst, "Au-delà de la peinture," *Max Ernst 1919-1936* (Paris: *Cahiers d'Art,* 1937), p. 20.

[9] In *La Pensée sauvage* (Paris: Librairie Plon, 1962), Claude Lévi-Strauss defines the activity of the *bricoleur*: "la règle de son jeu est de toujours s'arranger avec les 'moyens du bord', c'est-à-dire un ensemble à chaque instant fini d'outils et de matériaux, hétéroclites au surplus, parce que la composition de l'ensemble n'est pas en rapport avec le projet du moment, ni d'ailleurs avec aucun projet particulier, mais est le résultat contingent de toutes les occasions qui se sont présentées de renouveler ou d'enrichir le stock" (p. 27).

human, and the artifactual. In his indiscriminate use of materials from diverse areas like Heraclitus, Péret does not distinguish between the inner world of the self and the outer world of nature. The first sentence of *Histoire naturelle* spans three domains from which Péret draws a comprehensive anthropomorphie view of the universe:

> Le monde est fait d'eau, de terre, d'air et de feu et la terre n'est pas ronde mais a la forme d'un bol. C'est un sein du ciel; l'autre se dresse au milieu de la voie lactée.

This internally consistent depiction of the universe relies on poetic perception alone: an obvious association of the forms of bowl and breast with a further link between breast and the Milky Way overturns accepted points of view without recourse to any pre-existing scheme. [10] Taken out of their ordinary context of size and temporal situation, these components are endowed with a new freedom which has important implications for the entire system in which they conventionally participate. Once the accepted notions of the structure of the world are abandoned, the poet is free to proceed with his description of its parts and their origin. Again, a discussion of the world of Max Ernst is applicable: according to Breton, "c'était comme le jeu de patience de la création; toutes les pièces, invraisemblablement distraites les une des autres, cherchaient à se découvrir de nouvelles affinités." [11] A partial list of the products of the transformation of soil by various processes attests to the variety of its potential: lipstick, Turksh bath, frog, cello, glasses for the myopic, compass, saveloy sausage, boxer, match, preposition, gooseberry, tricycle, sieve, concierge, knitting needle, seagull, cradle, pea, motorcycle, fish-hook, urinal, moustache. The association of

---

[10] In *L'Un dans l'autre,* Breton recounts the following episode in the game, as proposed by Péret: "Je suis un très beau SEIN de femme, particulièrement long et serpentin. La femme qui le porte ne consent à le montrer que pendant certaines nuits. De ses innombrables mammelons jaillit un lait lumineux. Peu de gens, à l'exception des poètes, sont capables d'apprécier son galbe" (p. 32). The answer to this description, "la voie lactée," links it with the image at the beginning of *Histoire naturelle,* the first chapter of which was composed nine years earlier. In the rules of the game, Péret would only have provided the first element of the comparison; the second, "sein," is furnished by other members of the group.

[11] André Breton, "Avis au lecteur pour *La Femme 100 Tête,*" *Ernst,* p. 114.

these diverse objects and phenomena within groups suggests an automatic technique at work within a fixed structure, yet some explanations recall other works by Péret and can be followed rationally with success:

> On distingue deux sortes de rouges à lèvres: le rouge ondulé à longues vagues qui, par distillation, donne les drapeaux et le rouge léger dont la fleur produit le baiser. Ce baiser s'obtient d'ailleurs de deux manières différentes, soit par dessication de la fleur cueillie au moment de l'éclosion, soit par écrasement de la graine qui donne une essence très volatile et difficile à conserver.

Love and its physical expressions have become literally elemental; moreover, it is the first product mentioned as coming from the first element, earth.

As in previous works, connotations of the various elements are not limited in *Histoire naturelle* to any particular field and each contributes equally to the elaboration of the world of things. Often, the items enumerated reflect the contemporary world in its apparent gratuity, as in the example of petrol which, as a primary product of water, takes on many forms. In a gas-powered world, the importance of petroleum is unavoidable, but in Péret's world it is integrated with the animal and vegetable kingdoms: it feeds butterflies and, in granular form, stimulates the growth of elephants' tusks. Removed from the realm of modern technology, petrol is thus "naturalized" into the world of this history. The intangible undergoes similar treatment: "remontée à la surface du sol, l'eau de puits s'évapore rapidement, laissant au fond du récipient un résidu d'un beau vert clair: le principe de causalité qui, soluble dans l'huile, est le père de l'artichaut." This unqualified statement is in keeping with Péret's own use of the causality principle, but it also deprives causality of inviolate status by making causal relationships as susceptible to change as anything else seen or unseen in the world.

Mary Ann Caws states that "perpetual movement informs all possible perspectives on Surrealism," [12] and *Histoire naturelle* is a manifestation of this principle. Not only do elements change into

---

[12] Mary Ann Caws, "Motion and Motion Arrested: The Language of the Surrealist Adventure," *Symposium,* 24 (1970), 303.

things which are capable of further change, but also the identities of these phenomena and objects fail to coincide with the expected. The same petrol enjoyed by butterflies and elephants can become in high altitudes "chaise, lémurien d'aspect inoffensif mais dont la morsure très venimeuse peut même devenir mortelle." The relaxation which a chair implies is antipathetic to this world in movement, and warning is given that human behavior must take the reality of *Histoire naturelle* into account. New uses as well as new identities are revealed: air gives rise to "le chef d'orchestre, si utile aux paysans au moment de la moisson." Desirable qualities and the objects to which they are attached suffer from the same disjunction, so that fire, when handled with special tools, can be made into "planches si résistantes et si légères que les enfants en font des cerfs-volants." The fresh and unexpected quality of these descriptions gives the appearance of each object the quality of an event; new relations between disparate elements are disclosed.

That these transformations take place does not mean that they are necessary; they are merely presented as facts. In the first sentence of "Le Règne minéral," Péret states that creative energy was expended so that the elements might keep warm rather than out of the desire to make things. Some are designated as useless:

> l'air, à son état normal, secrète constamment du poivre qui fait éternuer la terre.... A deux mille mètres dans l'atmosphère, le poivre se condense également et retombe sur la terre en poussière si impalpable que personne ne s'en aperçoit, mais un beau jour apparaît le testament d'une inutilité si flagrante que les passants l'écrasent immanquablement.

Other elements fit well into Péret's informal scheme: fire, for example, is best when used "dans l'incendie des églises."

Although this first section is divided by chapters according to the element in question, all four often combine in the creation of something new, as in this example from the chapter of fire: "abandonnées à la pluie tout un hiver, les pierres de vent donnent un feu violent." The apparent incompatibility of fire and water is overcome in this interaction; words are absolutely free regardless of the characteristics of the objects they designate. The mixture of elemental components is, like the synthesis of causal sequences and lists, the result of a free play of chance and automatism rather than of a consciously causal structure. The conformation of reality is presented as analogous with poetic thought within the superstructure of scientistic phraseology.

After the four elements and their products are described, the second section, which comprises the three chapters on the kingdoms, begins with the elements in a miserable state; they are all freezing, and even fire, which ordinarily incarnates heat, is dying of the cold. The creation of the minerals is a chance occurrence: water blows on its hands to warm them and sulfur comes into being. Other elements imitate water, and their varying natures lead to the creation of different minerals. Yet all this activity is play rather than work: "l'eau, l'air, la terre et le feu commençaient à se divertir avec tant d'entrain qu'ils ne sentaient plus le froid." Although Péret labels their activity "l'invention des minéraux," they are not depicted as conscious of their inventive procedure. In keeping with the allusions to alchemy such as "Albert-le-Grand" and "bain-marie" in the first section, the appearance of mercury in this chapter is of great importance; once the elements recover from their astonishment at its character, they begin to create with it:

> Ils commencèrent alors à mélanger, au gré de leur fantaisie, tous les minéraux qu'ils avaient méprisés jusque là, sans oublier d'y ajouter toujours quelques gouttes de mercure, et l'on n'entendit plus que rires et cris de joie qui parfois s'envolaient à tire-d'ailes.

Again, the identities of these elements, like creations such as the chair, are the products of new descriptions rather than of habit, and each mineral has a distinct personality. Mica, for example, is "un commerçant prospère, bien peigné, rasé de frais et en habits de dimanche." Occasionally, chance and accepted reality coincide, as in the case of gold: it attaches itself so tightly to the earth that the element must carry the mineral about with it. In both these cases, the narrative is a reflection of reality: mica, perceived as the mineral incarnation of a businessman, is despised for its illusory brilliance, while the value of gold is conveyed in its natural rather than commercial aspect. The interaction of the elements with their mineral creations is not always to their advantage because, immediately after their creation, the minerals are endowed with powers of their own equal to those of the elements. The emerald, for example, does considerable damage to the air, but it is still admired by the other elements because of its great beauty. In the family quarrel that ensues, the minerals take sides. The results of the quarrel lead beyond the scope of the chapter: the first river is established, fire is hidden under the earth and, as the primordial situation of this chapter is reestablished, the first sunrise takes place.

Although eight years elasped between the composition of "Le Règne minéral" and the completion of *Histoire naturelle,* this chapter is closely linked with the following one through the final image of sunrise and solitude. "Le Règne végétal" begins with a single blade of grass alone in the vegetable realm and longing for company. By dividing itself and projecting the divided part onto mica, it makes a companion in the form of the pumpkin, but it does not recognize this new creation as being part of the same kingdom; rather, it says "encore un soleil qui se couche!" and thus recalls the end of the preceding chapter. Up to this point, the creative activity of the chapter has taken place in the daylight; in Péret's world, in view of the emphasis on dream in his theoretical work, it is to be expected that the oneiric climate of night would give rise to even greater movement. The enormous productivity of night is partially attributed to rain which, in falling, turns to seeds which vary in their growth according to the minerals touched in falling. Disorder marks the development of the plant world despite occasional attempts to create stability, and plants take shapes which show that they are in early stages of evolution:

> Quelques instants plus tard, de cet endroit naissait l'artichaut qui s'éleva bientôt jusqu'à dix mètres de hauteur puis, notant son erreur, redescendit prudemment jusqu'à atteindre sa taille normale.
> Ailleurs, l'iris s'était commodément installé au sommet d'un hêtre, mais son triomphe fut bref.

Because the minerals still have seniority in this new world, it is the tournaline, a stone, which attempts to find a way of stopping the disorder by creating cacti which impede the freedom of movement of the plants. This stasis is only temporary because a storm comes up which blows the vegetation about and adds to the confusion by creating more varieties through the generative power of lightning.

Another interruption in the displacement of flowers, trees, and vegetables is brought about by the multiplication of fig trees, but this stasis is also broken. The desire for order is increased toward the end of the chapter before it is finally installed: "enfin, la désolation était générale et c'était vraiment triste de voir le désordre. . . . Rien qui fut à sa place."

The text of *Histoire naturelle* increasingly takes on the allocutions of fable, most significantly in the attributions of etiologies to the configurations of various members of the plant world. The rose, for example, acquires its thorns in order to protect itself from the bombardment of the nut-tree; another event in the style of fable is "une rixe sanglante au cours de laquelle la carotte, écorchée vive, fut jetée dans un trou et le platane fut si bien rossé qu'il resta couvert d'ecchymoses." The naïvete of this point of view is reinforced by the emotions attributed to the plants and minerals which interact in this chapter like small boys at play. [13] Occasional narrative interventions in the text associate it further with fable:

> le laurier abusait du lilas qui se vengeait sur le buis. Celui-ci devint timide et il lui fallut longtemps pour oublier l'outrage qu'il avait subi, mais l'oublia-t-il vraiment? Il est permis d'en douter.

The humanization of a world devoid of human presence characterizes Péret's work from a very early stage, and the persistence of this technique is part of the marked consistency of his prose and poetry. The attitude toward nature in the 1924 collection *Immortelle Maladie* is expressed thirty-four years later in the final chapters of *Histoire naturelle*.

The link between the vegetable and animal kingdoms is made by the fly-trap, a plant which has the animal attribute of eating. Willed causality is, as usual, detached from effect:

> au-dessus de lui, le flamboyant agitait ses longues gousses dans un bruit de castagnettes, comme pour le railler. D'une gousse, une graine s'échappa . . . et bientôt des milliers de mouches et de moustiques sillonnaient l'air.

---

13 André Breton, *Le Surréalisme et la peinture* (Paris: Gallimard, 1965), p. 165: "les Grands Naïfs: on reconnaît les deux Rousseau (Jean-Jacques et Henri), Jean-Paul Brisset, Benjamin Péret, au centre Max Ernst."

Eating is again involved in the creation of the next animal life; the surplus of flies and mosquitoes threatens the balance of nature, so birds, beginning with the warbler and one of Péret's favorite birds, the titmouse, are brought into being in answer to the question "qui nous débarrassera de cette saleté?" Disorder threatens in the proliferation of ants, which arise from the dead bodies of flies, but an anteater is created by the agave to take care of this problem. This plant takes a magisterial position in the following pages; among its creations are the otter, the cricket, the woodpecker, the mole, and the earthworm. But the scope of the elaboration of the animal kingdom quickly escapes the bounds of natural order and the text returns to the multiplicity of reference which characterizes *Histoire naturelle*. The first example of this appears when the agave

> saisit son violon, l'accorda et des lombrics par vagues s'en échappèrent, puis il entreprit de jouer une valse et le porc sauta de l'archet en grognant, suivi du cheval qui s'enfuit bouleversé par les grognements du porc.

A deck of cards is the next creative vehicle, and while the agave is expounding upon its potential, he states in passing the current location of the imminent creatures "qui, pour l'instant, se morfondent dans un bain turc."

When the giraffe is created, the link with the elemental sections of the text is even stronger; various treatments for the giraffe are explained along with the products they yield: in white sauce, the cormorant when warm and the ibis when cold; in thin strips, lobsters and bears. The same multiplication through the introduction of ancillary factors leads to the creation of various breeds of dogs:

> combinant, mélangeant avec des ingrédients divers — trapèze, litote, poudre à éternuer, patrie, plume, sergent-major, etc. . . . — l'agave réussit à extraire tous les chiens de la queue du premier, mais aucun n'aboyait, à l'exception de celui-ci; aussi saisit-il un alexandrin avec lequel il entreprit de fustiger la meute qui bientôt aboyait.

Two of the elements in this sequence belong to literary terminology; the use of abstractions is common in the chapter, and their presence in juxtaposition with diverse objects deprives them of privileged status; the rule of three, flowers of rhetoric, and a psychological treatise take their place as parts of the world of phenomena. The creative combinations of the agave recall Breton's "l'un dans l'autre" game in that anything can by made from anything else through the imaginative use of analogy. [14] After stating that "tout est possible," the agave continues his activity by casting it in the form of cognition: "je connais les cétacés. . . . Je connais aussi des félins. . . . D'ailleurs, on connaît diverses panthères." The account of the agave continues to draw on abstract and concrete words; the tortoise is made from Archimedes' principle and frozen tomato sauce and the pelican comes from "un sophisme battu en neige." Care to detail is present despite the quantity of creatures; the agave is troubled, for example, by the beak of the toucan, the plumage of the pelican and the provision of a skeleton for a limp elephant.

According to the agave's narrative, the final event in his career is the creation of man. In the poetic context of *Histoire naturelle,* the unique human verbal capacity is emphasized:

> J'avais distribué un peu partout la parole mais elle était encore confuse. . . . C'est pourquoi j'ai taillé l'homme dans un pruneau. Il était encore minuscule mais j'avais confiance dans le temps qui lui permettrait de grandir, d'ailleurs il me l'avait promis.

The universal personification of the text is finally extended to time itself. Just as *Histoire naturelle* began with a depiction of the kiss and of the universe as a female body, so it ends on the theme of love. Man's first words are "et ma femme? Où est-elle?" When the agave responds that it is up to man to find her, the newly-created

---

[14] Fourier appears again in the context of analogies; a number of his investigations of this mode of thought sound very much like Péret's although they obviously belong to another time. The following example from *Le Nouveau monde industriel* (1848) is typical of this aspect of Fourier's thought: "le chou est emblème de l'amour mystérieux. . . . Le chou-fleur, qui est contre-partie du chou, dépeint la situation opposée, l'amour sans obstacles." André Breton draws on Fourier's use of analogy to create images some of which are remarkably like those of *Histoire naturelle*: "entre en se dandinant la molécule de caoutchouc." See Breton's *Ode à Fourier* (Paris: Klincksieck, 1969), especially pages 22-23 and 73.

male makes his own female from honey. The world is now complete and the text ends on this note of harmony and wholeness.

Histoire naturelle is unique; it draws on texts in the natural sciences and alchemy, as well as on the automatism of which Péret was a fervent exponent. [15] The verbal puns which characterize such early works as *152 proverbes mis au goût du jour* (1925) are expanded into physical metamorphoses; but this is not the first appearance of this technique in Péret's work. Change in things characterizes all the prose tales and, more generally, many of his poems. As Nicholas Calas states in a chapter of *Confound the Wise* dedicated to Péret, "without change no creation is possible; poetry is metamorphosis." [16] No stronger illustration of this principle can be found than *Histoire naturelle*. Heraclitus, whose name appears first on a reading list compiled by Breton, [17] states a principle which is basic to this work and to all of Péret's Surrealism: "Ils ne comprennent pas comment les contraires se fondent en unité: harmonie des forces opposées comme de l'arc et de la lyre." [18]

Max Ernst's *Histoire naturelle* (1926), a series of *frottages,* is an example of the coalescence of visual and verbal art forms in Surrealism. René Crevel comments on this title in relation to Ernst's works in a manner which is equally descriptive of Péret's *Histoire naturelle*: "l'histoire du rêve, l'histoire SURRÉELLE est bien, comme l'a dit Max Ernst, une HISTOIRE NATURELLE." [19] The illustrations of Péret's *Histoire naturelle* are by the Czechoslovakian Surrealist Toyen; this choice is indicative of a remarkable similarity between Péret's and Toyen's respective outlooks. In "Au Monde nouveau: maison fondé par Toyen," Péret uses terms to describe her work which apply to his own productions:

> Toute l'œuvre de Toyen ne vise pas à autre chose qu'à corriger le monde extérieur en fonction d'un désir qui s'alimente et s'accroît de sa propre satisfaction . . . aujourd'hui,

[15] Raymond Queneau's treatment of the same subject matter in *Petite cosmogonie portative* (Paris: Gallimard, 1950) adheres more closely to the discoveries and vocabulary of the sciences.

[16] Nicholas Calas, *Confound the Wise* (New York: Arrow Press, 1942), p. 44.

[17] Maurice Nadeau, *Histoire du surréalisme,* p. 384.

[18] Yves Battistini, "Héraclite d'Ephèse," p. 31, fragment 57.

[19] René Crevel, "Max Ernst," *Ernst,* p. 95.

on assiste dans chacun de ses tableaux à une phase donnée d'une incessante métamorphose, l'ensemble formant un monde entièrement neuf. [20]

Péret's article on Toyen was published during the period in which *Histoire naturelle* was written, and "Le Mythe de la lumière," its closing passage, is complementary to the longer work and shares its orientation towards the explanation of basic phenomena.

Although *Le Gigot: sa vie et son œuvre,* the volume which collects Péret's prose tales, was not published until 1950, the majority of its contents dates from the 1920s. Most of the tales were published in reviews between the twenties and the appearance of *Le Gigot,* and some of Péret's tales are not included in this volume. [21] Chronologically, Péret proceeds from effects to causes, from a description of activities in his world to a delineation of the generative and creative principles on which it is constructed. An exploration of Péret's tales shows that they take place in the world described in *Histoire naturelle.* In the finished context in which the tales operate, as in the world in the process of creation, life is everywhere, and the population of a city street is as diverse as that of the primordial world. Man is not the king of the universe; he constantly encounters other forms of existence in places where human beings are expected. Courtot describes this state in the following manner:

> Les éléments universellement répandus et séparés par nul cloisonnement sont communs à tout ce qui est.... Les règnes végétal, minéral, animal et humain sont tous également doués d'une même vie qui les parcourt et les fait vibrer d'un même frisson. [22]

---

[20] "Au Monde nouveau: maison fondée par Toyen," *Toyen,* by André Breton, Benjamin Péret and Jindrich Heisler (Paris: Editions Sokolova, 1953), is an introduction to an exposition of Toyen's work. Péret's characterization of Toyen's point of view in this essay illustrates the close relationship between her work and his own: "le monde à ses yeux demeure indéfiniment perfectible et il suffit de l'aiguillonner un tant soit peu pour qu'il se remette en mouvement comme aux premiers âges, alors qu'un semblant d'ordre s'ébauchait peu à peu dans le désordre des quatre éléments se livrant un combat impitoyable. Rien n'était encore stable et, d'un œuf de poule pouvait aussi bien naître un singe qu'une agate" (pp. 23-24).

[21] For further bibliographical information, see Appendix.

[22] Claude Courtot, *Introduction,* p. 171.

In the earliest tale, "Au 125 du boulevard Saint Germain," the protagonist is on the trail of a criminal when he knocks on a door and hears successively the cock's crow, a sheep, and a gust of wind. The civilized Jardin des Plantes is the site of another series of invasions in the same tale; there, the king of Greece is diverted from his search by a heron, an antelope, and a crab. When the elusive Monsieur Séraphin is finally run to ground, he invites the amateur detectives to dinner, noting that they must be hungry since their bodies, split down the center, reveal organs covered with butterflies. Whenever possible, the untamed replaces the civilized; in "Une Vie pleine d'intérêt," the hapless Madame Lannor finds her cherry trees exchanged for "des girafes naturalisées," while in "Les Vagues Ames," the result of a revolution is the appearance of an enormous leg in the place of the column in the Place de la Bastille.

This proliferation of life, like that in *Histoire naturelle,* is capable of unexpected growths. In *Le Gigot,* "Les Malheurs d'un dollar" includes a typical example:

> lorsque, de la vase, jaillit, vous entendez bien jaillit, un gigantesque chapeau melon qui, arrivé à trois mètres de hauteur, se retourna et laissa tomber dans la vase une charmante jeune fille blonde et rose.

People are especially susceptible to inordinate development. Madame Lannor finds her feet covered with cherry leaves and fruit, and in "Une ornière vaut une jument," a female character "se gonfla rapidement, devint gluante, puis poisseuse et s'étala enfin comme une large tache de sang sur le gazon." However strange the growth of people and things may be, it tends to follow a logic which is part of the tale. "Et les seins mouraient" illustrates this logic when the growth of aquatic plants in the pavement of a city street is attributed quite simply to a strong rain. On other occasions, the phenomenon relies on a motivation which is presented as general knowledge, as in the case of the "frequent" growth of geranium sprouts on pregnant women which makes them give birth prematurely in "Corps à corps." Causality is sufficient for the tale when two events can be temporally juxtaposed:

> à cet instant, un chêne perdra tous ses glands et un petit gyroscope, tournant au milieu de tes intestins, donnera naissance à un roseau lequel, réflexion faite, deviendra un dra-

> peau grâce à la présence d'un verre rempli d'eau addition-
> née de sang de canard.

Nothing appears in a void; things are the products of transformations of one material into another. As in *Histoire naturelle,* the appearance of something new in the tales depends on the existence
of a substance which has the inherent capacity for change. For
Péret, anything has this potential, and the specific changes that are
made are determined by the course of the narrative, which they in
turn direct.

Elsewhere there is complete metamorphosis which is not accompanied by the growth which characterizes the passages just cited.
According to Courtot, this is an essential part of human freedom:
"pour que l'être puisse s'épanouir pleinement, il doit posséder cette
faculté onirique et poétique (mais n'est-ce pas un pléonasme?) de
la métamorphose immédiate et sans limites." [23] The results of change
are unknown until they appear, like the interior of the houses in
such tales as "Au 125 du boulevard Saint Germain," which reveal
streams, vegetable and animal life, and unexpected villains. Often
the changes which occur recall those of the early chapters of *Histoire naturelle* in that they are performed by the combination of
several elements:

> Une montagne de ferraille sur laquelle elle jeta la peau d'une
> orange qu'elle venait de manger . . . une faible lueur permit
> à Sonia de voir le tas diminuer avec une inquiétante rapi-
> dité et un manceniller entouré d'un cercle d'agaves s'élever
> à sa place.

Throughout Péret's work, death is presented as the passage from
one form of existence to another, so it is not surprising to one who
has read *Immortelle Maladie* that in "Il était une boulangère," the
dead Poincaré becomes an oak. The intangible is as capable of metamorphosis as any other phenomenon: "l'histoire qu'elle lui raconta
lui planta dans la tête toutes les fleurs des champs" ("La Maladie
no. 9"). No element of Péret's world is too humble to participate
in the beauty and freedom of change; even the lowly toe in "Le
Pont des soupirs" is transformed into jasmin trees which are also

---

[23] *Ibid.,* p. 169.

butterflies. What appears to be unique is merely one form of an essence which can assume a wide vaiety of shapes: "n'as-tu pas compris qu'en changeant de climat, la Roche Tarpéienne s'est modifiée? Roche Tarpéienne à l'équateur, ours blanc au pôle, voilà la vérité" ("Et les seins mouraient").

The technique of naming the successive incarnations of an element of the world in sequence is used frequently in the tales and parallels the use of this stratagem in *Histoire naturelle*. The life of man is thus summed up in "Sur le passage d'un panier à salade":

> Dans sa jeunesse, l'homme sans inquiétude pour lui-même se borne à regretter que les animaux domestiques ne soient pas des bottes de sept lieues; à trente ans, il soupçonne qu'il n'a été qu'un homard; à quarante ans il le sait et pense à se manger lui-même à l'américaine; à cinquante ans, il cesse de se raser, il fait avaler ses dents par les poules qui, le soir même, meurent sur leur perchoir et il meurt à son tour en souhaitant que ses enfants renversent la colonne Vendôme.

The woman who makes this statement is a seer who appears as a rather ridiculous figure despite her professional connection with the marvelous. Another example of the sequence technique as a means of revealing the relatively low position of man in the world is the genealogy of Napoleon in "La Fleur de Napoléon," which proceeds from the abstractions of uniformity and boredom through artichokes and cows to the general himself. The life of the nine of clubs in "Et les seins mouraient" is even more involved in its mutations: "d'abord pâte à rasoir, puis grain de sel, puis frôlement, rayon X, savon minéral, coquillage, poisson, etc. . . ." Similarly, less concrete elements of this world organize themselves in successive incarnations; there are, for example, three distinct manifestations of earthquake in "Ne pas manger de raisin sans le laver." Sometimes, as in the genealogy of Napoleon, these lists may be associated with a specific meaning, but most often they are merely illustrations of the diversity and interpenetration of life.

It is not coincidental that many of Péret's tales take the form of detective stories or children's novels. This is a world of unknown and to some extent unknowable phenomena which transform themselves in full sight of the protagonists, belying normal expectations. One of the traditional keys to the understanding of change is alchemy, and Péret's awareness of its pertinence to his subject matter is shown in his use of alchemical references in *Histoire naturelle*: "Albert-le-Grand," "bain-marie," and the multiplying powers of mercury are examples. "Et les seins mouraient" continues this tendency, but whereas in *Histoire naturelle* alchemy participates in the text as a technique, in the tale it is present in its goal, the philosopher's stone. Péret does not claim that his characters discover the stone, but rather that the stone exists in his world in the same potential state in which all things have ontological presence:

> Mais à l'instant où les pierres deviennent philosophales, les fétus de paille se jettent dans les puits de mercure et demandent aux étoiles le chemin de Nijni-Novogrod.
>
> Trois mille Patagons à la recherche de la pierre philosophale qu'ils trouveront dans la poche d'un Arabe.

The philosopher's stone is juxtaposed with two objects which undeniably exist in the present world: the road to a Russian city and the pocket of an Arab, a member of an ethnic group which is associated with the development of the science of which the philosopher's stone is the goal.

Other mysteries are explored in the tales and, like the heros of *romans policiers,* Péret's protagonists often arrive at their resolution. In "La Fleur de Napoléon," the *feu central,* the awesome center of the world, is discovered; it is immediately described with reference to the known world: "A un détour du chemin ils aperçurent le feu central où nagaient des cygnes noirs hauts de trois mètres, qui chantaient *La Madelon* et s'envolaient comme des éléphants." Nothing is to be taken for granted; not only can mysteries be solved, but the unknown is present in phenomena which are presumed to conform to ordinary expectations. In "Il était une boulangère," the wife of General Boulanger discovers that Rome is inhabited by spirals which excrete green flame. The quality of surprise is as universal as those of speech and thought in the tales and *Histoire naturelle*: "Une branche morte tombe d'un arbre et lui dit: 'J'ai faim.' Elle lui donna sa bouche à baiser et la branche reprit sa place dans l'arbre au grand étonnement de ce végétal." In "Les Malheurs d'un dollar," the mysteries revealed in the adventures of the heroine, Baba, have political and religious implications.

Her love affair with a character who introduces himself as the dollar results in the birth of a child who is not, as he promised, "en or avec des yeux en mœlle de sureau," but rather of coal with sugar eyes. After a voyage in the claws of an eagle, she awakens to find herself in the tomb of Jesus, reads his will, and is finally mistaken for the resurrected Christ when she emerges from the cave.

The greatest mystery in the tales is the place of man in the world, specifically in this world which repeatedly fails to fulfill human expectations and in which the non-human has such incommensurate power. In order to show himself worthy of full participation in the interactions of this world, man must be as open to change as every other element in the world and make full use of his poetic powers. The most definitive statement of this imperative is in "Et les seins mouraient": "à quoi te sert d'être un homme si tu ne peux pas changer le plomb en liège et le liège en plomb." Those childlike figures who have never been made to believe that they could not perform such feats are the most successful in these tales, and the textbook approach in *Histoire naturelle* suggests that it was also for them that the later work was written. As Herbert Gershman notes, "for adults . . . Péret's tales are neither terrifying nor amusing. . . . there arises the suspicion that . . . he was deliberately engaged in writing new fables for old children." [24] It is they who are free to participate in the poetic process of change which is the key to Péret's world.

B. THE UTOPIA OF TRANSFORMATION: FOOD AND PLAY

Benjamin Péret's world is one of abundance in which people, plants, and animals coexist and play together. Whether it is the primordial realm of *Histoire naturelle* or the modern world of the poetry and tales, it fulfills the qualifications for Herbert Marcuse's definition of utopia:

> Such a hypothetical state could be reasonably assumed at two points which lie at the opposite poles of the vicissitudes

---

[24] Gershman, p. 44.

of the instincts: one would be located at the primitive beginnings of history, the other at its most mature stage. [25]

The freedom which characterizes the structure of this utopia is a form of protest against prevailing conditions which points to possibilities and asks why they are not realized. Péret's characters move in a world which shares many elements with the more familiar forms of society. The two salient features of the world of change as evoked in Péret's poetry and tales are the abundance of food and the prevalence of play. These aspects diverge from their commonplace counterparts in an inversion which distinguishes the fictional from the factual world. The fantastic aspects of this frame of reference do not cut it off from the realm in which Péret and his readers live; as Marcuse notes, "in its refusal to accept as final the limitations imposed upon freedom and happiness by the reality principle, in its refusal to forget what *can be* lies the critical function of phantasy." [26] Péret's poetry and prose carry on this criticism in the context of Surrealism.

Various aspects of the alimentary process take place constantly and simultaneously; they obey no particular order except that imposed by the eater in his social and economic situation. Eating internalizes the external world, yet in Péret's work the world remains unconquered by human will. Food acts as an autonomous agent apart from the desire of men, even when it is explicitly designated as prospective human nourishment. Play, in contrast, is a universal attribute of human life which is generally external to human reality; in Péret's Surrealist world it is internalized.

Because the formulae and descriptions of *Histoire naturelle* refer to experience beyond the range of daily life, they are easily relegated to the realm of pure fantasy. For the Surrealist, however, belief in his perception of nature will come with time: "the revolutionary meaning of this depiction of nature may seem absurd at first, but it may become more comprehensible with the presence of analogous results in modern microphysics." [27] Within the scope

---

[25] Herbert Marcuse, *Eros and Civilization* (New York: Random House, 1962), p. 137.

[26] *Ibid.,* p. 135.

[27] Max Ernst, "What is Surrealism," trans. Gabrièle Bennet, *Surrealists on Art,* ed. Lucy Lippard (Edgewood Cliffs, N.J.: Prentice-Hall, 1970), p. 135.

of normal existence, there are experiences of metamorphosis which make the universality of change more acceptable. In Péret's poetry and prose, one of those most frequently referred to is the production and consumption of food: "car la *nourriture* tient une place importante dans l'univers mental du poète, et les nourritures une non moins grande dans ses poèmes et ses contes." [28] Whether plant or animal, food undergoes a series of changes from the point of the reproductive seed, which becomes a living individual, to the time of slaughter and processing for consumption, and finally to the process of eating, digestion and excretion. All of these phases are constantly being enacted, and they are necessary to human life. Food unites the dualities of interior and exterior, height and depth, as well as fusing the animal, vegetable, and mineral kingdoms in the process of nutrition. The most humble aspect of daily life is inherently marvelous for Péret; his prolific use of alimentary imagery adds a quality of credibility to his work which counterbalances the perpetual intrusion of the marvelous.

The use of food in Péret's Surrealist work is a political as well as a poetic statement. His travel and political involvement made him personally and philosophically aware of the problems of food distribution in the world, and of the fact that many go hungry. In using the imagery of nutritional plenty, he pursues the critical work of fantasy within the images of poetry; according to one Marxist critic, "the Surrealist image is thus a convulsive effort to split open the commodity forms of the objective universe by striking them against each other with immense force." [29] The creation posited by Péret is one of plenty in which food is everywhere and no one goes hungry. For Jean-Christophe Bailly, whose study of Péret is highly influenced by political ideology, this is "l'incarnation d'une abondance fabuleuse, d'une dépense heureuse qui serait comme un défi irrévérencieux jeté au malheur dont la forme la plus courante est encore la Faim." [30] The world itself, along with its inhabitants, is full of nutrition and thus of energy to be used in vital transformations. Although Péret's sphere exists in contrast to the consumer society, it is nonetheless a society of consumption; nothing is safe

---

[28] Jean Louis Bédouin, *Benjamin Péret*, p. 35.
[29] Frederic Jameson, *Marxism and Form*, p. 96.
[30] Jean-Christophe Bailly, *Au-delà du langage*, p. 91.

from becoming fuel for something else. As Banquaert puts its, Péret wishes to "rendre le monde comestible." [31] Change is potentially complete exchange as one thing serves as food for another and thus loses its original identity.

Food is important in Surrealist pictorial art; its properties of immediacy and potential decomposition make it ideal for inclusion in works which are to be presented as art while they deny the traditional standard of conscious control and the masterpiece. Salvador Dalí notes this tendency in an essay on the Surrealist object: "the predominance of eatables or things that can be ingested is disclosed to analysis in almost all the recent surrealist articles." [32] For Dalí, the edible quality of a work is very important; even a serious painting like his 1936 "Premonition of civil war" is subtitled "Soft construction with boiled beans." Like Péret, Dalí finds eating intrinsic to human interaction with the world and, more importantly for him, with the art object: "as we think it over, we find suddenly that it does not seem enough to devour things with our eyes and our anxiety to join them actively brings us to want to *eat them*." [33] Dalí extends his definition of eating in relation to the work of art to include other methods of consumption: "burning a thing is equivalent, *inter alia*, to making it edible." [34] Although he does not relate this process to that of cooking, the association is clear in Péret's work; things burned are often edible, as in the example of "l'incendie d'un magasin de confections" in "Quatre à quatre," the first poem in *De derrière les fagots*. Aside from the connotations of cooking food in the context of civilization, it is a means of change which places upon a substance the mark of human presence. Burning desire, in a literal sense, is an important adjunct of the desire for union with another and for the change which characterizes Péret's world.

Le Gigot, sa vie et son œuvre, the volume of collected tales, and *Trois Cerises et une sardine*, a long poem published separately in 1936, have titles which place articles of food in positions of

---

[31] Marie-Odile Banquaert, "Le Mythe de l'amour sublime dans *Feu central* de Benjamin Péret," 63.

[32] Salvador Dalí, "The Object as Revealed in Surrealist Experiment," trans. David Gascoyne, in Lippard, p. 95.

[33] *Ibid.*

[34] Dalí, p. 96.

primary importance. The former title exemplifies one facet of Péret's use of imagery derived from food: the article in question, the leg of lamb in this case, assumes a very dignified human state through the attributes of "vie" and "œuvre," which are usually associated with a great and learned man. The title is also intentionally misleading, as the tales in this collection are not about the life or works of a *gigot*. [35] Food is also alluded to in the titles of three of the tales: "Il était une boulangère," "Sur le passage d'un panier à salade," and "Ne pas manger de raisin sans le laver." [36] In all three instances, references to food appear in the titles of tales as they do in ordinary French life. *Trois Cerises et une sardine,* which carries on the imagery of foodstuffs in the choice of the two nouns of its title, creates an image of incongruity rather like a humorous still life. In contrast with *Le Gigot,* in which the leg of lamb of the title would feed several people, the title of the poem alludes to a meager collection of four small things.

Titles of poems within *Le Grand Jeu* and *De derrière les fagots* include references to vegetables such as tomatoes, artichokes, carrots, figs and, above all, olives. Bread figures frequently in Péret's works in all its forms; it is refused in *Je ne mange pas de ce pain-là* and appears elsewhere in crumbs, stale, and in rye, black, and white varieties. Meat most often takes the form of the steak and lobster, two foods which show the amphibious nature of nourishment, but the title of a text from *Le Grand Jeu,* "Charcutons *charcutez,*" is evidence of the active presence of other meats. Alcoholic drink is also quite common; in *Le Grand Jeu* alone, three texts show the diverse possibilities of the imagery of alcohol: it is referred to as a physical substance in "Ma Main dans la bière," as something to be drunk in "Avez-vous du whisky," and as an agent for unexpected change in "La Forêt saoûle." The variety of comestible ingredients in the titles alone indicates their importance in the context of Péret's work, but in the body of poetry and prose they are even more common than in the titles.

---

[35] The verb *gigoter* does bear some relation to the text, with its implication of constant movement.

[36] Even these references are ambiguous, since the "boulangère," the wife of General Boulanger, does not make bread and the "panier à salade" is a colloquial expression referring to a paddywagon.

An examination of the various roles played by food images in *De derrière les fagots* (1934) shows that such substances are active, participating members of the world of change. Food is capable of autonomous action or of interaction with other elements in Péret's universe of things, and it performs functions which are conventionally reserved for human or animal agents. On a number of occasions, for example, an edible article is placed in a position of dialectic opposition with another item, and the two are fused to create a new third element:

> La querelle entre la poule au pot et le ventriloque
> nous a valu un nuage de poussière
> qui est passé au-dessus de la ville
> en sonnant de la trompette
> > ("Braves Gens")

> Mille parapluies et mille bouteilles de Pippermint
> se battant autour d'un alambic
> engendront plus ou moins fatalement une avalanche de pelotes
> > d'épingles
> > ("Un de plus un de moins")

The first example leads from a quarrel and a cloud of dust to the appearance of a novel creature who is the product of the interaction of a chicken whose mode of preparation recalls Henri IV, a ventriloquist, a cloud of dust and a human being with the ability to play a musical instrument. An alembic, part of the equipment of alchemy, is the catalytic agent for the second union, and the multiplicity of umbrellas and bottles of peppermint is continued in the mass of pincushions which create an avalanche. The dichotomy need not be resolved in the creation of a third element. It is typical of the process of eating that one substance is absorbed into another, but the identities of the two items are not predictable in Péret's world: "plonger dans le pain rassis / voilà ce qui attend les pierres plates" ("Rendre l'âme"). Ingestion follows its normal course in these poems, but the identity of the articles eaten is surprising even when the process followed is the standard one: "les arrêts facultatifs se mangent mutuellement le nez" ("Déjeté").

Like other participants in the process of change, food refuses to remain in its customary associational context. In *De derrière les fagots,* examples abound of the association of an article of food with something else which may be as ordinary as food, but which is not expected in juxtaposition. Jean-Louis Bédouin offers an explanation of this technique: "ce qui se savoure ou, plus prosaïquement, se mange, n'est nullement inférieur, poétiquement parlant, à ce qui se voit, se respire, se caresse ou s'entend." [37] In the poem "Ça continue," two examples of this equalization appear: between an old suitcase and a sock, an endive arrives at the rendez-vous of two blades of grass, and later the poem recounts the establishment of a lending society which "prête des oignons pour recevoir des fauteuils." Often an even closer association is indicated by explicit statement of resemblance or by prepositional alliance:

> Je m'étonne de l'orthographe de *fois*
> qui ressemble tant à un champignon
> roulé dans la farine
>> ("Chasse à courre")

> Pince l'œil pour appeler le violon de beurre
> et la mayonnaise chantera
>> ("Une Nuit comme une autre").

The infinite potential for association is such that when any two things fail to come together, the poet is disappointed; the possibility is, however, realized in its negative statement: "il n'y a pas de galéries dans les pommes" ("Vous n'irez plus au bois").

In these cases, food appears in its original state, but in others it undergoes the transformations which are characteristic of Péret's world of change. This metamorphosis can be indicated by grammatical structure; the alimentary image is juxtaposed with the thing it becomes:

> La tour s'allonge comme un pain de seigle
>> ("Au petit jour")

> plongeant dans des rivières de purée de pomme de terre
>> ("A un millimètre près").

The process of becoming is also indicated explicitly, as in the case of springs which flow from spice bread ("Qui est-ce"), and a salad

---

[37] Bédouin, p. 37.

which becomes a child's umbrella ("Dans le blanc des yeux"). In the context of food imagery, the process of transformation which is generally used is cooking, and this ordinary variety of metamorphosis is present in *De derrière les fagots*. The final text in the collection, "Variable," contains three references to cooking: "le homard qui n'est pas encore tout à fait cuit / à l'américaine," "un petit pois cuit à l'étouffé," and "une sole tellement frite / qu'elle demande son chemin à un passant." The references to the modes of preparation of lobster, peas and sole add to the descriptions of these situations a precision which belies their apparent gratuity. Péret in his poetic kitchen, like the alchemist in his laboratory, cooks things to transform them: in "A demain," a bouillon is made from Citroëns, while in "Prête-moi ta plume," cloves become stars in a sky made of coffee. In the scope of alimentary imagery, even the marvelous aspects of transformation are reduced to their most ordinary, universal manifestations.

Histoire naturelle presents elements, minerals, plants, and animals which act like human beings. This anthropomorphism is carried on in *De derrière les fagots*: a steak can whistle for its dog ("Défense d'afficher") or lose its wedding ring ("Les loups ne se mangent pas entre eux"). Specifically human activities are not limited to human beings, but are rather extended throughout the edible world to include a French fry which is in the Tour de France, a sugar cube which wears "un dégoûtant chapeau de curé" ("Déjeté"), and a leek which meets with buttons and gooseberries on the corner of the Avenue Matignon. Jean-Louis Bédouin finds that this use of alimentary imagery has ancient analogues: "la nourriture, au sens le plus concret du terme, revêt à ses yeux cette sorte de dignité que lui reconnaissent tant de peuples sauvages." [38] Man's role in this world is again called into question in such examples; even food, which is defined in human terms, is capable of filling his shoes. But human activities are not the only functions which foods overtake: in "En voiture Messieurs Dames," a pig's foot is the sun, [39] and in *Le Grand Jeu*, olives take over the world, becoming sea, forest, rain and finally the death of the person addressed. The

---

[38] *Ibid.*, p. 38.
[39] This image can be compared with fragment 3 of Heraclitus: "le soleil, large comme un pied d'homme" (Battistini, p. 25).

idea of collage reappears in this context: images of the world are constructed with components which are unrelated to the thing depicted, and the contrast leads to the experience of an event as new relationships are realized.

"Qui perd gagne," the fourth chapter of *Mort aux vaches et au champ d'honneur* (dated 1923, published in 1963), is almost entirely concerned with eating. What the narrator and his companion, Monsieur Charbon, want most to eat is "le cœur de la nature." Monsieur Charbon, who behaves like a magician, [40] can call forth roast chicken from the weeds and a basket of fruit from the river, but his power is frustrated by that of the elusive heart, which in this case is held accountable for a series of metamorphoses. When he finally captures the heart of nature, he swallows it in the dual form of an egg and a handkerchief. But his trials are not over: "nous reprîmes notre marche vers la Marne. Une centaine de pas plus loin, Monsieur Charbon se liquéfia brusquement." It is impossible for a character, even so extraordinary a personage as Monsieur Charbon, to engage in the intimate interaction of eating with something as potent as the heart of nature without being affected by the substance eaten. In Péret's world, what is eaten always affects the eater: you are what you eat.

Consumption of things is a form of union with them by which man can participate in the interaction and change which characterize non-human processes. The corollary to this principle is, for Péret, that food is never refused no matter what its source, as long as it is not contaminated by human connotations. In the tales there are many illustrations of this idea of universal edibility; Dalí's integration of eating with art is carried one step further, since eating in an art form is no longer the expression of a perverse desire but rather something entirely natural. In the innocent world of the tales, the precautions taken by the author of *Je ne mange pas de ce pain-là* are not necessary:

> Arrivé à l'angle de la pièce mon chien disparut. Je vis à cet endroit un trou circulaire ... au moment où j'allais y plonger le bras, une huitre énorme prête à être dégustée

---

[40] Monsieur Charbon's name indicates that he belongs to the world of metamorphosis. Coal is an example of dramatic change in nature, as it is made from plant life and can potentially become diamond.

me fut présentée sur un plateau d'argent sur les bords
duquel on lisait "la mobilisation n'est pas la guerre." Na-
turellement je ne fus pas assez sot pour refuser un aussi
agréable hors-d'œuvre.

("Un Plaisir bien passager")

Il ne sait plus quoi faire de ses dix doigts. Il aborde le
premier passant venu: "Monsieur, j'ai dix doigts. C'est pro-
bablement trop. Mangez-moi un doigt."

("Ne pas manger de raisin sans le laver")

Like Alice in Wonderland, the characters in Péret's tales eat what
is before them in a spirit of adventure and experiment.

The poetry of desire in *Je sublime* is situated in the same world
where the tales and such poetry as *De derrière les fagots* take place.
The use of food imagery in the love poetry indicates that it is not
romantic in the traditional sense. In *Je sublime,* food is analogous
with abstractions such as desire: "parmi les désirs simples comme
une salade qui se dresse au-dessus des grands arbres" ("Je"), and
it also plays the multiple roles which appear in the poetry not
directly concerned with the theme of, *l'amour sublime.* As in *De
derrière les fagots,* the edible substance can act independently: "une
asperge qui sort de terre / et demande s'il est l'heure de dormir"
("Egaré"). Food is also compared with diverse items, both abstract
and concrete: "la nuit de beurre sortant de la baratte" ("Nébuleuse"); "Non n'est qu'une botte de radis" ("Nébuleuse"); "Un
frein qui grince une chanson de chou-fleur" ("Ah"). In the highly
personal context of love poetry, the basis for comparison is frequently the self or the object of love, and food is often related to
the speaker and his subject. [41] Among the sequential images of
"Allo," for example, there are comparisons of a woman with Rhine
wine, snails, and cassis. These complex images are in keeping with
the exalted tone of a work shaped by desire. The relationship between man and woman is given an oral dimension by the reference
to eating, and the violence of this desire is transformed into de-

---

[41] The first of the following examples illustrates the identification of alimentary imagery with women, while in the second, the poet responds to a command
addressed to wine and thereby identifies with it: "Les éperviers de ton regard /
pêchent sans s'en douter toutes les sardines de ma tête" ("Homard"); "attends
vin de falaise qui vient d'éraser un patronage ... / J'attends" ("Le Carré de
l'hypoténuse").

structive images which are based on the consumption of one thing by another.

Allusions to food and eating often have political overtones which perform the necessary union of amorous and political desire: "un amas de flics dans la neige / qui voudrait les manger" ("A quand"); "qui fait sauter la banque comme une crêpe qui se colle au plafond" ("Ah"). For the police and banks, which are the agents of repression in Péret's work, the natural process of consuming food is as dangerous as the free working of desire. In contrast, Péret as lover finds gratifying the metaphorical consumption of some part of himself by the woman. The following lines from "Je" are comparable with those which depict her as an unconscious sparrowhawk in "Homard":

> deux yeux de pierre bleuie par le dernier quartier mangent lentement les champignons qui croissent paisiblement à l'intérieur de la petite mappemonde.

This dual role of eating is not paradoxical, as Marie-Odile Banquaert explains: "on avale ce qu'on n'aime pas pour le faire disparaître et on mange ce qu'on aime pour s'incorporer sa substance dans une tentative de fusion primitive." [42] The shape of the world, as well as the poet's personal life, can be changed by the aspect of eating.

For Roland Barthes, as for Dalí, the relationship between modern poetry and the reader is analogous with that between eater and eaten:

> Chaque mot poétique est ainsi un objet inattendu ... il est donc produit et consommé avec une curiosité particulière, une sorte de gourmandise sacrée.... Cette faim du mot, commune à toute la poésie moderne, fait de la parole poétique une parole terrible et inhumaine. [43]

In order to overcome this verbal terrorism, the reader of Péret's work must accept the food and the adventure it potentially entails. Like all elements of Péret's world, the edible must be granted its otherness and its equality to man, who is but another object in this universe. The text *Trois Cerises et une sardine* illustrates this

---

[42] Banquaert, 63.
[43] Roland Barthes, *Le Degré zéro de l'écriture* (Paris: Seuil, 1953), p. 45.

principle; nothing is to be taken for granted: "Ce qui s'élève d'un champ de blé ne ressemble pas forcément à un pot à eau / pas plus que ce qui mange les trônes ne ressemble à un wagon-lit." The process of ingestion and the substances consumed will be unexpected no matter how bizarre the assumptions of the reader. When these isolated phenomena are incorporated into their proper world and context, their alienation disappears. If the reader's appetite is complete, he will find the hunger for the poetic word assuaged, for no one goes hungry in Péret's Surrealist world.

Along with food, the dominant element of Péret's world which characterizes it as a utopia is the game. The activity of his characters is play, not work, or rather, failing to conform to conventional ideas of work, it appears to be play. Herbert Gershman finds the idea of play to be central to Surrealism:

> The triumvirate of automatic writing, spiritism and love stormed the gates of Wonderland directly. Play was more oblique . . . perhaps it would be more accurate to say that automatic writing and its two avatars wooed *le merveilleux,* while play created it anew at each moment. [44]

The use of games in Surrealism is so important to Breton that, as late as 1953, he feels the need to defend it:

> S'il est, dans le surréalisme, une forme d'activité dont la persistence a eu le don d'exciter la hargne des imbéciles, c'est bien l'activité de *jeu* dont on retrouve trace à travers la plupart de nos publications de ces trente-cinq dernières années. [45]

Breton's praise of Johan Huizinga's study of play, *Homo ludens,* makes the Dutch scholar's definition relevant to the context of Surrealism; for Huizinga, play is "an activity which proceeds within certain limits of time and space, in a visible order, according to rules freely accepted, and outside the sphere of necessity of material utility." [46] In Péret's work, play reverses this definition, for it is universal in its temporal and spatial situation and takes place ac-

---

[44] Gershman, pp. 10-11.
[45] André Breton, *Perspective cavalière* (Paris: Gallimard, 1970), p. 50.
[46] Johann Huizinga, *Homo ludens* (London: Paladin, 1970), p. 154.

cording to an order and rules which are intrinsic to the universe in which the poetry and the tales take place. Pleasure as stimulated by playing is the basis for the satisfaction of material needs; nothing is useful unless it can be used for play. Péret, then, both participates in and goes beyond the Surrealist use of play.

In the general activity of the Surrealist group, the definition of the world as a place for playing has two phases. First, games are played within the group; techniques are invented and experiments are performed in a manner which characterizes play. According to Breton, "bien que ... parfois cette activité ait été dite par nous 'expérimentale,' nous y cherchions avant tout le divertissement." [47] The first production to be called Surrealist, *Les Champs magnétiques,* follows the principles of games. Breton and Soupault decided upon the manner in which the text was to be executed and wrote it in a spirit of experimentation which demanded no more of the result than that it be a novel revelation of the workings of the human mind. A child-like insistence on obeying the rules of the game is revealed when Breton criticizes Soupault for furnishing titles for some of his contributions to the work. [48] As the group expanded, other games were invented and explicitly designated as such; the verbal and pictorial *cadavres exquis,* the parody of grading *littérateurs* and the games of definitions are examples. [49] Paul Eluard's description of the mental state enjoyed by the players typifies the feeling of a separate reality attached to games: "plus aucun souci, plus aucun souvenir de la misère, de l'ennui, de l'habitude. Nous jouions avec les images et il n'y avait pas de perdants." [50] In view of the diversity among the members of the Surrealist group, the games performed the important function of unifying them in common activity. In the Premier *Manifeste,* Breton outlines other games which are capable of being played by anyone because they have fixed rules which can be followed without disrupting the daily life of the player. These are ironically called "Secrets de l'art magique surréaliste," [51] and within their explication Breton calls them "jeux

---

[47] Breton, *Perspective cavalière,* p. 50.
[48] Breton, "Premier Manifeste," p. 37.
[49] Other games are listed by Breton in *Perspective cavalière,* p. 51.
[50] Paul Eluard, "Donner à voir," *Œuvres complètes,* I, 990-91.
[51] Breton, "Premier Manifeste," pp. 42-43. For further discussion of Surrealist games, see Phillipe Audouin's "Le Surréalisme et le jeu," *Le Surréalisme,* ed. Ferdinand Alquié (Paris: Mouton, 1968), pp. 455-85.

surréalistes." [52] Later in the *Premier Manifeste,* Breton displays the results of a game which consists of cutting out fragments of advertisements and assembling them to form an objective poem. Even in this game, where chance is the ruling element, adherence to rules is suggested: "observons, si vous voulez, la syntaxe." [53]

These activities diverge from the general definition of game in one important sense: whereas "le jeu ne vise pas à une modification utile du réel," [54] the Surrealist games are undertaken in order to reveal this reality, which is modified by being brought into the light of conscious thought. The triumph of pleasure over reality, of play over work is a state which the Surrealists who play these games wish to extend to all of life. At the same time, they undertake a dialectic task in unifying opposites:

> Par ailleurs, l'impérieux besoin que nous éprouvions d'en finir avec les vieilles antinomies . . . nous invitait à ne pas épargner celle du sérieux et du non-sérieux (jeu) qui commande celle du travail et des loisirs, de la "sagesse" et de la "sottise," etc. [55]

Hence the second phase of the Surrealist game is the extension of the play-state to include a relationship with society. In one sense, this implies that a true Surrealist will never work seriously; like the young Aragon, he should be able to say "je ne travaillerai jamais, mes mains sont pures." [56] On a larger scale, the Surrealist, viewing his relationship with society as that of a player with his antagonist, insists on the obedience of rules. [57] Infractions of the rules by which established society operates are all the more intolerable to the self-appointed referrees because the rules were established by the same institutions which break them. For Péret, hypocrisy of this sort

---

[52] Breton, "Premier Manifeste," p. 45.

[53] *Ibid.,* p. 56.

[54] Roger Callois, "Le Jeu et le sacré" (Appendice II), *L'Homme et le sacré* (Paris: Gallimard, 1970), p. 200.

[55] Breton, *Perspective cavalière,* p. 50.

[56] Louis Aragon, "Fragments d'une conférence prononcée à Madrid à la 'Residencia des Estudiantes'," Nadeau, p. 76.

[57] The following quotation from "Déclaration du 27 janvier 1925" (Nadeau, p. 68) illustrates this position: "nous lançons à la société cet avertissement solonnel. Qu'elle fasse attention à ses écarts, à chacun des faux pas de son esprit, nous ne la raterons pas."

ranks with murder as a cardinal sin; in *Je ne mange pas de ce pain-là,* the Eucharistic Congress of Chicago and the League of Nations are guilty enough to stand on a par with "l'assassin Foch."

Poetry is a manifestation of the instinct to play: "*poeisis,* in fact, is a play-function." [58] Traditionally, this means that the poet acts within a self-contained context by referring to external reality on the poem's own terms. In Péret's work, these terms are those of the marvelous as it is distilled from everyday life into images. These components of the poem are then combined: "what poetic language does with images is to play with them." [59] The status of the poet according to Péret reinforces the idea of the poet as player. He shares in the separateness that characterizes the participant in game in relation to his society: "on sait que la condition de poète place automatiquement celui qui la revendique en marge de la société et cela dans la mesure exacte où il est plus réellement poète." [60] The basic rules of his games are outlined in the text "L'Ecriture automatique" (1929), and the guidelines for his behavior are detailed in *Le Déshonneur des poètes.* Despite these analogies with the play-state as described by Huizinga and others, there is, again, the major difference that Péret does not act apart from reality; rather, he creates new myths in an attempt to change man's view of this reality. As Jean-Christophe Bailly states, "la poésie de Péret dépense la matière verbale sans compter et dans sa folie elle nie le monde des faits, dans sa course elle se déroule hors de toute loi admise. Mais cette fabulation qui nie le monde affirme en même temps qu'elle ne fait pas que nier, puisqu'elle est la vraie vie." [61]

At the same time, Péret is not content to play with words and images; on the contrary, he focuses on constructing a situation in which the components of the poem play freely among themselves. Breton, in his introduction to *Trois Cerises et une sardine* in the *Anthologie de l'humour noir,* remarks on the "détachement" which this freeing of language presupposes and contrasts it with the conventional restriction of language which, in Breton's words, "ne laisse pratiquement aucun jeu à leurs associations." [62] Birds provide an

---

[58] Huizinga, p. 141.
[59] *Ibid.,* p. 156.
[60] "La parole est à Péret," p. 50.
[61] Bailly, p. 68.
[62] André Breton, ed., *Anthologie de l'humour noir,* p. 385.

appropriate metaphor for the freedom of this verbal interplay: among the inhabitants of the ideal house in the *Premier Manifeste* is "Benjamin Péret dans ses équations d'oiseaux." [63] The shifting configurations alluded to by this image are like the changing combinations which are the result of game. The operation of chance governs many games, especially those of children, but the structure of these forms of play is so arranged that chance may take its course within them. The same technique of setting a trap for chance characterizes theories of the image which influenced Péret's Surrealism, as well as many of the Surrealist games. "L'un dans l'autre," for example, is a game in which two objects, persons, or activities are chosen arbitrarily and one is described in terms of the other; the object of the game is to guess the identity of the second element. [64]

The operations of play in poetry are most evident in the use of word games in Péret's work. Although Robert Desnos is better known for playing with individual words in such texts as *L'Aumonyme* and *Rrose Sélavy,* this technique is limited to his poetry of the early twenties. For Péret, words are capable of playing throughout his life. As early as 1921, he uses the potential for metamorphosis inherent in verbal structure in texts within *Passager du Transatlantique*: "Petit hublot de mon cœur" and "Passerelle du commandant" are examples of poems based entirely on the transformation of words. The most consistent use of this method appears in *152 Proverbes mis au goût du jour,* written in 1925 in collaboration with Paul Eluard: the saying "un chat sans un os fidèle," for example, becomes "fidèle comme un chat sans os." [65] "Passerelle du commandant" also plays on proverbs useing the form "Il faut être": the text ranges from "Il faut être chaste pour être bon" to "Il faut être deux pour être trois." In the *152 Proverbes mis au goût du jour,* the two poets explore the possibilities inherent within common proverbs, and new phrases are presented

---

[63] Breton, "Premier Manifeste," p. 30.

[64] As Breton states in *Perspective cavalière,* "Nous n'en étions déjà plus à penser que tout objet peut se décrire à partir de tout autre mais encore toute *action* et aussi tout *personnage,* même placé dans une situation déterminée, à partir de tout *objet,* et inversement" (p. 53). It is interesting to note that in Breton's account of the contributions to the game by various individuals, those by Péret outnumber even Breton's own.

[65] Paul Eluard and Benjamin Péret, "152 proverbes mis au goût du jour," *Œuvres complètes,* I, 1581.

as coming from within their source rather than being dependent upon the will of the writer. Words and phrases are capable of playing autonomously; game is discovered to exist within the texture of reality, rather than being constructed outside the real world. Thus the use of word-play is an integral part of the text: "il y a chez Péret des exemples de jeux de mots formels, mais ils sont toujours pris dans une continuité sémantique qui les englobe et n'interviennent que comme recours lorsque la vitesse d'émission poétique semble devoir ralentir." [66] An example of this slowing effect appears in the tale "Le Conte voué au bleu et au blanc": "Quel temps! Il fait une chaleur merveilleuse et toutes les horloges marquent sept heures." The doubling of the meaning of *temps* to include both weather and the time marked by clocks intensifies the descriptive consistency of the passage.

Rhyme and scansion are clues to the hidden relationships of words for Péret from his earlies work to the end of his life; the lines "le bœuf à fermeture éclair / ressemble à ton grand-père" were written shortly before his death, yet they display the same lightness of tone and reliance upon the power of words on their own as do texts written more than thirty years earlier. "Petit hublot de mon cœur," published in 1921, depends on a confusion of the Canada apple with the country of the same name. The word-play is more complicated in "S'essouffler," the first text in *Le Grand Jeu,* where the same set of words is used in three stanzas; the poem's humor depends on changing the order of the words. Another early text, "Chanson de la gardeuse de kangourous" (1923), is a rare example of rhyme-play in which words are used by virtue of their rhyming. Each stanza of this text begins with verses relating to a lady in a tower, and the rhyming lines which follow are closely linked with the opening by the word "que"; the last stanza serves as an example:

> La dame était si petite
> la tour était si grande
> que les amandes
> et les amantes
> s'aimaient dans les soupentes.

---

[66] Bailly, p. 58.

In "26 Points à préciser," the abstraction of words in games reaches an extreme point, as fundamental aspects of Péret's life are expressed in increasingly complex mathematical formulae. Among the later poetry, three texts are characterized by the editors of the *Œuvres complètes* as "le fruit de jeux collectifs auxquels Benjamin Péret aimait à se livrer avec des amis." [67] The first of these "Trois Poèmes-gages," entitled "Hymne," is another illustration of the departure from standard verbal expression occasioned by playing:

> Et patati et patata
> Et tapati et tapata
> Et patiti et patoto
> Et titipa et totopa
> Et pititi et pototo
> Et titipi et totopo
> Ah!

Other texts display affinity with game in their use of the riddle. [68] Again, these forms of play appear over a number of years from early examples in *Passager du Transatlantique* to the last poetry. Péret asks fundamental, enigmatic questions which indicate once again the seriousness of his play. In "Pont aux cygnes," the riddles concern human time, while in "Emigrant des mille milles," they are even more mysterious:

> Qu'est-ce qu'un cancer
> qu'est-ce que le génie
> C'est la même chose
> et le caoutchouc aussi
> mais dites-moi ce qu'est le caoutchouc.

"J'irai veux-tu" in *Le Grand Jeu* is a long, involved riddle; a house and its master are described in apparently contradictory terms, the master is given sixteen different identities and the question is then posed: "Dites-moi dites-moi où est la grande maison." A later poem,

---

67 Benjamin Péret, *Œuvres complètes*, II, 333.

68 According to Huizinga, "what poetic language does with images is to play with them. It disposes them in style, it instils mystery into them so that every image contains the answer to an enigma" (p. 156). The internalization of the answer within the text is most evident in "La Baisse du franc": "Petit franc petit franc qu'as-tu fait de tes os / qu'en aurais-tu fait sinon le *poker dice* qui projette ces mots sur le papier."

"La Baisse du franc" in *Je ne mange pas de ce pain-là,* presents an economic question of an equally basic nature, but the answers are always implicit in the context of the poem.

This sort of riddle is also quite common in the tales collected in *Le Gigot*: "Corps à corps," for example, has an extended riddle posed by a pig:

> Je vis dans les cabanes des cantonniers, je mange des traî-
> neaux, je lis Paul Bourget en commençant par la fin de
> chaque ligne, je joue de la musique de table de nuit, je
> caresse les doigts des mariées et j'héberge un homme poli-
> tique dans la forêt de mes soies. Quel est-il et qui suis-je?

The narrator, who is trying to get rid of the pig, responds with an evasive question: "avez-vous dû faire la queue?" Two days later, after a frenetic trip in a sled, the pig still is preoccupied with his riddle, and repeats the question "quel est-il et qui suis-je?" Whereas the pig's riddle is apparently unanswerable, in "Aglaë s'ennuie devant une fraise des bois," there is an answer, apparently to a riddle, without a question: "Corne, cornichon, cornemuse. Voilà! Com-prends-tu?" It is interesting to note that this riddle-less answer relies on another sort of play in its punning, and that two of the three words in the pun are used in similar fashion in "De la corne du sommeil," the first poem in *Dormir dormir dans les pierres.* In the tale "Ces Animaux de la famille," a cobra poses a series of riddles to a young man and, after his correct response, decorates him with "l'ordre du casoar qui a avalé un rocking-chair." [69] Riddles are not limited to animate creatures: in "Les Vagues Ames," the age of the letter *n* is asked by "l'horloge pneumatique du carrefour Drouot." In these takes, an ordinary question can take the enigmatic contours of a riddle, as in "Ne pas manger de raisin sans le laver":

> Moi. — Ce n'est rien, mais regardez vos souliers. Qui donc
> s'en est servi comme d'un violon? Et pourquoi la tête d'un
> renard surgit-elle à leur extrémité?
> Le Gentleman Excentrique. — Un franc cinquante ... C'est
> parce que le renard n'a d'yeux que pour ses lunettes ...

---

[69] Benjamin Péret, "Ces Animaux de la famille," *La Révolution Surréaliste,* 6 (1 March 1926), 14.

The internalization of question and answer in Péret's poetry and tales parallels that of game, which is, according to Roger Callois, "forme pure, activité qui trouve en soi sa fin." [70]

In Péret's work, humor shares with game the status of being a key to the comprehension of the real world, and neither pastime is frivolous. The relationship between play and *l'humour noir* is very close; Surrealist black humor depends on the discovery of analogies and connections through the free play of images. In Michel Carrouges' definition, "l'humour ... extrait un fait ou un ensemble de faits de ce qui est donné comme leur normale pour les précipiter dans un jeu vertigineux de relations inattendues et surréelles." [71] This displacement is the same method used to create the Surrealist image: "accouplement de deux réalités en apparence inaccoupables sur un plan qui en apparence ne leur convient pas." [72] The process of poetry, like that of humor, depends on arbitrary rules, detachment from everyday reality, and visible order within disorder; all of these are characteristic of play. As a practicioner of Surrealist black humor, Péret extracts pleasure from the bleakest of situations and characters. Perhaps the finest example of this practice is his treatment of the unfortunate Pope Pius VII in "Il était une boulangère": the Pope is shown as capable of normal human desires and impulses and is more real in his incarnation as the object of humor than as the cloudy figure of history. Black humor in Péret's work shows the play element inherent in every aspect of reality; like game, it is a means of rediscovering the joy of childhood and, concomitantly, of freedom:

> Ansi l'homme retrouve l'incroyable liberté de l'enfance à l'égard de la réalité et, si noire que soit l'humanité, il est possible de goûter le miel phosphorescent du wonderland, nourriture magique de tous les désirs. [73]

The poet who plays with words and images is free of constraint with regard to their meaning; they belong first to his game and only coincidentally to conventional reality. The dominance of play

---

[70] Callois, p. 207.

[71] Michel Carrouges, *André Breton et les données fondamentales du surréalisme* (Paris: Gallimard, 1966), p. 122.

[72] Ernst, pp. 28-30.

[73] Carrouges, p. 131.

in Péret's work marks the world to which it refers as one in which
the pleasure principle has triumphed; it is a utopia in Fourier's
terms, the world of a perfected, satisfied humanity. Norman
O. Brown's designation of play as "the erotic mode of activity"[74]
implies that a state in which game dominates is one in which death,
the force of repression and stasis, has been overcome. Everything
is given freely for the play of the inhabitants of this world, as in
the following illustration from "A petits pas" (1959):

> chargés de présents scintillants du point du jour
> au rire de petites filles décoiffées
> dans l'excitation du jeu
> où l'une agrandit la bouche de l'autre
> avec une branche d'amandier en fleurs
> qui s'empressent de donner leur fruit
> chantant
> et turbulent
> de sucre d'orge qu'on tourne entre les lèvres.[75]

The utopian vision of this text merges the elements of eating and
game; significantly, the participants in this wonderland are children
whose freedom from adult standards is indicated by their being
"décoiffées." "A petits pas" ends with a line which fuses images
of movement and stasis in a depiction of the delicate balance of a
world of which children are the most appropriate inhabitants: "comme une toupie presque immobile sur son axe." In *Je ne mange pas
de ce pain-là,* the triumph of the people is represented by Péret as
the persistence of life after the death of the oppressor; with the
bones of "Macia désossé," for example, revolutionary whistles are
made. According to Brown, the primacy of dream and play describe
a primitive rather than a civilized culture; in this sense, Péret's
world resembles that of the native Americans with whom he felt
great sympathy.[76] At the same time, the pleasure principle in sub-

---

[74] Norman O. Brown, *Life Against Death* (New York: Random House,
1959), p. 33. Herbert Gershman says of Brown that "without alluding to the
surrealists, he manages to describe the world as they would see it" (p. 180).

[75] "A petits pas" appears in *Œuvres complètes,* II under the collective title
Dernièrement; also see Appendix.

[76] According to Brown, "primitive is that level of culture in which the
rhythm of what Freud calls the primary processes — the rhythm of dreams and
childhood play — is predominant. Civilized is that level of culture which

limated form gives rise to both political action and *l'amour sublime* and, in a wider sense, to the entire corpus of Péret's written work. As Brown puts it, "the play element in culture provides a prima facie justification for the psychoanalytical doctrine of sublimation, which views 'higher' cultural activities as substitutes for lost infantile pleasures." [77] Ideally, the process is reversed in Péret's world: the sublimated images of freedom and pleasure are finally supplanted by the utopia in which they are realized. The form of this ideal community of things is defined by a continual breaking of forms in the ongoing process of change.

C. The Syntax of Dream

Péret is emphatic about the importance of dream in his Surrealist approach to the world. In the context of the bitterly rational "Le Déshonneur des poètes" (1945), he finds a place for a defense of dream against those who would repress it:

> Ils méprisent le rêve au profit de leur réalité comme si le rêve n'était pas un de ses aspects et le plus bouleversant, exaltent l'action au dépens de la méditation comme si la première sans la seconde n'était pas un sport aussi insignifiant que tout sport. [78]

The binary construction of this sentence equates dream with meditation and opposes to them the unthinking activity which is the structure of the established view of reality. Péret's use of the word *leur* to designate this version of the reality principle separates it from himself; rather, he advocates another world-view. This new reality involves a synthesis of opposites which he finds rigorously held apart in modern society: meditation and action, dream and waking reality.

In "La Parole est à Péret," the introduction to the *Anthologie des mythes, légendes et contes populaires d'Amérique,* he describes a mode of thought in which these elements coexist:

---

effectively represses the rhythm of the primary processes in favor of rationality and the reality principle" (p. 37).

[77] *Ibid.*

[78] "Le Déshonneur des poètes," p. 73.

> Pour le primitif il n'y a pas encore de rêves; cette mysté-
> rieuse activité de l'esprit lui révèle que son "double" veille
> sur lui, qu'un ancêtre pèse sur sa destin, ou, plus tard,
> qu'un dieu ... veut le bonheur du peuple en échange d'un
> tribut d'adoration.[79]

Without advocating a return to the primitive variety of superstition,
Péret applauds in it the complete fusion of information gathered
from waking life with that conveyed by the dream.[80] This conver-
gence of his prose with the integrated state of consciousness is
evident to Ferdinand Alquié as he describes Péret's prose:

> Benjamin Péret n'hésite pas à prêter à ses personnages de
> véritables soucis logiques, à introduire en ses récits les plus
> égarés les détails les plus exacts ... le langage est ici à
> fleur de rêve, et devient semblable au discours que l'on se
> tient parfois en une très grande fatigue. Et l'on sait que
> les données de l'automatisme se coulent le plus souvent,
> chez les surréalistes, en une syntaxe cohérente et correcte.[81]

In his poetry, Péret is even more insistent upon the need for union
of the diurnal and nocturnal modes of existence. The important
text "Atout trèfle"[82] gives instructions for an adventure which goes
beyond dividing lines: "Doute de l'horizon de l'autre côté de tes
yeux / et va-t-en à travers les montagnes blanches de fougères." The
separation of day from night is, for Péret, as artificial as the punctuation which he scorns in his poetry; he envisions "cette avenue
plantée de seins bleus / où le jour ne se différencie de la nuit que
par une virgule" ("Prête-moi ta plume"). Herbert Gershman remarks
upon Péret's emphasis on dream in stating that "Benjamin Péret ...
more consistently than any other, with the possible exception of
Breton, mingled in his work the two realities of dream and conscience."[83]

---

[79] "La parole est à Péret," p. 25.

[80] Péret explores the subject of superstition in "Le Sel répandu," *Le Surréalisme en 1947* (Paris: Pierre à feu, 1947), pp. 21-24.

[81] Ferdinand Alquié, *Philosophie du surréalisme* (Paris: Flammarion, 1955),
p. 189.

[82] For further discussion of this text, see Elizabeth Jackson Hanchett,
"Poésie activité de l'esprit: A Study of 'Atout trèfle' by Benjamin Péret,"
French Review, 44 (1971), 1036-47.

[83] Gershman, p. 190.

Dream is a universal experience and thus a potential unifier of humanity. It is also a locus of perpetual change: according to Heraclitus, "les hommes, dans leur sommeil, travaillent fraternellement au devenir du monde." [84] In Péret's tales, the distinction between dreamed events and those carried out in the waking world is obliterated. The world of dream is a revelation of the freedom necessary for the liberated functioning of the force of change, as it denies boundaries of time and space, as well as those of objective identity. The freeing of the unconscious as it is expressed in dream is a form of Surrealist subversion:

> Hence Surrealism's reliance on dreams and related, undirected reverie, which will presumably lull the Censor into carelessness, and so permit one to observe what lies below the surface ... which Breton saw as undermining our conventional, taboo-ridden society. [85]

Péret's work, like that of most Surrealists, illustrates the theories of Freud, who recognizes the need for unifying waking and sleeping states in *The Psychopathology of Everyday Life*:

> The peculiar mode of operation, whose most striking function we recognize in the dream content, should not be attributed only to the sleeping state of the psychic life, when we possess abundant proof of its activity during the waking state. [86]

This text defends the idea echoed by Péret that dream-like activity persists in the daylight hours and is a normal human experience, not "determined by deep-seated decay of psychological activity or

---

[84] Battistini, p. 35, fragment 87, Heraclitus tends, however, to denigrate the value of this sleep-work because of its individualism, as for example in fragment 101: "les hommes, à l'état de veille, ont un seul monde, qui leur est commun. Dans le sommeil, chacun s'en retourne à son propre monde" (p. 36).

[85] Gershman, p. 36.

[86] Sigmund Freud, *The Psychopathology of Everyday Life, Basic Writings of Sigmund Freud,* ed. A. A. Brill (New York: Random House, 1938), p. 177. Péret says of Freud that although "Freud lui-même éprouve le besoin de s'opposer au merveilleux, dans les dernières pages de la *Psychopathologie de la vie quotidienne,* par exemple," this is a "vaine précaution: le merveilleux jaillit, puits artésien, entre toutes les lignes de son livre" ["La pensée est UNE et indivisible," *VVV,* 4 (1944), 10].

by morbid state of function." [87] On the contrary, for Péret the unconscious has a highly positive value; his essay "La pensée est UNE et indivisible," the title of which reveals his unified view of human thought, refers to "l'inconscient, individu cosmique, souverain phénix qui s'engendre indéfiniment de son propre feu." [88] Two facets of human experience are so completely integrated that the succession of events in the tales can be followed only if they are accepted with the inevitability of dream-events. Yet, the apparent incoherence of the prose contained in *Le Gigot, sa vie et son œuvre* is not to be rejected as "only a dream"; it is a vision of a wider reality, a surreality in which the generative force of change is liberated of constraints imposed upon it by waking rationality. Freud's theories, while providing an interesting grid through which to view Péret's work, are ultimately insufficient as an approach. In his tales, as in his poetry, Péret has proceeded beyond the interpretive presentation of dream to a concretization of the dream state in textual reality.

In the early stage of the Surrealist movement, the induction of dream-like states and the reciting of the contents of dream was an important activity. In his *Vague de rêves* (1924), Aragon describes the "épidémie de sommeils" which overtook the group; they had been introduced to the technique of *séances* by René Crevel in late 1922. [89] "L'Entrée des médiums" is Breton's account of the experiments of the group in this realm. For the early Surrealists, dream was all-important; the very word *surréalisme,* Breton notes, has come to mean "un certain automatisme psychique qui correspond assez bien à l'état de rêve." [90] The dream state, then, is the most commonly shared version of the attitude cultivated by the Surrealists. Péret was one of the members of the group who was capable of entering at will into a trancelike approximation of dream. Breton names him, along with Desnos and Crevel, as being on the active side of the dream sessions, while Eluard, Ernst, Morise, and Breton himself looked on. [91] In his *Entretiens,* Breton speaks of

---

[87] Freud, p. 177.

[88] "La pensée est UNE et indivisible," p. 12.

[89] This period in the life of the group is discussed by Nadeau in his chapter entitled "L'Epoque des sommeils" (pp. 49-54) and, more significantly, by Aragon in "Une Vague de rêve" [*Commerce*, 2 (Fall, 1924), 89-122].

[90] André Breton, *Les Pas perdus* (Paris: Gallimard, 1969), p. 124.

[91] *Ibid.,* p. 122.

"Péret, qui s'endort au cours d'une des séances et tient des propos d'un caractère plutôt jovial, dont le prétexte et le ton s'apparentent à ceux des contes." [92] Yet another friend of Péret testifies that "la voix est apparemment plus familière, mais ce n'est pas non plus celle du poète, son débit est beaucoup plus accéléré et la drôlerie dont elle fait preuve . . . beaucoup plus désloquante et ravageuse que la voix de l'homme que nous connaissons." [93]

In the tales, the union of dream and waking life is evident in the role of night as a time for change. The world neither vanishes from human consciousness nor enters into somnolence at night. When a character is not present in the night, he or she is likely to find things radically altered upon returning to familiar phenomena. The case of Madame Lannor in "Une Vie pleine d'intérêt" is typical; when she goes out to look at her beloved cherry trees in the morning, "Madame Lannor vit que ses cérisiers, la veille encore couverts de beaux fruits rouges, avaient été remplacés pendant la nuit par des girafes naturalisés." The speaker in the poetry of *Je sublime* uses the example of the woman's influence on his waking to indicate her omnipresence:

> Aujourd'hui je regarde par tes cheveux
> Rosa d'opale du matin
> et je m'éveille par tes yeux.

The same association between love and the special state of consciousness associated with waking is made in *La Brebis galante* with regard to natural phenomena: "le vent se lève comme un femme après une nuit d'amour. Il ajuste son binocle et regarde le monde avec ses yeux d'enfant." Waking is a mysterious process, a passage from one world to another, and as such it is associated with absolutes in the same prose text:

> J'apporte avec moi la couleur originale, celle qui nous a valu les violoncelles crevés et leurs suaves mélodies dont tu te repais chaque matin en levant la tête au-dessus des barreaux de vapeur que tu n'as jamais songé à briser et que tu imagines être des cerveaux d'enfants.

---

[92] André Breton, *Entretiens,* p. 84.
[93] Alain Jouffroy, "Discours," *Surréalisme,* ed. Ferdinand Alquié, p. 139.

The world of night is different from that of day, and closer to the element in which dreams take place. As J. H. Matthews notes, "Péret's is a universe in perpetual creation. Everything finds new and unforeseen life from the moment the writer takes pen in hand, and no concessions can be made to the memories we bring with us from the world we know." [94] Night, like the tale itself, is a site of metamorphosis:

> Cette nuit tous les nègres sont éveillés et mangent des rats . . . la nuit les rats ont des têtes de nègre et je pourrais bien confondre un bananier avec une brosse à reluire.
> ("Ne pas manger de raisin sans le laver")

In "Aglaë s'ennuie devant une fraise des bois," the mystery associated with night is present despite the dormant state of the participants in the adventure, which is in this case a frantic chase in a bus after an evasive baobab tree. While day is completely given over to this activity, night is a time for the secret workings of events: "une rafale de sable passait puis le calme revenait et c'était comme une lettre qui, tombant d'une enseigne, rend le mot illisible."

Night is by its very nature a threat to the organization of life based on daytime phenomena. "Minuit, l'heure du crime" is one of the enigmatic statements of the pneumatic clock at the Drouot intersection in "Les Vagues Ames"; night is, by extension, a crime against day in this commonplace expression. The same association of night with crime is made in the 1942 tale "Le Dégel": "la pluie de vin rouge tombait drue et rendait plus proche la venue de la nuit couleur de sang." In *La Brebis galante,* an explanation is given for this freedom of behavior during the night: "les rues désertes de votre ville natale à l'heure nocturne où, seuls, les pieuvres et les bien-heureux moustiques osent se promener et respirer un air que n'alourdit plus aucune respiration humaine." Night is dangerous for those who proceed unwarily within it: "Et les seins mouraient" which, atypically, begins at night, shows the hero Marcarelle who "marcha si longtemps que la lune lui caressa les pieds." This leads him to sigh "si longtemps que ses pieds devinrent bleus comme une pioche maniée par un homme de haute taille qui démolit une

---

[94] J. H. Matthews, "The Mechanics of the Marvelous: The Short Stories of Benjamin Péret," *L'Esprit Créateur* (Spring 1966), 27.

église célèbre." Again, the activity of night itself, here represented by the moon, is destructive of established society.

Nocturnal activity is also common to the poetry of *De derrière les fagots* and the nature of night has important consequences. Things move about in ways which are unseen during the day:

> si les lacets de souliers ne guident pas les papillons
> le soir
> quand la pluie tombe comme un pendu
>
> ("A demain")

> Minuit ou une heure du matin
> les pillules Pink ont fini leur journée
> et rentrent dans leur caverne.
>
> ("A dormir debout")

Their secret lives are evealed to the poet who is able to accomodate himself to the mode of existence which characterizes the night. As in the tales, in these poems night is associated with crime through the color red:

> comme des sous-marins
> sur des oreillers
> blancs parce que la nuit est rouge.

Je sublime also abounds in imagery of night and in phenomena associated with night. The most striking poem in this respect is "Je ne dors pas"; this title indicates the speaker's presence in the night. After placing the poem in "ce soir," he alludes to cobalt, crows, and coal in the first three lines and intensifies the chromatic unity of these images through alliteration. The color black is combined with light at the approach of dawn in the images of "un rayon de lune" and of lava. The eclipse introduces darkness into the poetic world, whether it is of the sun as in "Parle-moi," or of the moon as in "A quand." Because the poet is preoccupied with woman in these texts, night tends to take gynecomorphic forms, and she is in turn identified with darkness: she has "chevelure de soleil noir" ("Nébuleuse") and "deux yeux de pierre bleuie par le dernier quartier" ("Je"). She has influence over the night because of her identification with it: the poet desires "que tu me regardes non comme un kilo de sucre / mais comme une nuit que tu as décousue."

But night is not always tied to either the poet or the woman of his
fantasy; it can participate in metamorphosis like any other element
of the universe: "quand la nuit de beurre sortant de la baratte /
noie les taupes des gares dont les yeux barissent" ("Egaré"). Likewise, in *La Brebis galante,* the stage is set for unusual happenings
in the night; the second sentence of the first chapter reads "C'était
une nuit sombre et pâle de romance méchanique." Night is a time
for love, and two elements of the tale, a Zouave and an acorn, are
given genealogies which involve nocturnal love and birth. The moon
is the major night-time presence in *La Brebis galante*: in the second
chapter, for example, the hero Nestor fills it with turnips and nails,
while later it is suggested that "la lune pouvait faire comme le
moustique qui se jette sur la lampe." The whole shape of earthly
life is thus changed through the force of desire in an elementary,
instinctual form.

The dreams of the characters in Péret's tales are never recounted
as such, but events which can be designated as para-dreams play
an important part in the stories. The most common of these concern
change which occurs when the subject has his or her eyes closed.
Many of the tales begin when a character awakens or opens his
eyes to find that the predictable world has changed while he was
asleep. To some extent, these episodes can be equated with dreams,
as they involve a transition from a system of expected events to
one in which the unexpected or marvelous predominates. Often,
this shift entails a change in the character's environment or situation;
it is as if he or she were awakening into dream. Madame Lannor,
for example, finds that "lorsqu'elle rouvrit les yeux elle était sus-
pendue par les pieds au sommet de l'obélisque de la place de la
Concorde." Lord Cheltenham in "Sur le passage d'un panier à salade" awakens to find himself in an equally unexpected position:
"Lord Cheltenham s'éveillait lentement lorsqu'il se sentit emporté
dans une valise. Il se rendormit et, en se réveillant, vit qu'il était
dans un pays aquatique." Not all of these awakenings involve an
exotic situation; in "Les Malheurs d'un dollar," Baba [95] finds that
"quand elle revint à elle, elle était couchée sur un monceau de
chemises d'homme." Yet in all of these instances of awakening,

---

[95] Baba's name recalls both the tales of Ali Baba and the dessert baba au
rhum.

something has changed which brings about the complete disorientation of the person in question. "Le Pays de Cocagne" [96] recounts the adventures of a child who, at one point in the narration, falls asleep in a closet; he awakens to find himself in the same closet, but "à son réveil, l'armoire était pourrie," and his immediate accession to manhood shows that an unexpected amount of time has elapsed while he was sleeping. In "Et les seins mouraient," the unexpected takes the form of an alteration in the normal course of reproduction: "O! pauvres haricots! C'est donc vrai que le serviteur de Napoléon vous enfanta à l'issue d'une nuit d'orgie." In "Ces animaux de la famille," a man gets up "au milieu de son sommeil" and throws all his furniture out the window. When he finds it again, although very little time has passed, "de l'armoire à glace éventrée sortent 1 000 flamants roses" and after his disappearance from the scene, "son meublier donne naissance à toute une faune pour laquelle une flore nouvelle se crée." [97]

In *De derrière les fagots,* sleep and dream are extended to non-human subjects which, like the people of the tales, awaken into whanged worlds. In "A cela près," an inanimate bowler hat has an experience which is both within and beyond normal human occurrences:

C'est ainsi que le chapeau melon graisseux comme il convient
s'est réveillé un beau matin sur une tête de pierre
qui se grattait les dents avec un chien empaillé.

In another instance, the participants in dream-like experiences are vaguely designated as "dormeurs"; while they sleep, they are accompanied by "des femmes nues qui disparaissent ensuite / dans la respiration des dormeurs," and they react with a semi-conscious "stupeur." But the effects of this phenomenon are not limited to the time of the dream; their stupor "leur fait dire une fois réveillée / tout tourne" ("S'ennuyer"). The same persistence of the effects of dream appears in another text in *De derrière les fagots* which

---

[96] Baudelaire's prose "Invitation au voyage" refers to a "pays de Cocagne"; see his *Petits Poèmes en prose* (Paris: Garnier, 1962), pp. 86, 87, and 89. This expression is quite common, and Péret's use of it is not necessarily a literary allusion.

[97] Benjamin Péret, "Ces animaux de la famille," 14.

suggests a connection with the nocturnal world by its title, "Une Nuit comme une autre":

Cependant ce roi a une collection d'éléphants
et les éléphants devront rêver pour lui
et les éléphants rêveront de meubles chinois avec des incrustations
de cyclones

et ils se réveilleront en disant
C'est la vie.

Again, dream is extended to non-human characters, and it is suggested that the dream of these elephants is actually superior to that of a king. The elephants identify dream with life in saying "c'est la vie" an recall Joseph's interpreting the dreams of Pharoah.

In *Je sublime,* sleep and dream are most frequently associated with the speaker-lover, as in the following examples:

je dormais en attendant que tu viennes
comme une forêt qui attend le passage d'une comète pour voir clair
("Ecoute")

jusqu'à ce que je m'endorme d'un sommeil Rosa vêtu de rêves Rosa
et l'aube Rosa me réveillera comme un champignon Rosa.
("Source")

The influence of the woman extends into the realm beyond consciousness, and the association of her with sleep is an indication of her total domination of his faculties. But sleep in *Je sublime* is also very much like that of Péret's other poetry: in the first poem of the collection, "Egaré," an asparagus comes out of the earth to ask if it is time to sleep, and sleep and wakening are characterized "comme une rivière qui saute à pieds joints." As the preceding examples show, dream is a source of revelation and change in the poetry and tales for both human and non-human characters.

Sometimes even vicarious contact withe the world of sleep is enough to bring about change; in the tale "Les Vagues Ames," the solitary narrator awakens a sleeping man, and the result is a complete revolution which changes the city and even the sky, rendering houses and chairs impalpable. Trance states which resemble sleep are equally capable of instilling an awareness of change in their subject: Baba in "Les Malheurs d'un dollar" is taken up in a cyclonic movement! "pendant des heures elle tourna. Le monde avait pris pour elle une forme octagonale et les êtres lui paraissaient se transformer indéfiniment." The threat posed by night to conventional identities and configurations in the world is an important part of the experiential base of the characters of the tales. The most menacing appearance of sleep is in its proximity to death; this is revealed through a medium, one who is capable of communicating with the realm of the dead. [98] When Sonia, the heroine of "Sur le passage d'un panier à salade," visits the medium Madame Daisy, she finds that her experience goes beyond the normal tricks of the seer's trade: the River Lethe runs through Madame Daisy's apartment. In the action which follows, "elles retirèrent leur autre chaussure et traversèrent le ruisseau . . . aussitôt la voyante grandit d'un mètre cependant que Sonia diminuait d'autant." The same desire for change which leads to Sonia's mystical investigation can, in another form, be an incitement to suicide, as explained in La Brebis galante:

> J'entends par suicide cette subite conscience de soi-même qui nous fait désirer devenir navet ou pelle à charbon, encore que j'aie une représentation insuffisante des métamorphoses que peut subir le corps d'un suicidé pour aboutir au stade définitif de navet ou de pelle à charbon . . . au milieu de son front apparaît un œil dont le regard commence par vous parler du malheur des pierres.

This text is contemporary with Dormir dormir dans les pierres (1926), in which the association between sleep, death and communication with nature is completed. In Péret's prose, a general equation is made of those states which do not relate to normal, waking reality, because dream, trance, and mystification entail a threatening challenge to the domination of rationality. De derrière les fagots extends this challenge to include the presumption that sleep is entirely passive: the final lines of the collection represent this passive state as the sleep of a conventional public and, ironically, suggest that they must remain awake to perpetuate productivity on their own terms in the world:

---

[98] The medium is a major theme in Breton's Nadja. The powers of the medium are closely linked with those of the poet; they share a capacity for communication with worlds beyond the reach of ordinary humans.

Assez
le public est fatigué et veut dormir
mais ce n'est pas moi qui favoriserait ce désir
car si le public dort
il n'y aurait pas de haricots cette année.

Sleep is often presented as a journey in the tales. These voyages
are marked by adventure and discovery; they are further manifestations of the equation of change with the sleep state. Gershman
notes that "Surrealist literature regularly appears as a pilgrimage
down to the underworld of desire unlimited." [99] In Péret's work,
the course of the journey often touches on mysteries and fundamental
questions. Napoleon and his entourage in "La Fleur de Napoléon"
travel through a series of tunnels to the center of the earth, while
the child-protagonist of "Le Pays de Cocagne" is carried off by
two white apes to a land of sensuality where he discovers that he
is a man. When Baba arrives at the end of a journey in an eagle's
beak, she finds herself in the cave of Joseph of Arimathea, in the
presence of the last testament of Jesus. The human agents in a tale
can also be responsible for journeys: in "Et les seins mouraient,"
Marcarelle enters into a mystery which is related to the world of
night and dream when "d'un coup de pied il fait un circuit fermé
ou la course vagabonde des animaux à l'aurore." The absence of
consciousness from these marvelous voyages is not necessarily complete; the participants are conscious of them as of dream events.
Nothing is surprising; the world is a system that must be re-learned
at every turn:

> Se réveiller au fond d'une carafe abruti comme une mou-
> che. . . . Cependant lorsque je m'éveillai j'imaginai pendant
> les premières minutes que j'avais toujours vécu au fond de
> la carafe et il est probable que je croirais encore si je n'avais
> aperçu de l'autre côté de la carafe une sorte d'oiseau qui
> la frappait rageusement à coups de bec. Grâce à lui je
> compris ce que ma situation avait d'accidentel et de fâcheux
> et je fus pris d'une grande colère.
>
> ("Corps à corps")

The child who spends his late childhood in a rotting closet, Madame
Lannor who learns not to expect to find herself in her bed upon

---

[99] Gershman, p. 37.

awakening, and the countless characters who encounter rivers and
tropical vegetation in anonymous city dwellings are also in the
process of learning this principle. In the context of dream, events
are inevitable no matter how unlikely, and rage against them is
both futile and ridiculous. In this respect, the events in Péret's tales
are like the Freudian dream-work, which "ne pense, ne calcule pas,
en règle générale ne juge pas; il se borne à transformer." [100] The
great principle of Péret's world is reaffirmed in the coalescence of
dream and waking reality; change is the combinant mode of existence
in this world, and those who live there must accomodate to change
in order to survive.

Dream and automatism are closely linked in that both overstep
the bounds of formal reason and create a syntax of events which
obeys an internal logic. The formal implications of Surrealism's high
regard for the unconscious are noted by Jameson: "it is precisely
the fact that the novel reproduces the discontinuity of waking life
which makes it worthless from the point of view of Surrealism, the
latter aiming at nothing less than the reconstruction of the unconscious itself." [101] In Péret's writing, the influence of automatism is
evident in the procession of phrases in the narration of tales or the
organization of poetry. Disgression into sequences of explanation of
unlikely length and obsessive concentration upon certain elements
of the text create a structure which depends on no pre-existing
givens but rather is derived from the images themselves. Breton,
whose relationship to automatism remains ambiguous, is nonetheless
aware of the artistic validity of this technique:

> Je soutiens que l'automatisme graphique aussi bien que
> verbal ... est le seul mode d'expression qui satisfasse plei-
> nement l'œil et l'oreille en réalisant *l'unité rythmique* ...
> la seule structure qui réponde à la non-distinction, de mieux
> en mieux établie, des qualités sensibles et des qualités for-
> melles, à la non-distinction ... des fonctions sensitives et
> des fonctions intellectuelles. [102]

---

[100] Jean-François Lyotard, "Le travail du rêve ne pense pas," *Revue d'Esthétique,* 21 (1968), 28.

[101] Jameson, p. 97.

[102] André Breton, "Génèse et perspective artistiques du surréalisme," *Le
Surréalisme et la peinture,* p. 66.

The rhythmic unity of Péret's tales depends on the readers' attitude of acceptance, which is analogous with the openness of automatic creation. In "Les Malheurs d'un dollar," for example, the sections of the text follow one another in terms of explicit connections, but the early portions of the narrative are unconventional in proportion and focus. This tale, which is predominantly the story of a girl named Baba, begins with the account of a mayor's tooth, then of the mayor's activities during a given day; he baptizes, among other things, a strange child with an insect head and a single leg ending in a wooden shoe. Then the child, the only object of interest thus far in the tales aside from the mayor's tooth, becomes the connector to a discussion of the circumstances of its conception: an athlete, having rescued a young girl, makes love with her. The shift in subject from the mayor and his baptism of the child to the circumstances of the child's conception can be explained in terms of Freudian analysis of dreams; the relations between clauses are expressed by "making the subordinate clause a prefatory dream and joining the principal clause to it in the form of the main dream." [103] Ignoring temporal logic, as in dream, the tale proceeds from a first subordinate "clause," the subject of which is the mayor, to a main "clause" with Baba as subject.

The focus of the story is in transition when the athlete, who is named Waldeck-Rousseau, [104] meets Baba, who is the protagonist for the remainder of the narration. She begins a tale without verbs which is nonetheless quite comprehensible; she was seduced by an individual who called himself the dollar and made false promises about the nature of the child she would have by him. After the deception of the child's birth, she has further adventures (meanwhile having had her verbs restored) and finally recounts her passage through the cave in which Jesus was buried and her emergence before a crowd which mistakes her for the risen Christ. From the mayor's tooth to the resurrection, the events of the tale follow in a progression which abandons one subject for the next while linking the sequence of happenings. The theme of birth ties the disparate elements of the narrations together; in order of their appearance,

---

103 Freud, *The Interpretation of Dreams,* Brill, p. 343.

104 René Waldeck-Rousseau (1846-1904) was, like Péret, a native of the Nantes area. As a legislator, he was largely responsible for the official separation of Church and State.

children are born of Baba and Waldeck-Rousseau and of Baba and
the dollar; Baba herself is finally taken for one who is reborn.

The same rhythmic unity in the syntax of events characterizes
the tales in general because they usually take the form of an adventure with a central protagonist. "Un Plaisir bien passager" (1924)
also begins with an atmosphere of banality: "Il m'advint un jour
de posséder un chien." The first section of the text is linked by the
narrator's search for his dog, which disappears after attacking a
woman in a green hat, reappears with a bunch of parsnips in his
mouth, and vanishes again while the narrator is looking for a special
kind of sheep at the La Villette market. Within the context of this
story of a man and his dog, the narrator takes on the characteristics
of a detective; after the dog's first disappearance, he says: "je
cherchai longtemps l'explication de cet étrange phénomène sans par-
venir à la découvrir. Le hasard — un hasard unique — devait me
mettre sur la piste." At the antipodes of Poe's ratiocination, Péret
as detective is aided by chance rather than by reason. His search
for the dog leads him through a mysterious hole in a wall, out of
which first a meal is served, then a hand appears. Kissing the hand,
he finds himself in an alley, still accompanied by the sheep from
La Villete. The hand, like something from Arthurian legend, appears
in a fountain, but the romantic aura surrounding it vanishes when
he finds it attached to a bunch of carrots. The tenacity of the
detective makes him persist in his investigation: "cependant, puis-
que la main était *chaude,* elle vivait nécessairement." He puts it
in his pocket and it drags him along; his identity as a follower of
clues helps him to predict the future: "dois-je dire que, cependant,
je ne fis pas montre d'une surprise excessive?" The appearance of
parts of the body alienated from thier normal physical context is
very common in Péret's work and represents another manifestation
of the relationship between the mode of existence in this work and
that of dream: "parts of the body are treated as objects, as is usually
the case in dreams." [105] This explanation also accounts for much of
the apparent violence in the tales; parts of the body thus objectified
cannot feel pain.

From this point to the end of "Un Plaisir bien passager," the
phases of the story are less intrinsically connected: the narrator

---

[105] Freud, *The Interpretation of Dreams,* Brill, p. 351.

finds himself on a bench in the Boulevard Sébastopol with a girl whose beauty instills desire in the passers-by, and the regiments of Napoleon pass above the rooftops. The tale ends in an atmosphere of calm following the holocaust; three sheep graze in a city returned to nature. The hand, which leads the narrator from the middle of the story to its termination, is a dream-like link between otherwise disconnected events. One image persists, that of the narrator in the company of a fairly large four-legged creature which unexpectedly changes identity from a Newfoundland dog to a sheep. In the language of dreams, this means that the creature could be either a dog or a sheep, as "dreams are quite incapable of expressive the alternative 'either-or'; it is their custom to take both members of the alternative into the same context." [106] Another example of the same duality is the appearance of both a bunch of leeks (in the dog's mouth) and a bunch of carrots (in the lady's hand). The double identity of the dog-sheep relates to another facet of dream language according to Freud: "the attitude of dreams to the category of *antithesis* and *contradiction* is very striking. This category is simply ignored." [107] Such paradoxes as that of the hand living apart from the body or that of the sheep grazing in an urban setting are not perceived as troublesome by the dream-like mind of the narrator. Two different mysteries, that of the dog and that of the hand, are pursued and solved to his satisfaction. The dog disappeared and the hand lives apart from a body because of the persistence in daily life of dream-like marvels which are finally embodied in a Napoleonic apocalypse.

A tale by Péret, like the tales of the sixteenth-century *conteurs,* is often interrupted by stories within stories; in Péret's tales, the break in narration is often given typographic concretization by the use of capitalized titles within the text. In "Corps à corps," for example, the "Histoire de la taupe blanche," recounted to the narrator of the tale when he finds himself alone in a wheat field, is itself interrupted by a letter concerning "Pipe en terre et les bouteilles vides." An extended metaphorical structure is created by the link between the latter tertiary story and the narrator's original situation of being imprisoned in a carafe. The linking of phases in

---

[106] *Ibid.,* p. 344.
[107] *Ibid.,* p. 345.

a story, which characterizes most of the tales, is apparent in "Corps à corps." The extreme confinement of the narrator at the outset is followed by various frenzied trajectories, first that of the mole in his story, then that of the narrator, who is transported in a sled with talking pigs who make an alliance with a forest and wage war against the narrator. After a row of dots, the tale ends on a note which continues the idea of boundless movement : "et depuis ce jour je parcours le monde."

The sequential syntax of events which characterizes these tales is also common in sentences within them. These are sometimes as long as entire poems and have the same breathless clausal structure which marks many of Péret's poems. Gerald Mead makes the following analysis of sequential expression in such a text:

> Sequences of relative clauses . . . create a kind of syntactic and conceptual momentum, and in the texts of Péret and Breton, this momentum reaches obsessive proportions, leading the reader on endlessly, it seems, until only an arbitrary period signals a stop. Thought is not really contained or centered in these texts, but only directed. . . . What we find here, I think, is a concrete illustration of that tendency or effort on the part of many Surrealists to identify and express the activity of the subconscious with a type of linguistic activity. [108]

The following sentence from "Et les seins mouraient" is typical of Péret's use of this style:

> Il regarda plus attentivement et vit que les arbres avaient des bras, ces bras des mains et ces mains tenaient maintenant le volant d'une auto qui roulait aussi rapidement que le lui permettait la fuite éperdue des hommes et des autos.

The absolute conjunction of syntax with meaning recalls the "unité rythmique" of which Breton speaks with reference to automatic writing. Language is not controlled by self-conscious, reasoned form, but rather joins the impulse of event. It is no longer possible to distinguish the phenomenal raw material of the text from its verbal

---

[108] Gerald Mead, "A Syntactic Model in Surrealist Style," *Dada/Surrealism,* 2 (1972), 35.

rendition; as Mary Ann Caws states, "language is seen as the imparter of consciousness." [109]

The chains of subordination which mark Péret's longer poems in the collection *De derrière les fagots* are divided into sentences by the use of capitalization in the majority of the texts, but it is not uncommon to find a poem which is one long, unbroken sentence. [110] The principal distinction between Péret's poetry and his prose is not so much the use of narrative sentence form as the shift of subject within the text as a whole. In the tales, a single hero, either the narrator or someone else, dominates the entire work although the appearance of the major character may be delayed by the dreamlike clausal technique. In the case of "Et les seins mouraient," the longest of the tales, this persistence of a protagonist is carried out for fifty pages and through two major divisions and eight minor interruptions by secondary tales, poetry, or dialogue with names. The poems which can be called thematic, such as *Air mexicain* or *Toute une vie,* maintain a subject which is basically the same throughout a lengthy text. But more frequently, the poems entail a community of subjects, none of which holds the stage for more than four lines. In general, the longer texts in *De derrière les fagots* have subjects which persist for longer chains of verses, while a short poem such as "Au bout du monde" changes subject almost with every line; only the "cheval de fiacre" rules the text for longer:

> Quand les charbons enflammés s'enfuient comme des lions
>   apeurés au fond de la mine
> les oiseaux de farine
> se trainent comme des timbres-poste sur des lettres
>   retournés à l'envoyeur
> et les escaliers branlants

---

[109] Mary Ann Caws, "Péret and the Surrealist Word," *Romance Notes,* 11 (1969), 237.

[110] The syntax of events in Péret's poetry is the subject of an entire chapter, "Une Branche morte croulante de son poids d'orchidées," in Courtot, pp. 131-54. Courtot notes the abundance of relatives and subordinates in Péret's poetry in comparison with that of earlier poets. What is more important then numerical superiority is the use Péret makes of this sort of word: "dans tous les autres cas la relative bouclait la boucle de l'image; chez Péret, elle s'envole, elle est décrochée de l'antécédent qui ne sert plus que de tremplin" (p. 148). The use of relatives is, for Courtot, Péret's automatic technique, as it provides a structure for the operation of the arbitrary and for the canalization of images.

bêtes comme des saucisses dont la choucroute a déjà été
                mangée
attendent qu'il fasse jour
que les pommes soient mûres
pour appeler le cheval de fiacre
qui joue à cache-cache avec son fiacre
et le détruira
avant que les orteils des concierges deviennent des rails de
                chemin de fer.

The syntactical chain is reflected in the image "les escaliers bran-
lants," which also appears in "Quatre à quatre," the first text of
the collection. These disorienting structures, which change, like the
subject of the text, while the one who uses them as structures is
trying to follow them, are called "bêtes"; they are removed from
conventional reasoning. They are part of a nocturnal schema, as
they "attendent qu'il fasse jour." The termination of a text is generally not a function of any formal order. Often, the last line of a
poem suggests an extension into non-verbal space after the conclusion by posing a new subject. In "Au bout du monde," for example, the last line reads "avant que les orteils des concierges deviennent des rails de chemin de fer"; this potential transformation is
preceded by a destruction which clears the way for something new:
"le cheval de fiacre / qui jour à cache-cache avec son fiacre / et le
détruira." Then a further transformation in terms of both meaning
and syntax is suggested by the future metamorphosis of the concierge's toes.

    In the longer poems of *De derrière les fagots,* a subject may
rule the development of as many as four lines or be confined to
a single line. While "Au bout du monde" has nine subjects in
twelve lines, "Mal rasé" has twelve in twenty-eight lines; like the
shorter text, "Mal rasé" is open-ended, finishing with the comparison "comme une pomme de terre frite," which could be developed
in the same sense as a comparison earlier in the poem:

        comme un paquet d'oignons au bord du toit
        pour chasser les hirondelles
        qui sans cela viendraient nous aboyer aux chausses.

The plurality of subjects is linked with both weak and strong con-
nectives: the relative pronouns *que* and *qui* are the most frequently
used, but *et* and *pour* are also common. The "strong" links include

adjectives and verbs which are further springboards to complication, as an adjective is either a basis for comparison ("édenté comme un ministre d'agriculture") or for the introduction of a new agent ("rongé par les mites"), while a verb brings another element into the network of events ("font une fois pour toutes rêver les vertueuses limaces").

Pierre Naville, who co-edited *La Révolution Surréaliste* with Péret during its first year of existence (1924), makes the following statement about Péret's state of mind during the writing of his works: "à travers cette buée où se perd toute mémoire, on devine que Péret conserve l'inconscience de sa conscience." [111] In his tales, as in his poetry, Péret tends to dissolve the links of compositional memory to a single subject. The paradoxical "inconscience de sa conscience" is an appropriate description of the problem of automatism from the critical point of view. In the final form taken by the printed work, the syntax of change is like that of dream: a succession of events which are not connected in the ways normally perceived by the waking mind, but which are nonetheless linked. Each image is a temporary obsession with is both total and transient in a structure which must be open to constant metamorphosis. Even in the tales, where a single character dominates the action, the subject can be transformed: the wife of General Boulanger in "Il était une boulangère" becomes a shrike at the end of the narrative, and the narrator of "Au 125 du boulevard Saint Germain," while retaining human form, is at the edge of a transformation when, at the end of the story, he is observed to have butterflies on his internal organs. The dream-principle of the coexistence of apparent antitheses holds true in these cases, as the characters are both what they originally were and something which contradicts this identity.

Dream is, then, the final unification of the force of desire, which can fulfill itself boundlessly in dream, with the generative function of change, which knows no limits of time, space, or identity in dream. Péret's works draw upon the universal resources of the dream, along with other states which contradict rational behavior. Yet his emphasis is always on the unification of dream and waking into a single surreality in which the liberation of dream would be

---

[111] Pierre Naville, "Benjamin Péret," *Œuvres complètes,* II, 19. Reprinted from *La Revue Européenne,* 26 (1 April 1925).

combined with the practical manifestations of the waking state. In order to make this surreality a meaningful replacement for the rational, waking state which governs modern Western civilization, a myth must be evolved to replace the Judeo-Christian and technological myths of our time.

IV

THE NEW MYTH OF CHANGE

In the Surrealism of Benjamin Péret, a new myth emerges in which change is the ruling force. Many of Péret's writings are directly concerned with the subject of myth; he reacts against the dominant myths of Western European civilization and favors primitive or Third World myth. Revolt against prevailing myth and study of other examples of mythological expression are two tendencies in Péret's work which can be interpreted as a thesis and an antithesis which are continually reaffirmed throughout his life.

Everything written by Péret expresses revolt against the myths of the culture in which he lives; texts which do so most explicitly include the poetry of *Je ne mange pas de ce pain-là,* "Le Déshonneur des poètes," and the important body of political writings, for the myths against which he speaks are political and military as well as religious. In honor of the myths of other peoples, which Péret collected in the *Anthologie des mythes, légendes et contes populaires d'Amérique,* he wrote *Air mexicain,* as well as the articles "Notes on Pre-Columbian Art," "Remembrance of Things to Come," "Arts de fête et de cérémonie," "Du fond de la forêt," and the long essay published as "La parole est à Péret." Automatism in the tales relates them to myth, for as Breton says with reference to automatic writing, "la confrontation des produits de cette écriture avait braqué le projecteur sur la région où s'érige le désir sans contrainte, qui est aussi celle où les mythes prennent leur forme." [1] According to Péret's own definition, his synthesis cannot be perfect

---

[1] André Breton, "Du Surréalisme en ses œuvres vives," *Manifestes du surréalisme,* p. 357.

because the society in which he lives is not completely free. In "La parole est à Péret," he postulates the advent of a new generation of mythographers in a society oriented toward complete liberty, rather than structured for repression like the present society:

> Si l'homme d'hier, ne connaissant d'autres limites à sa pensée que celles de son désir, a pu dans sa lutte contre la nature produire ces merveilleuses légendes, que ne pourra pas créer l'homme de demain conscient de sa nature et dominant de plus en plus le monde d'un esprit libéré de toute entrave? [2]

Péret's primary revolt against myth is directed toward God, and is Promethean and to some extent Oedipal, for myth-directed revolt is in itself part of mythology.[3] The structure of myth implies change and the replacement of one ruling force with another in an endless series; as Banquaert states, "le sacré appelle sa violation et confère la divinité à qui l'a osée."[4] The word "divinité" is misleading in the context of Péret's work because Péret denies the existence of God in unmistakeable terms: "l'idée d'un fantôme aussi sinistre est déjà une offense à l'humanité. Que ceux qui y croient nous démontrent son existence. Ce n'est pas à moi de prouver que je n'ai pas assassiné ma concierge."[5] Because God does not exist outside the human imagination, religion is inadmissible in its theocentric form; for Péret, it is a gratuitous tool of oppression. The Christian religion is presented as having been rejected in "Il était une boulangère," although one of the major characters is a Pope and the people will continue to frequent church buildings if given good reason. The populace is sensitive to the mythical potential of everyday objects, and miracles occur in the form of transformations of the ordinary to an extent which belies the apparent suppression of *le merveilleux quotidien*:

---

[2] "La parole est à Péret," p. 61. The association between myth and desire is also made by Northrop Frye in his definition of myth in *Anatomy of Criticism* (New York: Atheneum, 1966), p. 136.

[3] Both Promethean and Oedipal myths appear in nineteenth and twentieth-century French literature, especially in the revival of classical themes in the early decades of this century.

[4] Marie-Odile Banquaert, 66.

[5] Quoted from *Le Peignoir de bain*, 4 (1954) in Jehan Mayoux, "Benjamin Péret ou la fourchette coupante," 54.

La gouttière traversa la nef et vint remplacer le crucifix qui dominait le maître-autel. Alors, le peuple, que l'image du Christ avait, à jamais, rejeté hors de l'église, accourut en masse adorer la gouttière miraculeuse.

For Péret, valid myth is an expression of popular creativity, not the imposition of a credo by some higher power. Discovery and stimulation of the powers of the human imagination is his mythical premise.

This point of view has led in the past and present to various attempts to create religious myth without God or gods. Péret also rejects these religions: "on assiste dès maintenant à des tentatives de création des mythes athées privés de toute poésie et destinés à alimenter et canaliser un fanatisme religieux latent dans les masses." [6] As examples, he discusses the cults of Hitler and Stalin. Although he does not make the analogy, the structure of these "religions" is appropriate to the schema established by Péret in his "Notes on Pre-Columbian Art":

> the appearance of the grandiose in art marks the end of the creative period of mythical poetry ... when mythical poetry has lost its power to create divinities, it acquires the power to celebrate heroes and to deify them. [7]

The mystique and exaltation formerly attached to religious phenomena are transplanted into a context which is, in the two current examples, predominantly military. In the Mexican civilization analyzed in the "Notes on Pre-Columbian Art," this is the time of the alliance of priest and warrior which "leads to the moment when fear and horror completely dominate." [8]

Unless the Promethean figure can rid himself and his culture of the idea of a God or gods, as Prometheus himself failed to do, the result of revolt will be further repression rather than liberation. In psychoanalytical terms, the revolt against God is a dimension of revolt against the father and is thus Oedipal. According to Péret,

---

[6] "La Parole est à Péret," p. 58.

[7] Benjamin Péret, "Notes on Pre-Columbian Art," trans. Peter Watson, *Horizon,* 15 (1947), 370. Article appears originally in English.

[8] *Ibid.,* 371. The warrior-priest has been a topos in French literature since Turpin in *La Chanson de Roland.*

this is a significant theme in myth; the incest taboo "ressuscite dans le mythe, projectant sur l'infini des cieux l'image fini du père assassiné." [9] In terms of Greek mythology, the assassination of the father is a necessary preliminary to the construction of a new society: Zeus kills his father, Chronos, with the collaboration of his mother Gaea (Earth). Again, there is a danger to be averted by the study of ancient mythical models, for the society over which Zeus reigns is a military dictatorship with a hero-god as leader. By Péret's standards, the mythology of the Greeks suffers in contrast with that of the pre-Columbians because its events are calqued on social and political reality, which is a post facto basis for the myth. [10] "The pre-Columbian Indian speaks to the imagination in terms of its own language," [11] and this is for Péret more valid than "the Greco-Latin products which, by relegating imagination to a secondary place, overlook the principal source of all art." [12] Within his revolt against God and religion, then, there is a fundamental revolt against the cultural premises of Western civilization. This is the rebellion of the Surrealist movement itself: "l'opposition entre surréalisme et religion n'est ni relative ni partielle mais absolue; l'enjeu de la lutte est l'homme tout entier, que la religion veut asservir, que le surréalisme veut libérer." [13] This statement by Jehan Mayoux, derived from a study of Péret's work and life, is interesting in its use of the terms Surrealism and religion as alternative human choices or as adversaries in a war for man's mind.

Surrealism is itself a myth, but in a different dimension from that of older mythological expressions; it is an outline of a schema which leaves the filling in of details to the individual and, more importantly, to the people of the future. Péret's new myth of change

---

[9] "La parole est à Péret," p. 52.

[10] This is, for example, the case with Hesiod's *Theogony* as translated by Norman O. Brown (New York: Bobbs-Merrill, 1953): "Thus Greek culture was faced with two characteristic problems: how to find unity in diversity, and how to find a permanent principle in the midst of flux. These later became the classic problems of Greek philosophy; it was Hesiod's achievement to have formulated them first in mythic terms" (p. 46). Hesiod's description of society under Zeus is modelled on the structure of his own time; Brown calls the *Theogony* "Hesiod's vision of the realities of the Iron Age" (p. 48).

[11] "Notes on Pre-Columbian Art," 367.

[12] *Ibid.*

[13] Mayoux, 56.

differs from the mythology of Surrealism in general, as well as diverging from the myths proposed by individual Surrealists. As a myth, Surrealism can be shown to have its representative gods which, as is generally the case in myth, are abstract, for example dream, *le merveilleux quotidien,* madness, and childhood. The heroes, another important component of myth, are enumerated in the First Manifesto: many of these, like Rimbaud and Lautréamont, had existences which were markedly separated from the normal range of human experience, and they are much more highly valued as dead ancestors than they were as living poets. In the works of André Breton and Louis Aragon, the concept of mythology in the modern world acquires a specificity which leads to a creation that diverges from that of Péret. Breton saw the problem of prophecy in a mythic context, associating it with ancient examples: "la voix surréaliste qui secouait Cume, Dodone et Delphes n'est autre chose que celle qui me dicte mes discours les moins courroucés." [14] In the 1942 "Prolégomènes à un troisième manifeste du surréalisme ou non," Breton's mystical preoccupations of the period lead him to propose the existence of "les grands transparents," who would be the basis and justification of "un mythe nouveau." [15] For Aragon, the idea of myth is also accompanied by supernatural creatures of his imagination:

---

[14] "Premier Manifeste du surréalisme," p. 61. The question of prophecy makes three appearances in Péret's work. The earliest is a poem, "Importé du Japon," originally published in *Action,* 4 (July 1920) and reprinted at the end of the first volume of the *Œuvres complètes.* Because of its use of place name and allusion to brutality, this text appears to foretell the use of atomic force at the end of the Second World War: "Qui a sali les viandes de Nagasaki / Le vent perdit la fin de la chanson / Le papou était un chimpanzé." Pierre Naville, in his article on Péret reproduced at the beginning of the second volume of *Œuvres complètes,* gives a second example which can be related to prophecy: a few days after the publication of "Au 125 du boulevard Saint Germain," which begins with a bathtub thrown from the window of the building in question, "le journal nous apprit qu'une baignoire avait été projetée dans la rue, par l'éclatement d'un chauffebains, *au 125 du boulevard Saint Germain,* et qu'elle avait écrasé dans sa chute une femme enceinte" (p. 18). The third example of prophecy is recounted in detail by Péret himself: on the windows of his prison in Rennes, he saw episodes from his life and finally the number 22, which predicted the date of his liberation" ("La parole est à Péret," pp. 37-50).

[15] "Prolégomènes à un troisième manifeste du surréalisme ou non," *Manifestes du surréalisme,* p. 351.

> L'évolution de ma pensée était un méchanisme en tout point analogue à la génèse mythique. . . . Il m'apparut que l'homme est plein de dieux. . . . Ils sont les principes mêmes de toute transformation de tout. Ils sont la nécessité du mouvement. . . . Je me mis à concevoir une mythologie en marche. Elle méritait proprement le nom de mythologie moderne. [16]

The association made by Aragon between myth, transformation, and movement is similar to Péret's use of these concepts, but the creation of explicitly designated divinities is foreign to Péret. Aragon, like Péret, connects myth and poetry, but the emphasis is on the former term when he states that "le mythe est la seule voix de la conscience." [17]

Whereas Breton and Aragon base their mythologies on the perception of divine or supernatural creatures and discuss these beings in vaguely mystical terms, Péret presents his mytho-mimetic characters as living in the world, as potential incarnations of ourselves. Far from being "transparent," like Breton's hypothetical creatures, they encounter resistance in the world of things as do normal human beings. The great difference between Péret's characters and Breton's beings (among whom such a factual character as Nadja might be included) is found in their confrontation of the world and their overcoming it through the force of change. They do not float, detached and mysterious, through the world, and they are not subject, as is Nadja, to the banishment which is a corollary of their irreality.

Revolt against repressive mythology and creative aspiration toward a new mythology are combined in Péret's Surrealism:

> Quand Péret reprend ce qui, dans n'importe quel contexte, relève de la pensée créatrice, ou de la poésie, il ne fait que témoigner de son indépendance et participer à la lutte séculaire pour la libération de "toutes les forces de l'humanité aspirant à la vie" — contre la religion. [18]

---

[16] Louis Aragon, Le Paysan de Paris, p. 145.

[17] Ibid., p. 157. For Péret, the emphasis is on poetry, "le véritable souffle de l'homme" ("Le Déshonneur des poètes," p. 71).

[18] Mayoux, 58.

The sources of the process which leads to the creation of a new myth are multiple, and they include the names cited in the First Manifesto as Surrealist. For Péret, there is no doubt that the myths of poets, in the exemplary manners of Rimbaud and Lautréamont, are sources and inspirations. *Les Chants de Maldoror* are moral and mythical revolt; Lautréamont is quoted in the context of a discussion of myth in "La parole est à Péret," and the collaborative poetry which he demands in the *Poésies* is exemplified in Péret's collection of myths, legends, and popular tales: "la poésie doit être faite par tous. Non par un." [19] For Péret, myth and poetry are expressions of the same spirit; myth is the first state in which poetry appears "et l'axe autour duquel elle continue de tourner à une vitesse indéfiniment accélérée." [20] Again, this is a myth which is poetic, not religious. [21] Being identified with poetry, it also participates in the components of poetic expression, most notably in dream. In describing the Brazilian *capoeira* in "Du fond de la forêt," Péret notes that the spectator "aboutit à un état de rêverie où le monde matériel s'enfuit à tire-d'aile" and that "on accède au cœur même du rêve." [22] The analogy between this behavior and Péret's myth is evident both in their shared goals and in their use of poetry and dream.

The importance of poetry as the original expression or mythic thought is re-emphasized in the "Notes on Pre-Columbian Art": "poetry, therefore, precedes plastic art, for man uses his imagination before possessing the means permitting him to give a form to the creatures born of his desires and of his agonies." [23] Poetry is the starting point both of the codification of myth and of the formulation of religion. Because of its basic status, it is also intrinsically

---

[19] "La parole est à Péret," p. 59. The quotation is from Lautréamont's *Poésies* in *Œuvres complètes* (Paris: Garnier, 1969), p. 291.

[20] "La parole est à Péret," p. 24.

[21] "On remarquera que le mythe primitif, dépourvu de consolations et ne comportant que des tabous élémentaires, est tout exaltation poétique. . . . La religion s'évanouit, mais le mythe poétique n'en demeure pas moins nécessaire" ("La parole est à Péret," p. 57).

[22] Benjamin Péret, "Du fond de la forêt," *Le Surréalisme Même*, 2 (1957), 109. Northrop Frye uses dream as part of his definition of myth: "this union of ritual and dream in a form of verbal communication is myth" (*Anatomy of Criticism*, p. 106).

[23] "Notes on Pre-Columbian Art," 365. Huizinga makes the same equation in *Homo ludens*, p. 151: "Myth is always poetry."

connected with the rhythms and structures of ritual. The artifacts of primitive ritual, as a major influence on French art in the early part of this century, were well-known to Péret; although he was never wealthy enough to become a collector, his love of masks, figurines, and other elements of non-European rite is apparent in the "Notes on Pre-Columbian Art" and "La parole est à Péret," as well as in the commentary for a film entitled "L'Invention du monde." This film, made in collaboration with Jean-Louis Bédouin and Michel Zimbacca, displays a global variety of primitive objects which were borrowed from collectors ranging from Breton to Lévi-Strauss.

Another interesting contribution by Péret to the study of myth is his 1944 essay "Le Sel répandu." The sprinkled salt of the title alludes to a superstition; in this essay, Péret shows the intrinsic link between myth and superstition, and between both these modes of thought and poetry:

> un lieu commun unit toutes les superstitions: une conscience poétique du monde qui constitue la base même de la pensée humaine de son aurore jusqu'à nos jours puisque cette conscience poétique palpite sur toute la surface du globe quelqu'effort qu'aient entrepris les civilisations modernes pour l'étouffer. [24]

This essay concludes with a series of suggestions for new superstitions. Whereas modern rationalist thought attempts to rid the world of superstition, Péret promotes it as a means of instilling a poetic awareness of the world in the population as a whole. Breton lists Péret among "les esprits très dissemblables mais comptant parmi les plus lucides et les plus audacieux d'aujourd'hui" who respond to the question: "Que penser du postulat 'pas de société sans mythe social'; dans quelle mesure pouvons-nous choisir ou adopter, et *imposer* un mythe en rapport avec la société que nous jugeons désirable." [25] Myth is a social necessity for Péret, and the nature of a society depends in large part upon its underlying myth. It is the nature of myth to be generalized in an entire people and to correspond, like superstition, to a basic aspect of human thought.

---

[24] Benjamin Péret, "Le Sel répandu," p. 22.
[25] Breton, "Prolégomènes au troisième manifeste du surréalisme ou non," *Manifestes du surréalisme,* p. 344.

Péret, like Antonin Artaud,[26] was vitally interested in the civilization of ancient and modern Mexico. For Artaud, "il n'y a plus depuis longtemps en Europe de mythes auxquels les collectivités puissent croire. Nous en sommes tous à épier la naissance d'un Mythe valable et collectif."[27] But Artaud's interest in primitive culture is diluted by a diffuse range of preoccupations, and he was more concerned with Oriental and other mysticism than with the mythological productions of native Central and South Americans. Nevertheless, it is interesting to note that his "Notes sur les cultures orientales, grecques, indiennes" are immediately preceded in the Gallimard edition of his works by a section on Heraclitus; he shares this dual inspiration with Péret[28] and is aware of the relevance of Heraclitean thought to non-western myth. Such essays as "La Culture éternelle du Mexique"[29] are, however, vitiated by excursions into mysticism and such personal preoccupations as the comparative value of experimental and homeopathic medicine. In contrast, Péret only raises questions apart from the subject of primitive myth in order to show their basic pertinence and it is he, not Artaud, who offers the more productive study of Mexican myth.

Like the myths of the early Mexicans, the modern, synthetic myth suggested by Péret's work is based on the force of the imagination rather than on any rational social or political model. The following comparison between definitions of the Surrealist image and of mythical activity shows their similarity:

> In terms of narrative, myth is the imitation of actions near or at the conceivable limits of desire ... (it is) a world in which every thing is potentially identical with everything else, as though it were all inside a single, infinite body.[30]

---

[26] Artaud was a member of the Surrealist group from 1924 until 1929, when he was chastized in the "Second Manifeste du surréalisme" for the commercial compromise required by his theatrical ambitions.

[27] Antonin Artaud, "Venu au Mexique," *Œuvres complètes,* VII (Paris: Gallimard, 1971), 162.

[28] The importance of Heraclitus to the Surrealist movement has already been noted; for the Surrealists, he replaces Socrates and Aristotle as the leading Greek philosopher.

[29] Artaud, 265-70.

[30] Frye, p. 136.

> Tout devient mobile et fusible, équivalent et interchan-
> geable, aucune cloison ne sépare plus le concret de l'abstrait,
> l'univers physique de l'univers mental qui sont reliés par le
> magnétisme de l'image. [31]

The motivational force of desire in myth become the force of change
in the image; this interconnection is a primary element of Péret's
myth. Both of the characterizations of the world of myth and image
insist on the element of synthesis and identity; a typical example
of this principle in Péret's work is the first line of "Qui est-ce" in
De derrière les fagots: "J'appelle tabac ce qui est oreille." Actions
within the context of myth or image are extreme, beyond the bounds
of reason, like almost any activity in the poetry or tales of Péret:
literally anything is possible.

When Péret undertakes the pan-mythical analysis of "L'Invention du monde," he finds illustrations of these principles in such
aspects of mythical behavior as the mask, which ostensibly changes
the nature of its wearer from man to animal, ancestor or god, and
permits him a latitude of behavior which is otherwise not allowed.
The mask, as he states, "dissimule et stimule," but eventually man
becomes dissatisfied with the imitation of freedom and leaves on
an adventure to seek the source of power: "l'homme veut devenir
la force même." [32] As Péret explains, drawing primarily on native
American and Oceanic myth, snakes represent this power in its
terrestrial manifestations, while birds are the symbolic incarnation
of divine power. The expanded awereness which is the result of the
voyage reveals to primitive man a "vie frémissante qui jaillit de
toute part," and is not limited to his island, valley, or forest. In
L'Invention du monde, the remarkable images which conclude the
journey to mythological understanding represent the burning change
of a "monde en devenir" and the multiplicity of an animistic world-
view. This multiplicity is everywhere characteristic of myth, which
is "a new arrangement of elements." [33] Hence, when Péret analyzes

---

[31] Marc Eigeldinger, "Surréalisme et dynamisme de l'imagination," *L'Imagination créatrice,* ed. Roselyne Chenu (Neuchâtel: A la Baconnière, 1971),
p. 167.

[32] For a discussion of "L'Inmation du monde," see H. Matthews, *Surrealism and Film* (Ann Arbor: University of Michigan, 1971), pp. 116-19. I
was given a private showing of *L'Invention du monde* by Jean-Louis Bédouin
and Michel Zimbacca in May, 1972.

[33] Claude Lévi-Strauss, *The Savage Mind,* p. 21.

the *capoeira,* he poses the question "une lutte ou une danse?," "un ballet ou un rituel?" [34] Finally, the myths of primitive man are based on the most important things in their lives:

> les mythes primitifs sont en grande partie des composés et des résidus d'illuminations, d'intuitions, de présages confirmés jadis d'une manière si éclatante qu'ils ont pénétrés d'un trait jusqu'aux plus grandes profondeurs de la conscience de ces populations. [35]

According to this formula, these perceptions passed directly into the subconscious without being refracted by rational mental activity; they are, therefore, pure communications between the depths of man's mind and the world in which he lives.

The significance of names in myth is often a subject of discussion in scholarly treatment of primitive thought. [36] Péret's speculations on the foundations of mythology in "L'Invention du monde" show that ancestors play an important role in the original perception of the world, so it is to be expected that the names of those who are dead would appear in the mythological context of the tales. These names are common and generally belong to royalty, military heroes, and political figures. They act as touchstones within reality for the action which might otherwise be situated by the reader in another county, if not another world. Ironically, these characters may appear, in contrast with their consecrated historical identities, as figures of fun; in a mythical context, they are demystified. Examples of this type of character are Napoleon, who appears in "La Fleur de Napoléon" and "Ne pas manger de raisin sans le laver," Waldeck-Rousseau, the "athlète" in "Les Malheurs d'un dollar," and Pope Pius VII, a major character in "Il était une boulangère." The number of characters who are merely alluded to is even greated; included among them are Mahatma Ghandi, Czar Nicholas II, Charlot, Nero, Mussolini, and Mistinguett in "Il était une boulangère," Joffre and Clemenceau in "Un Plaisir bien passager," Christ and Camille Flammarion in "Les Vagues Ames," Théroigne de Méricourt, Cromwell, the Thermopolytes and the Spar-

---

[34] "Du fond de la forêt," 108.
[35] "La parole est à Péret," pp. 51-52.
[36] Brown's treatment of Hesiod, for example, concludes with an exhaustive catalogue of names (pp. 85-87).

tans, Christ again, and Damocles in "Et les seins mouraient," and
Le Poussin, Peter the Great, Richelieu, Louis XII, and Napoleon II
in "Au 125 du boulevard Saint Germain," to cite only a few examples. In "La Maladie no. 9," there is a considerable amount of
dialogue between Nicholas the wine merchant and Job, while "La
Fleur de Napoléon" includes, in addition to Bonaparte, the Unknown Soldier, whose presence recalls Péret's performance in this
role, and the Cid, complete with a photograph of Chimena. But the
allusive role of proper names is minimized in these tales; they are
words in the same sense as are common nouns, and all people tend
to behave in similar ways. The analogy between human conduct
and the behavior of words in their liberated state is especially striking in the examples of these historical figures.

Not all the characters in the tales have familiar names; when
the name is not drawn from the category of ancestors, it is generally indicative of fantasy. Monsieur Séraphin, the earliest example
of this current, shares the action in "Au 125 du boulevard Saint
Germain" with the king of Greece and the President of the Re-
public; [37] other fantasy names include several with humorous overtones, such as Zacharie Artichaut in "Le Pont des Soupirs" and
Monsieur Détour, the mayor in "Les Malheurs d'un dollar." In
"Pulchérie veut une auto," the name of the heroine, reminiscent of
Corneille, is juxtaposed with those of the heroic Glouglou and the
villains Pandanleuil and Mère Volauvent to humorous ends. Not
all the character have standard human names; this is also a characteristic which links the tales with myth, since the animistic context of myth leads to personifications of plant and animal life. "Ne
pas manger de raisin sans le laver" is an example of this sort of
tale: its principal characters have no given names but rather are
designated as a "petit bonhomme en plâtre," a "teinturier," and
the "ambassadeur-marchand du lard," who is never named but is
readily recognizable as Paul Claudel. Péret names himself in two
tales: in "Passage à niveau," he is powerful enough to cause a lapse
in the incessant hammer-stroke of time on his birthday, and in "La
Dernière Nuit du condamné à mort," he is himself the protagonist

---

[37] It is interesting to note that in the "mythe nouveau" which is Aragon's
Paysan de Paris, the figure of Imagination appears holding a copy of "Au 125
du boulevard Saint Germain" under his arm (p. 80); it is he who gives the
famous discourse in which Surrealism is described as a drug.

of the tale. Names in the tales have mythological implications even
when it is the author himself who is named.

These protagonists share many traits with mythical heroes, [38]
but they are definitely not gods for, like the new myth to which
Péret alludes in "La parole est à Péret,"

> ces mythes seront dépourvus de toute consolation religieuse
> puisque celle-ci sera sans objet dans un monde orienté vers
> la poursuite de la toujours provocante et tentatrice chimère
> de la perfection à jamais inaccessible. [39]

There are, therefore, imperfect heroes, but they are heroes nonetheless in their extensive activities beyond the limits of normally
perceived human experience. They are like the participants in the
capoeira:

> les "adversaires" possédant cette agilité étrangère à toute
> effort dont chacun est susceptible lorsque le sommeil le
> possède et qui, le soleil levé, porte cependant l'inconséquent
> à accuser les images de la nuit. [40]

This strength is outside the realm of sport, to which Péret's hostility is vehement; [41] it is the power which exists when awareness
of rational human limitations is overcome. The connection between
sleep and death which Péret posits in *Immortelle Maladie* and *Dormir dormir dans les pierres* continues to be valid in the context of
his mythic synthesis; as Phillip Wheelwright notes in his study
of Heraclitus, "in the universe as Heraclitus envisages it there is
nothing truly immortal in the literal sense — except, indeed, the
endless process of mortality itself." [42] Mortality is the immortal
malady, and as such it is also an intrinsic physical process in Péret's
myth of change.

---

[38] In Northrop Frye's definition, "if superior in kind both to other men
and to the environment of other men, the hero is a divine being and the story
about him will be a *myth* in the sense of a story about a god" (p. 33). Péret's
characters are not divine, but they fulfill Frye's qualifications in that they "do
whatever they like, which in practice means whatever the story-teller likes"
(p. 135).

[39] "La parole est à Péret," p. 62.

[40] "Du fond de la forêt," 109.

[41] For example, Péret fears the extinction of the *capoeira* "sans doute au
profit de quelque sport abrutissant" ("Du fond de la forêt," 109).

[42] Phillip Wheelwright, *Heraclitus,* p. 75.

The characters in the tales have the effortless influence of the participants in the *capoeira*. Waldeck-Rousseau in "Les Malheurs d'un dollar" is typical in his physical prowess which is explicitly athletic in his approach to the marvelous:

> Chaque matin il allait sur la route arracher un arbre, de préférence un vieux car il était de ceux qui croient que tout ce qui est vieux n'a plus de raison d'être. L'après-midi, il vidait un étang et, dans la vase qui tapissait le fond, il plantait des choux.

Later, he saves Baba from a strange fate at the hand of a bowler hat and is rewarded with her love. Like a surreal Paul Bunyan, he is beyond normal measure and quite unlike the political figure after whom he is named, but, unlike Breton's "grands transparents" or Aragon's phantom ideas, he is a real person with essentially human characteristics. With Waldeck-Rousseau's feat, the reader is still on fairly familiar ground. This is not the case with Francis Macarelle, the hero of "Et les seins mouraient":

> Ah! Garde-toi de rencontrer Macarelle, car il lui suffirait de remuer l'un après l'autre les cinq doigts de sa main gauche et la racine de réséda qui lui fait un sixième doigt pour que tu sois semblable à ces tessons de bouteilles qui décorent si agréablement le ventre des femmes enceintes vers le sixième mois de leur grossesse.

The common expression "il n'a qu'à remuer son petit doigt" is expanded in terms both of action, with the five fingers acquiring a sixth as an extension, and of effect, which is entirely unpredictable.

Even when the character in question is not the protagonist, he participates in an elevated, super-human context. In "La Dernière Nuit du condamné à mort," the defense attorney for the condemned man, who is identified as Péret, is won over to his client's ambition, a Lautréamont-like "*généralisation du crime.*" The non-human characters also act in the manner of the heroes of myth: the Amazon river in "Il était une boulangère" is told by Nicholas II that "tu as fait le monde avec tes cheveux qui sont ces mouches de sel visibles sur la peau des demoiselles à marier." The river also realizes what must have been a common masculine aspiration of the era contemporary with the writing of the tale: he receives a love letter from the aging dancer Mistinguett. The heroic stature of the Amazon is, like that of most of the protagonists, vitiated in an encounter with an insuperable obstacle when Mistinguett refuses to acknowledge her communication with the Amazon. It is interesting to note that this personage is not *an* Amazon, as might be expected in a traditional mythical context, but rather *the* Amazon.

In the action of the tales, the protagonists display an affinity with the heroes of myth in that they influence and interact with the order of nature. The easy transition of the Amazon river from natural to human existence is one example of this phenomenon. Another is in "Un Vie pleine d'intérêt," where the lovers can act without fear of harm from the helpless Madame Lannor because of the strength of their love:

> Madame Lannor saisit une énorme pierre et la jeta dans la direction des amoureux mais, arrivé à un mètre de la tête de François, la pierre s'arrêta dans sa course, une étincelle jaillit entre la pierre et la tête de François, cependant qu'on entendait un formidable bruit de vitres brisées. Le bruit s'était à peine apaisé que de la base de l'obélisque, sortait une troupe de jeune filles nues se tenant par la main.

Through the force of their desire, François and Gertrude create change in the course of the stone and liberation in the breaking of glass to free the young girls into a new collective joy. Even the unsympathetic characters like Lord Cheltenham in "Sur le passage d'un panier à salade" can enter into a state of grace through the process of change. After being transported over a triple curtain encountered in the middle of a London street, he finds himself in a new land where "quatre ibis l'attendaient pour lui dire combien son arrivée était souhaitée." The major affinity with the characters of myth is the capacity for transformation possessed by these actors in the tales. Aragon makes an explicit connection between myth and the property of metamorphosis: "des mythes nouveaux naissent sous chacun de nos pas. Là où l'homme a vécu commence la légende, là où il vit. Je ne veux plus occuper ma pensée que de ces transformations méprisées." [43] Examples of this phenomenon abound in Péret's prose; there is, in this context, nothing unusual about the

---

[43] Aragon, p. 15.

lovers François and Gertrude, who become a cloud "affectant la forme d'un saucisse munie à chaque extrémité d'une immense oreille s'agitant lentement comme une éventail." Transformations are the results of the mythical status of the hero:

> Bolo Pacha coupa la partie des intestins qui tenait encore à l'animal et prit leur place. Aussitôt le ventre se renferma et la poitrail de l'animal se couvrait de glycines, le cheval hennit et dit:
> — Droits de l'homme et du citoyen.
>
> ("Dans le cadre de nos mœurs")

Despite the proliferation of events which resemble the results of magic in the tales, the use of ritual in explicit form is rare. The transformations and miraculous deeds which take place are spontaneous and unpredictable, not the results of a predetermined formulation of cause and effect. The one person in the tales who is a sorceress, Madame Daisy in "Sur le passage d'un panier à salade," says "répétez les paroles que je vais prononcer et faites les gestes que je vais faire"; she implies a traditional form of action which is atypical in Péret's work. Her prediction of the future is accompanied by a further indication that she belongs to a rejected tradition of classical mythology: the River Lethe runs through her apartment. Her feats exceed those normally expected of a seer, but they belong to an entirely different realm from that of most of the characters in the tales. It is significant that the terror of the Lethe is domesticated and made part of the human urban setting; hence, it is removed from its original sacred context. An anonymous woman at the beginning of "Une ornière vaut une jument" can do more than Madame Daisy could hope:

> Un coup de pistolet donna le signal du départ et une dame blonde s'éleva verticalement dans les airs, puis glissa légèrement par dessus quelques bouquets d'arbres, franchit aisément une rivière et se posa le plus simplement du monde au pied d'un seringa fleuri.

According to Huizinga, the game aspect of myth is among its greatest powers: "myth, so playing, can soar to the heights of insight beyond the reach of reason." [44] Ritual action, to the extent

---

[44] Huizinga, p. 151.

that it does occur in Péret's writing, is interiorized in the form of game structures. These can have the power of incantations:

> Et quand je lui ai répondu 19
> il m'a répondu 19
> 22 si tu as le temps d'être riche
> 30 et 40 pour la comédie en deux temps
> 50 pour ton sale anniversaire
> 100 pour les commodités du printemps
> et pour le reste je suis pâle et hypnotique.
>
> ("Mystère de ma naissance")

They are also, as in this example, important keys to the mythical understanding of the hidden workings which govern man's life.

The immense flexibility of the characters in the tales means that, like figures in myth, they are able to exist in both supra- and sub-terranean environments without losing their identities. In this sense they recall the language of the early collections *Immortelle Maladie* and *Dormir dormir dans les pierres,* in which incorporation with nature beyond death does not necessarily imply a loss of consciousness. "La Fleur de Napoléon" is striking in its use of this theme; both the Cid and Napoleon make descents into the underworld and then, as if in parody of this action, make investigations of their physical selves. For the Cid, the action of descent begins with his kissing the photograph of Chimena and setting out for his office. After passing through a door, he goes down a staircase "et se trouva dans une vaste salle où brillaient des milliers de cierges fichés le long des murs." Napoleon has a similar experience: he is, of course, dead, and so he returns to his tomb. At once, he exits in the other direction and is inundated by a shower of rose petals. Then, followed by his entourage, he proceeds to the center of the earth, but the location of the entrance to this passageway is within himself:

> Il toussa et l'un des côtés tourna sur son axe, laissant voir une ouverture d'un mètre vingt environ par laquelle Napoléon se glissa. . . . Le couloir allait en s'exhaussant et au bout de cent mètres, s'étant redressé, il marchait à grands pas.

The Cid also undergoes this transformation from microcosm to macrocosm although in his case the consequences are not so drastic:

"ils trouvèrent le Cid examinant ses entrailles avec une loupe." A similarly extreme act of self-examination and introspection is performed by Zacharie Artichaut, the protagonist of "Le Pont des soupirs"; although he is not a historical ancestor, the words used to describe him give him a mythical aura: "Homme au masque pâle, aux yeux de plumes de paon, soulève ta tête comme un couvercle et regarde dans ton corps: tu y verras une toupie qui tourne, qui tourne." Early in "Il était une boulangère," the heroine has an experience of descent into interior spaces; her trajectory is more analogous with that of Napoleon than with that of Zacharie Artichaut:

> Elle descendit l'escalier du métro, mais que s'était-il passé? l'escalier n'en finissait plus, ce n'était plus un escalier, c'était un macaroni. Cependant, tout a une fin. A force de descendre, elle arriva sur les bords d'une rivière dont les eaux nacrées charriaient des perles qu'eussent enviées les élégantes des deux mondes.... Une chose l'étonna: l'absence totale de poissons.

The transformation of the staircase into a piece of macaroni suggests that this descent might be related to digestion. Within the interior or subterranean space, Madame Boulanger meets Pope Pius VII, who will accompany her throughout her adventures and become her lover as well. The heroes are presented as being in Paris and Rome and ascend to great heights, yet events of the story which follows Mme. Boulanger's descent are associated with the underground setting. Traveling through the underworld is not the dangerous task for these characters that it is for a traditional mythical hero like Orpheus. They participate in the triumph of the synthesis over that which has gone before and are at once more and less like human beings.

These examples show that the myth toward which Péret is working is based on an integration of the human body with the world; although not humanistic in the usual sense, it is based on human rather than methanical, scientific, or religious perceptions and phraseology. In his essay on Breton, Michel Beaujour proposes a definition of Breton's mythology which is also largely valid as a description of that of Péret:

le poète propose les bases d'une cosmologie renouvelée, où
la vision anthropocentrique dont relèvent toutes nos démar-
ches, se dépasserait dans une vision analogique au sein de
laquelle la nature humanisée et l'homme matérialisé dialo-
gueraient sans obstacle, dans une exaltante transparence. [45]

Whereas Breton "propose les bases" for this mythology, Péret illustrates it in a large and consistent body of work. The free dialogue
between man and nature is exemplified in *Histoire naturelle,* for
example, where man, in the form of the narrator's *on* can shape
the heart of nature while the natural elements take human form
and behavior. Yet in Péret's work, the interplay between "la nature
humanisée et l'homme matérialisé" always takes place in a situation which includes obstacles; the traditional separation must be
overcome at every turn. Péret's mythology is always in process, on
the way to perfection rather than being the perfect expression of
harmony, and it is thus that it is a mythology of continual change.

Once the poet has found a means for perceiving and conveying
change, he explores the workings of this universal phenomenon.
Like Heraclitus, Péret finds change to be intrinsic to the phenomenal
world, and the Heraclitean image of fire, which is basic to this
universe in flux, is common in his poetry and prose. Change is
depicted as a creative activity, both in serial transformations brought
about by an external agent and in autonomous metamorphoses. Like
the Mayan pyramid which he describes in the preface to his translation of *Le Livre de Chilám Balám de Chumayel* (1955), Péret
orients himself in a manner which not only allows him to intercept
and interpret change, but which also facilitates the externalization
and communication of the appearance of change.

Throughout Péret's work, change is presented in the structure
of desire; it is the function of such collections as *Je sublime* and
Un point c'est tout to define and explore its implications at every
level of human existence. As in the earlier works, in this poetry
it is the special gift of the poet to be able to see beyond the temporal and spatial limits of man's life on earth and to find desire in
the superhuman and the subhuman. Erotic love, a basic form of
desire, is extended to encompass and effect the entire experiential

---

[45] Michel Beaujour, "André Breton ou la transparence," *Arcane 17* by
André Breton (Paris: Union générale d'éditions, 1965), p. 183.

world through the process of sublimation, which is intrinsic to Péret's definition of love. Desire extends to history in the human search for unity among men and with nature; this manifestation of desire appears in the long poems *Air mexicain* (1952) and *Dernier Malheur dernière chance* (1945). It informs a political view which emphasizes the attempts of desire to eliminate all obstacles to the free expression of the marvelous; *Je ne mange pas de ce pain-là* and "Le Déshonneur des poètes" are most direct in their emphasis of this requisite, which is a strong element in all of Péret's work. The natural adversaries of the poet are those who have civilized themselves out of natural processes and those who work to keep others from free participation in the ecology of the marvelous. They represent the status quo in its widest manifestation, that is, those forces which maintain stasis in opposition to the dynamic force of desire. Among these are established religion and repressive government, which Péret sees as alienating men from their own natures and from Nature itself.

Once desire is described and evoked in its positive and negative aspects, Péret proceeds even deeper in his exploration of change in the world to define generation itself. Change is inherent in Péret's view of the mythical process of creation; everything in the world is both the product of transformations and potential material for further change. The force of desire, which provides the structure for change, is manifested in generative processes through the humanization of natural forces. The human point of view is the only possible vantage for the poet; the pretense of scientific objectivity, which fails to account for change in the observer, is abandoned for a continual redefinition of stance on the part of both subject and object in mythic interaction. In his attempts to formulate the ideal relationship between man and the world, Péret studies primitive myth and legend and finds in them guidelines which are less contaminated by the civilized European tradition. Péret finds the openness and vitality of primitive beliefs to be a more satisfying and valid response to the human need for physical and metaphysical interaction with the world than the religious and political dogmatism which separates man from nature.

Myth is not only a manifestation of the past; more important, myth is the product of creativity in Péret's work. The situation of his poems and tales is a world in which super- and sub-terranean elements are fused, as are all states of being and consciousness. It is a dynamic form of utopia in which the pleasure principle dominates in the omnipresence of food and the use of play as the primary form of action and interaction. The great ruling force in Péret's myth is not a social god like Quetzalcoatl or Zeus, whose powers are limited to action within worlds created before their arrival. Unlike earlier mythographers, Péret does not personify his omnipotent central concept; rather, he depicts it as it inheres in every action in human and natural life. From the shaping of the cosmos to the events of daily life, it is change which rules the world. Because many aspects of the work of change are not perceived in the normal context of human awareness, this mythology relies on the imagination as a sixth sense which unites the conscious with the unconscious, dream and death. The unified, expanded insight of the poet into the mythological structure of the world is expressed through poetry, the vehicle of the image, and through a prose which empties narrative forms of their dead content to revive them as expressions of poetic insight. The Surrealist works of Benjamin Péret reveal the significance and implications of the new myth of change.

WORKS BY BENJAMIN PÉRET

The following list of works by Péret is given in chronological order according to date of publication or of composition, when this date is known. It is arranged in five categories: poetry, prose, works in collaboration, non-fiction and journal contributions. Although this appendix is intended to be complete, the diversity of sources involved, especially under the heading of non-fiction, renders the task virtually impossible. The sources used in compiling this list include the notes to the *Œuvres complètes* prepared by Claude Courtot, Jean Schuster, Vincent Bounoure and others, the bibliography given in Jean-Louis Bédouin's *Benjamin Péret,* the Library of the Museum of Modern Art, Herbert Gershman's *A Bibliography of the Surrealist Revolution in France,* and the dates of composition indicated by Péret at the end of some of his works. Unless publication in the *Œuvres complètes* is the first printing of a work, this publication is not mentioned.

A. Poetry

1. Collections and Separately Published Works

1921 *Le Passager du Transatlantique.* Collection "Dada." Paris: Au Sans Pareil.

    1934 "Babord pour tous," in *Anthologie poétique du surréalisme.* Edited by Georges Hugnet. Paris: Editions Jeanne Bucher. Hereafter referred to as Hugnet.

1936   "Passerelle du commandant," in *Anthologie des poètes de la NRF.* Paris: Gallimard.
1964   Entire collection republished in *Le Grand Jeu, suivi du Passager du Transatlantique.* Collection "Poésie." Paris: Gallimard.

1924 *Immortelle Maladie.* Collection "Littérature." Paris: Gallimard.

1934   First section ("Sur la colline") in Hugnet.
1947   Reprinted in *Feu central.* Paris: K Editeur.
1961   "Sur la colline" and "Courir sur un miroir" reprinted in Jean-Louis Bédouin, ed., *Benjamin Péret.* Paris: Seghers. Hereafter referred to as *Poètes d'aujourd'hui.*
1964   "Sur la colline" reprinted in Jean-Louis Bédouin, ed., *La Poésie surréaliste.* Paris: Seghers. Hereafter referred to as Bédouin.

Translation:
1965   Sections 1, 2, 4, 5, and 6 in English in J. H. Matthews, *Vingt poèmes/Péret's Score.* Paris: Minard. Hereafter referred to as Matthews.

1926 *Dormir dormir dans les pierres.* Marseilles: Les Cahiers du Sud.

1927   Republished. Paris: Éditions Surréalistes.
1934   Second section ("Soleil route usé") in Hugnet.
1947   Reprinted in *Feu central.*
1961   "Soleil route usé" and "Nue nue comme ma maîtresse" in *Poètes d'aujourd'hui.*
1964   "Soleil route usé" in Bédouin.
1969   "Nue nue comme ma maîtresse" in J. H. Matthews, ed., *An Anthology of French Surrealist Poetry.* Minneapolis: University of Minnesota Press. Hereafter referred to as Matthews Anthology.

Translation:
1965   Third section in Matthews.

1928 *Le Grand Jeu.* Paris: Gallimard.

Texts published prior to 1928:
1922   "Ma Main dans la bière" and "Le Quatrième danseur." *Littérature,* nouvelle série 1 (1 March 1922).
1922   *La Mare aux mitrailleuses,* comprised of "Le Dernier Don Juan de la nuit," "Simplement," "Deux petites

mains," "La Grande Misère des derniers cailloux," "Le Langage des saints," and "Les Enfants du quadrilatère." *Littérature,* nouvelle série 7 (1 December 1922).

1922   Exerpts from "Le Quart d'une vie" and "La Pêche en eau trouble." *Les Feuilles libres,* 30 (December 1922 - January 1923).

1923   "Portrait de Paul Eluard," "Portrait de Louis Aragon," "Portrait de Max Ernst" (I), "Nuage," "Voyage de découverte," "Charcutons *charcutez,*" "Un oiseau a fienté sur mon veston salaud," and "Les Morts et leurs enfants." *Littérature,* nouvelle série 11-12 (15 October 1923).

1924   "La Mort du Cygne." *Manomètre,* 4 (February 1924).

1924   "Le Travail anormal." *Intentions,* 26 (July-August 1924).

1925   "La Chair humaine," "L'Arête des sons," and "La Lumière dans le soleil." *La Revue Européene,* 26 (April 1925).

1926   "La Femme à chose." *Proverbe,* 6 (1 July 1926).

Texts reprinted after 1928:

1934   "Mystère de ma naissance," "J'irai veux-tu," "Le Sang répandu," and "Les Puces du champ" in Hugnet.

1936   "Les Jeunes Filles torturées" in *Anthologie des poètes de la NRF.*

1937   "Portrait de Max Ernst" (I). *Max Ernst: Œuvres de 1919 à 1936.* Paris: Cahiers d'art.

Translations:

1935   "Quatre Ans après le chien" and "Le Sang perdu." Translated into Portuguese. *Gaceta de Arte,* 36 (Tenerife, October 1935).

1936   "J'irai veux-tu." Translated into English. *Contemporary Poetry and Prose,* 2 (London, June 1936).

1934   *De derrière les fagots.* Paris: Editions Surréalistes (José Corti).

Texts published prior to 1934:

1930   "Se laver les mains" and "S'ennuyer." *Le Surréalisme au Service de la Révolution,* 2 (1930).

1932   "A demain," "Ca continue," "A mi-chemin," and "Et ainsi de suite." *Nadrealism danas i ovde,* 3 (Prague, June 1932).

1933   "Au bout du monde," "Dans le blanc des yeux," "Et ainsi de suite," "Les lycées de jeunes filles sont trop petits," and "Bras dessus bras dessous." *Le Sur-réalisme au Service de la Révolution,* 6 (1933).

Texts reprinted after 1934:

1934 "Quatre à quatre," "Braves Gens," and "A cela près." *Documents 34. Intervention surréaliste.* Brussels (June 1934).

1934 "A cela près" in Hugnet.

1961 "Ça continue," "Mille fois," "Atout trèfle," "Qui est-ce," "Nuits blanches," "Chasse à courre," and "Pain rassis" in *Poètes d'aujourd'hui.*

1964 "Mille fois," "Quatre à quatre," and "Chasse à courre" in Bédouin.

Translations:

1965 "Qui est-ce," "Nuits blanches," and "Chasse à courre" in Matthews.

1970 "Sans tomates pas d'artichauts." Translated into English. *Radical America,* 4 (1970), 28.

1936 *Je ne mange pas de ce pain-là.* Paris: Editions Surréalistes.

Texts published prior to 1936:

1926 "La Mort de la mère Cognacq" and "La Mort héroï-que du Lieutenant Condamine de la Tour." *La Révo-lution Surréaliste,* 6 (1926).

1926 "Le Tour de France cycliste," "Le Congrès eucha-ristique de Chicago," "La Société des Nations," and "La Baisse du franc." *La Révolution Surréaliste,* 8 (1926).

1926 "Le Cardinal Mercier est mort." *Clarté,* 1 (19 June 1926).

1929 "Pour que M. Thiers ne crève pas tout à fait," "La Loi Paul Boncour," "La Stabilisation du franc," "Hymne des anciens combattants patriotes," and "Epitaphe sur un monument aux morts de la guerre." *La Révolution Surréaliste,* 12 (1929).

1930 "Vie de l'assassin Foch." *Le Surréalisme au Service de la Révolution,* 2 (1930).

1933 "La Conversion de Gide" and "Le Pacte des Quatre." *Le Surréalisme au Service de la Révolution,* 5 (1933).

1934 "Epitaphe sur un monument aux morts de la guer-re" in Hugnet.

Texts reprinted after 1934:

1961 "Louis XVI s'en va à la guillotine," "Hymne des anciens combattants patriotes," and "6 février" in *Poètes d'aujourd'hui.*

1964   "6 février" in Bédouin.

1935   *Je sublime* (date given in *Œuvres complètes,* II, 325). Paris:
Editions Surréalistes, 1936.

> 1947   Reprinted in *Feu central.*
> 1961   "Allo," "Clin d'œil," "Source" and "Nébuleuse" in
> *Poètes d'aujourd'hui.*
> 1964   "Allo" and "Source" in Bédouin.
> 1969   "Allo", "Clin d'œil," and "Attendre" in Matthews
> Anthology.
>
> Translations:
> 1935   "Source," "Allo," and "Parle-moi." Translated into
> Portuguese. *Gaceta de Arte,* 36 (October 1935).
> 1945   "Clin d'œil" and "Allo." Translated into Spanish.
> *El Hijo Pródigo,* 12 (May 1945).
> 1965   "Egaré," "Homard," and "Allo" in Matthews.

1936   *Trois Cerises et une sardine.* Paris: Editions GLM.

> 1964   Reprinted in André Breton, ed., *Anthologie de
> l'humour noir.* Paris: Pauvert.

1942   *Dernier Malheur dernière chance.* Paris: Editions Fontaine.

> 1943   Part Three ("Toujours plus noire jusqu'à la faim"),
> *VVV,* 2-3 (New York, March 1943), 94-95.

1946   *Un point c'est tout. L'Evidence surréaliste.* Special number
of *Les Quatre Vents,* 4 (1946).

> 1947   Reprinted in *Feu central.*
> 1961   "On sonne" and "Sais-tu" in *Poètes d'aujourd'hui.*
> 1964   "On sonne" in Bédouin.
> 1969   "A suivre" and "Tout à l'heure" in Matthews An-
> thology.
>
> Translation:
> 1965   "A suivre," "Où es-tu" and "Lundi" in Matthews.

1947   *A tâtons.* First published in *Feu central.*

> 1961   "Vent du nord" and "Le Premier Jour" in *Poètes
> d'aujourd'hui.*
> 1964   "Vent du nord" in Bédouin.

Translations:
1947 "Soupe" and "Virgule." Translated into Spanish. *Las Moradas,* 1 (Lima, 1947).
1965 "Une Tourbillon de poussière," "Virgule," and "Sans autre formalité" in Matthews.

1949 *Air mexicain.* Paris: Librairie Arcanes.

1961 Series of fragments beginning "Les hommes jaillissaient de l'ombre" in *Poètes d'aujourd'hui.*
1964 Fragment "Le feu vêtu de deuil" in Bédouin.

1949 *Toute une vie. André Breton: Essais et témoignages,* ed. Marc. Eigeldinger. Neuchâtel: A la Baconnière, 1950.

1961 Fragment, "Le temps était aux aurores boréales" in *Poètes d'aujourd'hui.*

2. POEMS ORIGINALLY PUBLISHED IN BOOKS OR JOURNALS

1920 "Importé du Japon." *Action,* 4 (July 1920).

1923 "Chanson de la gardeuse de kangourous." *Paris-Journal,* 20 April 1923.

1925 "Portrait de Saint-Pol-Roux." *Les Nouvelles littéraires,* 9 May 1925, 5.

Translation:
1970 Translated into English. *Radical America,* 4 (1970), 28.

1925 "Portrait de Max Ernst" (II). *Catalogue de l'exposition Max Ernst.* Paris: Van Leer.

1937 Reprinted in *Max Ernst: Œuvres de 1919 à 1936.* Paris: Editions des *Cahiers d'Art.*

1933 "Violette Nozières." *Violette Nozières.* Brussels: Editions Nicholas Flamel.

1934 "Minute." *Minotaure,* 6 (December 1934), 65.

1935 "Picasso." *Cahiers d'Art,* 7-10 (1935), 198-99.

1937 "Ubu Dieu." *Ubu enchaîné*. Paris: No publisher given, p. 10.

1941 "A garder précieusement." *NEON*, 4 (November 1948).

1942 "Premiers Résultats." *Leitmotiv*, 1 (1942).

1952-53 "Trois poèmes-gages." First published in *Œuvres complètes*, II, 288-91.

1957 "Des cris étouffés." First published in *Poètes d'aujourd'hui* (1961).

    1964 In Bédouin.

1959 "Plus bas." *Front unique*, nouvelle série 1 (Spring-Summer 1959).

1959 *Dernièrement*. Title given to poems composed by Péret during the two months preceding his death. Published for the first time in *Œuvres complètes*, II, 295-320 with the following exceptions:

> 1959 "A petits pas." *Arts*, 442 (30 September-6 October 1959), 3.
> 1959 "Dernièrement" and "Les Mains dans les poches." *Boite alerte: Catalogue de l'exposition internationale du surréalisme*. Paris: Galerie Daniel Cordier, pp. 16-17.
> 1959 "Du bout des lèvres" and "Signe du temps" with English translation in Matthews.
> 1963 "Dans le vent." *De la part de Péret*. Paris: Association des Amis de Benjamin Péret.
> 1965 *Les Mains dans les poches*. Montpellier: M. L. Feraud.

3. COLLECTED TRANSLATIONS

1936 *Remove Your Hat*. Translations into English by Humphrey Jennings and David Gascoyne. London: Roger Roughton Contemporary Poetry and Prose Editions. (Not seen.)

1965 *Vingt Poèmes/Péret's Score*. Translations into English in bilingual edition by J. H. Matthews. Paris: Minard, 1965.

B. Prose Tales

1922 *Au 125 du boulevard Saint Germain.* Collection "Littérature." Paris: Gallimard.

> 1946 Reprinted in *Main forte.* Paris: Editions Fontaine.
> 1957 Reprinted in *Le Gigot, sa vie et son œuvre.* Paris: Le Terrain Vague.

1922 "Les Malheurs d'un dollar." Collection "Les Pages libres." Paris: La Main à Plume, 1942.

> 1957 Reprinted in *Le Gigot.*

1922 "La Fleur de Napoléon." *Littérature,* nouvelle série 8 (1 January 1923), 22-23.

1922 "Pulchérie veut une auto." *Littérature,* nouvelle série 10 (1 May 1923), 17-23.

1922 "Une Vie pleine d'intérêt," "Sur le passage d'un panier à salade," and "Le Pays de Cocagne." First published in *Le Gigot.*

1922 "L'Enfant au ventre blond." *Mécano,* 3 (Leiden, 1922).

1922 "L'Auberge du cul volant." *Littérature,* nouvelle série 3 (1 May 1922), 16-17.

1923 "Dans le cadre de nos mœurs," "Une ornière vaut une jument," "Le Conte voué au bleu et au blanc." First published in *Le Gigot.*

1923 *Mort aux vaches et au champ d'honneur.* Paris: Editions Arcanes, 1962.

> 1925 Chapter 4. *La Révolution Surréaliste,* 4 (15 July 1925), 12-15.
> 1961 Chapter 4 in *Poètes d'aujourd'hui.*
> 1967 Republished. Paris: Le Terrain Vague.

1924 "La Dernière Nuit du condamné à mort." (Undated; date given in notes to *Œuvres complètes,* III). *La Révolution Surréaliste,* 7 (15 June 1926), 26-27.

1946   Republished in *Main forte.*
1957   Republished in *Le Gigot.*

1924   *Il était une boulangère.* Collection "Les Cahiers nouveaux."
Paris: Editions du Saggitaire, 1925.

1946   Republished in *Main forte.*
1957   Republished in *Le Gigot.*

1924   "La Maladie no. 9." *La Révolution Surréaliste,* 11 (15 March
1928), 24-26.

1946   Republished in *Main forte.*
1957   Republished in *Le Gigot.*

1924   "Corps à corps." *La Révolution Surréaliste,* 9-10 (1 October
1927), 33-36.

1946   Republished in *Main forte.*
1957   Republished in *Le Gigot.*

1924   "Une étoile vaut une autre" and "Un Plaisir bien passager."
First published in *Le Gigot.*

1924   *La Brebis galante.* Paris: Editions Premières, 1949.

1949   Reprinted. Paris: Losfeld.
Extracts published before 1949:
1924   Chapter 3. *La Révolution Surréaliste,* 1 (1 December 1924), 9. Published as *texte surréaliste.*
1925   Chapter 12. *Le Disque Vert,* troisième année, 1 (January 1925).
1925   Chapter 10. *La Révolution Surréaliste,* 3 (15 April 1925), 12-13. Published as "L'Amour des heures, la haine du poivre."
1927   Chapters 1, 2, 3, 4, 5, 6, 11, and 12. *Commerce,* 13 (Fall 1927).
1929   Chapter 7. *Variétés,* Special Number "Le Surréalisme en 1929." Published as "Les Végétations factices."
1946   Chapter 19 republished in *Main forte.*
1949   Chapter 12 (fragment). *NEON,* 5 (1949).
1961   Fragment "La cruche était pleine de linges." *Poètes d'aujourd'hui.*
Translation:
1969   Chapter 4. Translated into English. *Radical America,* 2, 42-44.

1922-25   "La Mort par la feuille," "Le Nègre et la soucoupe en-
flammée," "La Casquette du Père Bugeaud," "Songe! " and "Sur
la route de la fortune." First published in *Œuvres complètes*, III
with the notation "on peut rapporter leur composition au début
des années 20."

1925   "Le Passage à niveau," "Aglaë s'ennuie devant une fraise
des bois," "Le Pont des soupirs," and "Les Vagues Ames." First
published in *Le Gigot*.

> 1961   "Aglaë s'ennuie devant une fraise des bois" in
> *Poètes d'aujourd'hui*.

1925   "Ces animaux de la famille." *La Révolution Surréaliste*, 5
(15 October 1925), 24-25 and 6 (1 March 1926), 14-15.

1926   *Et les seins mouraient*. Marseilles, Editions des *Cahiers du
Sud*, 1928.

> 1946   Republished in *Main forte*.
> 1957   Republished in *Le Gigot*.
> 1961   Fragment of first part in *Poètes d'aujourd'hui*.

1927   "Ne pas manger de raisin sans le laver." First published in
Le Gigot.

1929   "L'Ecriture automatique." Written for *Diario da Noite*
(Brazil) but unpublished before *Œuvres complètes*, IV.

1930   "Morts ou vifs." *Le Surréalisme au Service de la Révolution*,
1 (1930), 24-26.

1933   "Au paradis des fantômes." *Minotaure*, 3-4 (December 1933),
29-35.

> 1938   Republished. Collection "Un Divertissement." Paris:
> Henri Parisot.

1936   "Entre chien et loup." *Minotaure*, 8 (15 June 1936), 19-24.

1938   "A l'intérieur des armures." *Minotaure*, 11 (1938), 54, 56.

1939   "Ruines: ruine des ruines." *Minotaure*, 12-13 (1939), 57-
59, 61.

1942   "Le Dégel." First published in French in *Le Gigot*.

First published in English in *VVV*, 1 (June 1942), 14-16.
Other translations:
1943   Translated into English. *New Road.* London: 1943.
1970   Translated into English. *Radical America,* 4 (1970), 25-27.

1950   "Midi." First published in *Le Gigot.*

1951   "La Semaine dernière." *L'Age du Cinéma,* special Surrealist number, 195.

1952   "Un Eternel Eté traversé d'éclairs." *Arts* (1952).

1954   *Les Rouilles encagées.* Paris: Losfeld. Includes poems originally published in *1929* (see Works in Collaboration) and new prose text.

    1970   Reprinted. Collection "Le Désordre." Paris: Losfeld.

1958   *Histoire naturelle.* Ussel: Privately printed. The first four chapters are dated 1945, the fifth is dated 1954, and the sixth and seventh are dated 1958.

    1947   Chapters 1-4. *Les Quatre Vents,* 8 (1947). Published as "Les Quatre éléments."
    1961   "La Terre" and "Le Feu" in *Poètes d'aujourd'hui.*

C.   Works in Collaboration

1922   "Préférences." With André Breton, Paul Eluard, Louis Aragon *et al. Littérature,* nouvelle série 2 (1 April 1922), 4.

1923   *Comme il fait beau. Littérature,* nouvelle série 9 (February-March 1923), 6-13. With Breton and Robert Desnos.

1925   *152 Proverbes mis au goût du jour.* With Paul Eluard. Paris: Editions Surréalistes.

    1968   Reprinted in Paul Eluard, *Œuvres complètes,* II. Paris: Gallimard, 155-61.

1925-27   "Revues de la presse." With Eluard. *La Révolution Surréaliste,* 5 (15 October 1925), 30; 6 (1 March 1926), 7; 8 (1 December 1926), 1-2; 9-10 (1 October 1927), 63-64.

1927 "Hands Off Love." With Breton, Aragon, Eluard *et al.* *La Révolution Surréaliste,* 9-10 (1 October 1927), 1-16.

1927 *Au grand jour* (pamphlet). With Breton, Aragon, Eluard and Unik.

1928 "Recherches sur la sexualité." With Breton, *et al.* *La Révolution Surréaliste,* 11 (15 March 1928), 32-40.

1928 "Le Dialogue en 1928." With Breton *et al.* *La Révolution Surréaliste,* 11 (15 March 1928), 7-8.

1929 *1929.* Premier sémestre. Under the pseudonym "Satyremont"; with Aragon. Paris: Editions de *La Révolution Surréaliste.*

ca. 1929 "L'Enfant planète." Synthesis of two poems, one by Péret and one by Desnos. First published in *Œuvres complètes,* IV.

1936 Viteslaz Nezval. *Antilyrique.* Translated, and with an introduction by Péret. Paris: Editions GLM.

1950 "Calendrier tour du monde des inventions tolérables." With Breton. *Almanach surréaliste du demi-siècle.* Special number of *La Nef.* Paris: Editions du Saggitaire.

1952 "Les Syndicats contre la Revolution." With George Munis. *Le Libertaire.*

> 1968 Reprinted in book form with preface by Jehan Mayoux. Paris: Le Terrain Vague.

1959 *L'Invenzione del mondo.* Album for the film *L'Invention du monde;* commentary by Péret. Milan: Galeria Schwartz. With Jean-Louis Bédouin and Michel Zimbacca. Translated into Italian by S. Quasimodo.

1962 Octavio Paz. *Pierre de soleil / Piedra de sol.* Translation by Péret. Paris: Gallimard.

1964 Enrico Baj. *Dames et généraux.* Translation by Péret. Milan: Galeria Schwartz; Paris: Berggruen.

no date Aimé Césaire. *Retorno al país natal / Cahier d'un retour au pays natal.* Preface by Péret. Havana: Molina y compañía.

D. ESSAYS AND OTHER NON-FICTION

1920 "Assassiner" (chronique). *Littérature,* 15 (July-August 1920), 19-20.

1920 "Revue de Odéo: *L'Homme cochon* (Casino de Paris) et *Carte blanche* (Cocteau)." *Littérature,* 16 (September-October 1920), 21.

1922 "L'Exposition Chirico." *Littérature,* nouvelle série 4 (September 1922), 24.

1922 "A travers mes yeux." *Littérature,* nouvelle série 5 (October 1922), 13.

    1961 Republished in *Poètes d'aujourd'hui.*

1922 Review of *Westwego* by Philippe Soupault. *Les Feuilles libres,* 26 (April-May 1922), 219-20.

ca. 1922 "Dada."

    1965 Published in *Dada à Paris,* ed. Michel Sanouillet. Paris: Pauvert, pp. 575-76.

1925 Preface. *Catalogue de l'exposition Joan Mirò.* Paris: Galérie Pierre.

1925 "Lettre à Madame de Bassino." *La Révolution Surréaliste,* 3 (15 April 1925), 32.

1931 "Les Sœurs Papin." *Le Surréalisme au Service de la Révolution,* 5 (1931), 27-28.

1935 "Le Surréalisme internationale." *Cahiers d'Art,* 5-6 (1935), 138.

1937 "La nature dévore le progrès et le dépasse." *Minotaure,* 10 (1937), 20-21.

1940 "André Masson." *André Masson.* Rouen: no publisher given.

1942 "Tanguy." *View,* second series 2 (1942), unpaginated.

1942 *La parole est à Péret.* New York: Editions Surréalistes, 1943.

1960 Republished with some changes as the introduction to the *Anthologie des mythes, légendes et contes populaires d'Amérique*. Paris: Editions Albin Michel.
1961 Fragment in *Poètes d'aujourd'hui*.
1965 Republished in *Le Déshonneur des poètes, précédé de La parole est à Péret*. Paris: Pauvert.
Translations:
1943 Extract translated into English. *View*, third series 2 (1943).
1970 Extract translated into English. *Radical America*, 4 (1970), back cover.

1943 "La pensée est UNE et indivisible." *VVV*, 4 (1944), 6-13.

Translation:
1966 Translated into English. *Surrealism and Revolution*. Chicago: Solidarity Press.

1945 *Le Déshonneur des poètes*. Mexico City: Poésie et Révolution.

1961 Fragment in *Poètes d'aujourd'hui*.
1965 Republished. *Le Déshonneur des poètes, précédé de La parole est à Péret*. Paris: Pauvert.
Translation:
1970 Translated into English. *Radical America*, 4 (1970), 15-20.

1947 "Notes on Pre-Columbian Art." Translated by Peter Watson. *Horizon*, 15 (1947), 364-74.

1947 "Le Sel répandu." *Le Surréalisme en 1947*. Paris: Pierre à feu, pp. 21-24.

1948 Preface. *Catalogue de l'exposition Indrich Styrsky*. Paris: La Dragonne.

1950 "La Soupe déshydratée." *Almanach surréaliste du demi-siècle*. Special number of *La Nef*. Paris: Editions du Saggitaire.

1951 "La Révolte du dimanche." *Révolte sur mesure*. Special number of *La Rue*.

1951 "Contre le cinéma commercial." *L'Age du Cinéma*, 1 (March 1951).

1951 "De derrière les fagots." *L'Age du Cinéma*, 4-5 (August-November 1951).

1952   "Remembrance of Things to Come." Translated by Martin James. *Trans/formation,* 1 (1952), 173-75.

1953   "Au monde nouveau: maison fondée par Toyen." In Breton, Péret, and Jindrich Heisler. *Toyen.* Paris: Editions Skolova.

1954   "Paillasse." *Médium,* deuxième série, 2 (1954), 11.

1955   *Le Libre de Chilàm Balàm de Chumayel.* Translated, with an introduction by Péret. Paris: Editions Denoël.

> 1950   Fragments. *Almanach surréaliste du demi-siècle.* Special number of *La Nef.* Paris: Editions du Saggitaire.

1955   "Le Noyau de la comète."

> 1956   *Anthologie de l'amour sublime.* Anthology edited by Péret and introduced by "Le Noyau de la comète." Paris: Albin Michel.
> 1961   Fragment in *Poètes d'aujourd'hui.*

1957   "Du fond de la forêt." *Le Surréalisme même,* 2 (Spring 1957), 105-09.

1958   "Arts de fête et de cérémonie." *L'Œil,* 37 (1958).

1958   *La poesia surrealista francese.* Selection and presentation by Péret. Milan: Editions Schwartz.

1958   "La Poésie au-dessus de tout." *Bief, Jonction Surréaliste,* 1 (15 November 1958).

> Translation:
> 1970   Translated into English. *Radical America,* 4 (1970), 23-24.

1960   *Anthologie des mythes, légendes et contes populaires d'Amérique.* Edited, and with an introduction by Péret. Paris: Editions Albin Michel.

1962   "L'Œuvre cruelle et révoltée de Luis Buñuel." *La Méthode,* 7 (January 1962).

1963   "Pierre Reverdy m'a dit." *Mercure de France,* 1181 (January 1962), 36-40.

E. CONTRIBUTIONS TO JOURNALS

Péret contributed to Surrealist journals from the beginning to the movement until his death. The following list indicates the names of these journals and the dates of his contributions.

Littérature. 15-16 (1920). Nouvelle série 1, 2, 3, 4, 5, 6 (1922); 8, 9, 10, 11-12 (1923).

La Révolution Surréaliste. Co-Director, 1-3 (1924-25). Contributions in all issues through 12 (1928).

Le Surréalisme au Service de la Révolution. 1 (1930), 5 (1931).

Minotaure. 3-4 (1934), 6 (1935), 8 (1936), 10 (1937), 11 (1938), 12-13 (1939).

VVV. 1 (1942), 4 (1944).

NEON. 4, 5 (1948).

Médium. Nouvelle série 2 (1954).

Le Surréalisme Même. 2 (1957).

Bief, Jonction Surréaliste. 1 (1958) and 2 (1959).

BIBLIOGRAPHY

Alquié, Ferdinand. *Philosophie du surréalisme.* Paris: Flammarion, 1955.

Angenot, Marc. "Le Surréalisme noir." *Les Lettres romanes,* 26 (1972), 182-92.

Aragon, Louis. *Le Paysan de Paris.* Paris: Gallimard, 1966.

──────. "Une Vague de rêve." *Commerce,* 2 (1924), 89-122.

Artaud, Antonin. *Œuvres complètes* VIII. Paris: Gallimard, 1971.

Audouin, Philippe. "Le Surréalisme et le jeu." *Le Surréalisme.* Entretiens dirigés par Ferdinand Alquié. The Hague: Mouton, 1968, pp. 455-85.

Bailly, Jean-Christophe. *Au-delà du langage: une étude sur Benjamin Péret.* Collection "Le Désordre." Paris: Losfeld, 1971.

Balakian, Anna. *Literary Origins of Surrealism: A New Mysticism in French Poetry.* New York: New York University Press, 1966.

──────. *Surrealism: The Road to the Absolute.* New York: Noonday Press, 1959.

Bataille, Georges. "La Veille Taupe et le préfixe 'sur' dans les mots *suhomme* et *surréaliste.*" *Tel Quel,* 34 (1968), 5-17.

Battistini, Yves, ed. and trans. "Héraclite d'Ephèse." *Trois contemporains.* Paris: Gallimard, 1955, pp. 13-77.

Beaujour, Michel. "André Breton ou la transparence." In André Breton. *Arcane 17.* Paris: Union générale d'edition, 1965, pp. 161-83.

Bédouin, Jean-Louis. *Benjamin Péret.* Collection "Poètes d'aujourd'hui." Paris: Seghers, 1961.

──────, ed. *La Poésie surréaliste.* Paris: Seghers, 1964.

──────. *Vingt ans de surréalisme. 1939-1952.* Paris: Denoël, 1961.

Benayoun, Robert. *Erotique du surréalisme.* Paris: Pauvert, 1965.

Berl, Emmanuel; Audiberti, Jacques; Breton, André; Revel, Jean-François; Gracq, Julien; Schéhadé, Georges; Pieyre de Mandiargues, André; Benayoun, Robert; Bédouin, Jean-Louis; Lebel, Jean-Jacques; Isvic, Radovan; Legrand, Gérard; and Alleau, René. "Hommages à Benjamin Péret." *Arts,* 442 (1959), 3-4.

Blanchot, Maurice. "Le Demain joueur." *Nouvelle Revue Française,* 15 (1959), 863-69. Reprinted in *L'Entretien infini.* Paris: Gallimard, 1969, pp. 597-619.

──────. *Lautréamont et Sade.* Paris: Editions de Minuit, 1963.

Bosquet, Alain. Review of *Œuvres complètes I. Le Monde des Livres,* February 14, 1970, v.

Breton, André. *L'Amour fou.* Paris: Gallimard, 1937.

──────, ed. *Anthologie de l'humour noir.* Paris: Pauvert, 1964.

──────. *Arcane 17, enté d'ajours.* Paris: Pauvert, 1965.

Breton, André. *La Clé des champs*. Paris: Editions du Saggitaire, 1953.

――――. *Entretiens avec André Parinaud et al., 1913-1952*. Paris: Gallimard, 1952.

――――. *Manifestes du surréalisme*. Paris: Pauvert, 1962.

―――― and Paul Eluard. *Notes sur la poésie*. Paris: Editions GLM, 1936.

――――. *Ode à Fourier*. Commentée par Jean Gaulmier. Paris: Klincksieck, 1961.

――――. *Les Pas Perdus*. Collection "Idées." Paris: Gallimard, 1969.

――――. *Perspective cavalière*. Paris: Gallimard, 1970.

――――. *Point du jour*. Paris: Gallimard, 1934.

――――. *Le Surréalisme et la peinture*. Paris: Gallimard, 1965.

――――. *L'Un dans l'autre*. Collection "Le Désordre." Paris: Losfeld, 1971.

――――. *Les Vases communicants*. Paris: Gallimard, 1967.

Brown, Norman O. *Life Against Death*. Vintage Books. New York: Random House, 1959.

Calas, Nicholas. *Confound the Wise*. New York: Arrow Press, 1942.

Callois, Roger. *L'Homme et le sacré*. Collection "Idées." Paris: Gallimard, 1970.

Carrouges, Michel. *André Breton et les données fondamentales du surréalisme*. Collection "Idées." Paris: Gallimard, 1966.

――――. "L'Empreinte de Péret." *Preuves*, 9 (1959), 82-83.

Caws, Mary Ann. *The Inner Theater of Recent French Poetry*. Princeton: Princeton University Press, 1972.

――――. "Motion and Motion Arrested: The Language of the Surrealist Adventure." *Symposium*, 24 (1970), 301-07.

――――. "Péret and the Surrealist Word." *Romance Notes*, 11 (1969), 233-37.

――――. "Péret's *amour sublime*: Just Another *amour fou?*" *French Review*, 40 (1966), 204-12.

――――. "Benjamin Péret: A Plausible Surrealist." *Yale French Studies*, 31 (May 1964), 65-7.

――――. *The Poetry of Dada and Surrealism: Aragon, Breton, Tzara, Eluard, Desnos*. Princeton: Princeton University Press, 1970.

Courtot, Claude. *Introduction à la lecture de Benjamin Péret*. Paris: Le Terrain Vague, 1965.

Desnos, Robert. "Pénalités d'Enfer." *Littérature*, nouvelle série, 4. Exerpted in Pierre Berger, ed., *Robert Desnos*. Paris: Seghers, 1949, pp. 107-09.

Eigeldinger, Marc, ed. *André Breton: Essais et témoignages*. Neuchâtel: A la Baconnière, 1950.

――――. "Surréalisme et dynamisme de l'imagination." *L'Imagination créatrice*. Edited by Roselyne Chenu. Neuchâtel: A la Baconnière, 1971, pp. 165-71.

Eluard, Paul. *Œuvres complètes*. 2 vols. Paris: Gallimard, 1968.

――――. *Poèmes pour tous*. Paris: Editeurs français réunis, 1959.

Ernst, Max. *Ecritures*. Paris: Gallimard, 1970.

――――, et al. *Max Ernst: Œuvres de 1919 à 1936*. Paris: Editions des Cahiers d'art, 1937.

Fauchereau, Serge. "Le Vrai Visage de Benjamin Péret." Review of *Œuvres complètes I* by Benjamin Péret. *La Quinzaine Littéraire*, 90 (1970), 8-10.

――――. Review of *Œuvres complètes II* by Benjamin Péret. *La Quinzaine Littéraire*, 128 (1971), 15.

Fowlie, Wallace. *Age of Surrealism*. Bloomington: Indiana University Press, 1960.

Freud, Sigmund. *Basic Writings of Sigmund Freud.* Edited by A. A. Brill. New York: Random House, 1938.

Frye, Northrup. *Anatomy of Criticism: Four Essays.* New York: Atheneum, 1966.

Gauthier, Xavière. *Surréalisme et sexualité.* Collection "Idées." Paris: Gallimard, 1971.

Gershman, Herbert. *The Surrealist Revolution in France.* Ann Arbor: University of Michigan Press, 1969.

Hanchett, Elizabeth Jackson. "The Cosmic Imagination of Benjamin Péret: A Reading of 'Une Ile dans une tasse'." *Dada/Surrealism,* 2 (1972), 41-44.

―――. "Poésie activité de l'esprit: A Study of 'Atout trèfle' by Benjamin Péret." *French Review,* 44 (1971), 1936-47.

―――. Review of *Œuvres complètes II* by Benjamin Péret. *French Review,* 26 (1972-73), 230-31.

Hesiod. *Theogony.* Translated, with an introduction by Norman O. Brown. New York: Bobbs-Merrill, 1953.

Het franse boek. Review of *Œuvres complètes I.* April 1970, 118-24.

Hugnet, Georges. "Paul Eluard." *Arts,* 891 (1965), 5.

―――. *Petite Anthologie du surréalisme.* Paris: Jeanne Bucher, 1934.

Huizinga, Johann. *Homo ludens.* London: Paladin, 1970.

Isaacs, Roger M. Review of *Le Grand Jeu* by Benjamin Péret. *French Review,* 46 (1972-73), 229-30.

Jameson, Frederic. *Marxism and Form.* Princeton: Princeton University Press, 1971.

Jean, Raymond. "La grande force est le désir." *Europe,* 46 (1968), 25-34.

――― and Arpad Mezei. *Histoire de la peinture surréaliste.* Paris: Editions du Seuil, 1959.

Josephson, Matthew. *Life Among the Surrealists.* New York: Holt, Rinehart, Winston, 1962.

Jouffroy, Alain. Discours. *Le Surréalisme.* Entretiens dirigés par Ferdinand Alquié. The Hague: Mouton, 1968, pp. 134-42.

Kelly, Edward. "The Theater of Terrestrial Astronomy." *Io,* 4 (1967), 45-60.

Laponge, Gilles. "Retour de Benjamin Péret." Review of *Œuvres complètes I,* by Benjamin Péret. *Le Figaro littéraire,* 1226 (1969), 31.

Lautréamont, Comte de [Isidore Ducasse]. *Œuvres complètes.* Edited, with an introduction by Marguerite Bonnet. Paris: Garnier, 1969.

Leiris, Michel. *Nuits sans nuit et quelques jours sans jour.* Paris: Gallimard, 1961.

Lévi-Strauss, Claude. *La Pensée sauvage.* Paris: Librairie Plon, 1962.

Lippard, Lucy, ed. *Surrealists on Art.* Edgewood Cliffs, NJ: Prentice-Hall, 1966.

Lyotard, Jean-François. "Le travail du rêve ne pense pas." *Revue d'Esthétique,* 21 (1968), 26-61.

Marcuse, Herbert. *Eros and Civilization.* Vintage Books. New York: Random House, 1962.

―――. *An Essay on Liberation.* Boston: Beacon Press, 1969.

Martin, P. Review of *Œuvres complètes II,* by Benjamin Péret. *Cahiers du Sud,* 8 (1971), 152-54.

Matthews, J. H. *An Anthology of French Surrealist Poetry.* Minneapolis: University of Minnesota Press, 1969.

―――. "Invective et merveilleux dans *Je ne mange pas de ce pain-là* de Benjamin Péret." *Kentucky Romance Quarterly,* 18 (1971), 409-21.

Matthews, J. H. "The Mechanics of the Marvelous: The Short Stories of Benjamin Péret." *L'Esprit Créateur,* 61 (1966), 23-30.
――――. *Surrealism and Film.* Ann Arbor: Univ. of Michigan Press, 1971.
――――. *Surrealist Poetry in France.* Syracuse: Syracuse University Press, 1969.
――――. *Vingt poèmes / Péret's Score.* Collection "Passeport." Paris: Minard, 1965.
Mayoux, Jehan. "Benjamin Péret, ou la fourchette coupante." *Le Surréalisme même,* 2 (Spring 1957), 150-58, and 3 (Autumn 1957), 53-58.
Mead, Gerald. "A Syntactic Model in Surrealist Style." *Dada/Surrealism,* 2 (1972), 33-36.
Michaux, Henri. *Passages.* Paris: Gallimard, 1963.
Mussacchio, Danièle. "Le Surréalisme dans la poésie hispano-américaine." *Europe,* 46 (1968), 258-84.
Nadeau, Maurice. *Histoire du surréalisme.* Paris: Editions du Seuil, 1964.
Patri, Aimé. "Légende et réalité de Benjamin Péret." *Preuves,* 9 (1969), 83-84.
Paz, Octavio. "Benjamin Péret." *Les Lettres nouvelles,* 7ième année, 24 (1959), 36-37.
Peyre, Henri. Review of *Surrealist Poetry in France,* by J. H. Matthews. *Symposium,* 24 (1970), 381.
Pierre, José. "Benjamin Péret ou le feu central." Review of *Œuvres complètes I* by Benjamin Péret. *La Magazine littéraire,* 36 (1970), 27-29.
――――. "Benjamin Péret." *Le Monde des livres,* February 14, 1970, V.
Prigioni, Pierre. *Conte populaire et conte surréaliste. Approche structuraliste d'un conte de Benjamin Péret.* Urbino: Argalia Editore, 1970.
――――. "Péret: Das Gewissen seiner Zeit." *Germanische-Romanische Monatschrift,* 14 (1964), 188-97.
Raymond, Marcel. *De Baudelaire au surréalisme.* Paris: Corti, 1940.
Revel, Jean-François. "La Mort de Péret." *Cahiers des Saisons,* 19 (1960), 414-15.
Riffaterre, Michael. "La Métaphore filée dans la poésie surréaliste." *Langue française,* 3 (Sept. 1969), 46-60.
Rosemont, Franklin. "An Introduction to Benjamin Péret." *Radical America,* 4 (1970), 1-13.
Sanouillet, Michel. *Dada à Paris.* Paris: Pauvert, 1965.
Séjourné, Laurette. *La Pensée des anciens mexicains.* Paris: Maspero, 1966.
Serge, Victor. "Letter from Mexico." *Horizon,* 15 (1947), 65-69.
Soupault, Philippe. "Benjamin Péret: audace, fidélité, surréalisme." *Arts,* 446 (1960), 4.
Soustelle, Jacques. *Daily Life Among the Aztecs.* London: Weidenfeld and Nicholson, 1961.
Spada, Marcel. Review of *Introduction à la lecture de Benjamin Péret,* by Claude Courtot. *Cahiers Dada Surréalisme,* 2 (1968), 218-27.
Wedell, Georg Wolfgang. "An Introduction to Alchemy." Translated by Richard Grossinger. *Io,* 4 (1967), 35-44.

NORTH CAROLINA STUDIES IN THE ROMANCE LANGUAGES AND LITERATURES

I.S.B.N. Prefix 0-8078-

Recent Titles

EL CRONISTA PEDRO DE ESCAVIAS. *Una vida del Siglo XV,* por Juan Bautista Avalle-Arce. 1972. (No. 127). *-927-8.*

AN EDITION OF THE FIRST ITALIAN TRANSLATION OF THE "CELESTINA," by Kathleen V. Kish. 1973. (No. 128). *-928-6.*

MOLIÈRE MOCKED. THREE CONTEMPORARY HOSTILE COMEDIES: *Zélinde, Le portrait du peintre, Élomire Hypocondre,* by Frederick Wright Vogler. 1973. (No. 129). *-929-4.*

C.-A. SAINTE-BEUVE. *Chateaubriand et son groupe littéraire sous l'empire.* Index alphabétique et analytique établi par Lorin A. Uffenbeck. 1973. (No 130). *-930-8.*

THE ORIGINS OF THE BAROQUE CONCEPT OF "PEREGRINATIO," by Juergen Hahn. 1973. (No. 131). *-931-6.*

THE "AUTO SACRAMENTAL" AND THE PARABLE IN SPANISH GOLDEN AGE LITERATURE, by Donald Thaddeus Dietz. 1973. (No. 132). *-932-4.*

FRANCISCO DE OSUNA AND THE SPIRIT OF THE LETTER, by Laura Calvert. 1973. (No. 133). *-933-2.*

ITINERARIO DI AMORE: DIALETTICA DI AMORE E MORTE NELLA VITA NUOVA, by Margherita de Bonfils Templer. 1973. (No. 134). *-934-0.*

L'IMAGINATION POETIQUE CHEZ DU BARTAS: ELEMENTS DE SENSIBILITE BAROQUE DANS LA "CREATION DU MONDE," by Bruno Braunrot. 1973. (No. 135). *-934-0.*

ARTUS DESIRE: PRIEST AND PAMPHLETEER OF THE SIXTEENTH CENTURY, by Frank S. Giese. 1973. (No. 136). *-936-7.*

JARDIN DE NOBLES DONZELLAS, FRAY MARTIN DE CORDOBA, by Harriet Goldberg. 1974. (No. 137). *-937-5.*

MYTHE ET PSYCHOLOGIE CHEZ MARIE DE FRANCE DANS "GUIGEMAR", par Antoinette Knapton. 1975. (No. 142). *-942-1.*

THE LYRIC POEMS OF JEHAN FROISSART: A CRITICAL EDITION, by Rob Roy McGregor, Jr. 1975. (No. 143). *-943-X.*

THE HISPANO-PORTUGUESE CANCIONERO OF THE HISPANIC SOCIETY OF AMERICA, by Arthur Askins. 1974. (No. 144). *-944-8.*

HISTORIA Y BIBLIOGRAFÍA DE LA CRÍTICA SOBRE EL "POEMA DE MÍO CID" (1750-1971), por Miguel Magnotta. 1976. (No. 145). *-945-6.*

LES ENCHANTEMENZ DE BRETAIGNE. AN EXTRACT FROM A THIRTEENTH CENTURY PROSE ROMANCE "LA SUITE DU MERLIN", edited by Patrick C. Smith. 1977. (No. 146). *-9146-0.*

THE DRAMATIC WORKS OF ÁLVARO CUBILLO DE ARAGÓN, by Shirley B. Whitaker. 1975. (No. 149). *-949-9.*

A CONCORDANCE TO THE "ROMAN DE LA ROSE" OF GUILLAUME DE LORRIS, by Joseph R. Danos. 1976. (No. 156). *0-88438-403-9.*

POETRY AND ANTIPOETRY: A STUDY OF SELECTED ASPECTS OF MAX JACOB'S POETIC STYLE, by Annette Thau. 1976. (No. 158). *-005-X.*

FRANCIS PETRARCH, SIX CENTURIES LATER, by Aldo Scaglione. 1975. (No. 159).

STYLE AND STRUCTURE IN GRACIÁN'S "EL CRITICÓN", by Marcia L. Welles, 1976. (No. 160). *-007-6.*

MOLIERE: TRADITIONS IN CRITICISM, by Laurence Romero. 1974 (Essays, No. 1). *-001-7.*

CHRÉTIEN'S JEWISH GRAIL. A NEW INVESTIGATION OF THE IMAGERY AND SIGNIFICANCE OF CHRÉTIEN DE TROYES'S GRAIL EPISODE BASED UPON MEDIEVAL HEBRAIC SOURCES, by Eugene J. Weinraub. 1976. (Essays, No. 2). *-002-5.*

When ordering please cite the *ISBN Prefix* plus the last four digits for each title.

Send orders to: University of North Carolina Press
Chapel Hill
North Carolina 27514
U. S. A.

NORTH CAROLINA STUDIES IN THE
ROMANCE LANGUAGES AND LITERATURES

I.S.B.N. Prefix 0-8078-

Recent Titles

STUDIES IN TIRSO, I, by Ruth Lee Kennedy. 1974. (Essays, No. 3). *-003-3.*

VOLTAIRE AND THE FRENCH ACADEMY, by Karlis Racevskis. 1975. (Essays, No. 4). *-004-1.*

THE NOVELS OF MME RICCOBONI, by Joan Hinde Stewart. 1976. (Essays, No. 8). *-008-4.*

FIRE AND ICE: THE POETRY OF XAVIER VILLAURRUTIA, by Merlin H. Forster. 1976. (Essays, No. 11). *-011-4.*

THE THEATER OF ARTHUR ADAMOV, by John J. McCann. 1975. (Essays, No. 13). *-013-0.*

AN ANATOMY OF POESIS: THE PROSE POEMS OF STÉPHANE MALLARMÉ, by Ursula Franklin. 1976. (Essays, No. 16). *-016-5.*

LAS MEMORIAS DE GONZALO FERNÁNDEZ DE OVIEDO, Vols. I and II, by Juan Bautista Avalle-Arce. 1974. (Texts, Textual Studies, and Translations, Nos. 1 and 2). *-401-2; 402-0.*

GIACOMO LEOPARDI: THE WAR OF THE MICE AND THE CRABS, translated, introduced and annotated by Ernesto G. Caserta. 1976. (Texts, Textual Studies, and Translations, No. 4). *-404-7.*

LUIS VÉLEZ DE GUEVARA: A CRITICAL BIBLIOGRAPHY, by Mary G. Hauer. 1975. (Texts, Textual Studies, and Translations, No. 5). *-405-5.*

UN TRÍPTICO DEL PERÚ VIRREINAL: "EL VIRREY AMAT, EL MARQUÉS DE SOTO FLORIDO Y LA PERRICHOLI". EL "DRAMA DE DOS PALANGANAS" Y SU CIRCUNSTANCIA, estudio preliminar, reedición y notas por Guillermo Lohmann Villena. 1976. (Texts, Textual Studies, and Translation, No. 15). *-415-2.*

LOS NARRADORES HISPANOAMERICANOS DE HOY, edited by Juan Bautista Avalle-Arce. 1973. (Symposia, No. 1). *-951-0.*

ESTUDIOS DE LITERATURA HISPANOAMERICANA EN HONOR A JOSÉ J. ARROM, edited by Andrew P. Debicki and Enrique Pupo-Walker. 1975. (Symposia, No. 2). *-952-9.*

MEDIEVAL MANUSCRIPTS AND TEXTUAL CRITICISM, edited by Christopher Kleinhenz. 1976. (Symposia, No. 4). *-954-5.*

SAMUEL BECKETT. THE ART OF RHETORIC, edited by Edouard Morot-Sir, Howard Harper, and Dougald McMillan III. 1976. (Symposia, No. 5). *-955-3.*

DELIE. CONCORDANCE, by Jerry Nash. 1976. 2 Volumes. (No. 174).

FIGURES OF REPETITION IN THE OLD PROVENÇAL LYRIC: A STUDY IN THE STYLE OF THE TROUBADOURS, by Nathaniel B. Smith. 1976. (No. 176). *-9176-2.*

A CRITICAL EDITION OF LE REGIME TRESUTILE ET TRESPROUFITABLE POUR CONSERVER ET GARDER LA SANTE DU CORPS HUMAIN, by Patricia Willett Cummins. 1977. (No. 177).

THE DRAMA OF SELF IN GUILLAUME APOLLINAIRE'S "ALCOOLS", by Richard Howard Stamelman. 1976. (No. 178). *-9178-9.*

A CRITICAL EDITION OF "LA PASSION NOSTRE SEIGNEUR" FROM MANUSCRIPT 1131 FROM THE BIBLIOTHEQUE SAINTE-GENEVIEVE, PARIS, by Edward J. Gallagher. 1976. (No. 179). *-9179-7.*

A QUANTITATIVE AND COMPARATIVE STUDY OF THE VOCALISM OF THE LATIN INSCRIPTIONS OF NORTH AFRICA, BRITAIN, DALMATIA, AND THE BALKANS, by Stephen William Omeltchenko. 1977. (No. 180). *-9180-0.*

OCTAVIEN DE SAINT-GELAIS "LE SEJOUR D'HONNEUR", edited by Joseph A. James. 1977. (No. 181). *-9181-9.*

When ordering please cite the *ISBN Prefix* plus the last four digits for each title.

Send orders to: University of North Carolina Press
Chapel Hill
North Carolina 27514
U. S. A.

NORTH CAROLINA STUDIES IN THE
ROMANCE LANGUAGES AND LITERATURES

I.S.B.N. Prefix 0-8078-

Recent Titles

When ordering please cite the *ISBN Prefix* plus the last four digits for each title.

Send orders to: University of North Carolina Press
                    Chapel Hill
                    North Carolina 27514
                    U. S. A.